ACADEMIC AND STUDENT AFFAIRS IN COLLABORATION

Academic and Student Affairs in Collaboration provides a comprehensive and evidence-based understanding of the partnerships necessary to achieve an institutional culture devoted to student success. Chapter authors explore how to design, implement and assess collaborative efforts between Student and Academic Affairs in support of increased student success. This book provides best practices for fostering and enhancing campus dialogue, career development pathways, academic support services, and other important initiatives to increase retention and learning outcomes, improve motivation and goal attainment, and enhance institutional accountability. This book is a must-read for scholars, faculty, leaders and practitioners in Student Affairs and Higher Education interested in achieving student success at their universities and colleges.

Mitchell A. Levy is a Higher Education consultant and Vice President of Student Affairs and Branch Campus Management at Atlantic Cape Community College, USA.

Bernard A. Polnariev is Administrative Executive Officer for Academic Affairs at CUNY LaGuardia Community College, USA.

ACADEMIC AND STUDENT AFFAIRS IN COLLABORATION

Creating a Culture of Student Success

Edited by
Mitchell A. Levy and
Bernard A. Polnariev

Routledge
Taylor & Francis Group

NEW YORK AND LONDON

First published 2016
by Routledge
711 Third Avenue, New York, NY 10017

and by Routledge
2 Park Square, Milton Park, Abingdon, Oxon, OX14 4RN

Routledge is an imprint of the Taylor & Francis Group, an informa business

© 2016 Taylor & Francis

Library of Congress Cataloging in Publication Data
Names: Levy, Mitchell A., editor. | Polnariev, Bernard A., editor.
Title: Academic and student affairs in collaboration :
creating a culture of student success / edited by Mitchell A. Levy
and Bernard A. Polnariev.
Description: New York, NY : Routledge, 2016. |
Includes bibliographical references and index.
Identifiers: LCCN 2015049696| ISBN 9781138913295 (hardback) |
ISBN 9781138913301 (pbk.) | ISBN 9781315691565 (ebook)
Subjects: LCSH: Student affairs services. | College student development
programs. | Counseling in higher education.
Classification: LCC LB2342.9 .A43 2016 | DDC 378.1/97—dc23
LC record available at http://lccn.loc.gov/2015049696

ISBN: 978-1-138-91329-5 (hbk)
ISBN: 978-1-138-91330-1 (pbk)
ISBN: 978-1-315-69156-5 (ebk)

Typeset in Bembo and Stone Sans
by Florence Production Ltd, Stoodleigh, Devon, UK

Mitchell's dedication

To my wife Marcy and our son Daniel, the best teammates anyone can ask for. My contribution to this project would not have been possible without their unconditional love and support.

To my colleague Bernard, a true friend and first-rate colleague.

To our colleagues in this book and across the world who commit to student success everyday with professionalism, integrity and accountability.

Bernard's dedication

To my wife, Ilana, and our two amazing kids, Eva and Russel, who played nicely while I wrote before they woke up, after they went to sleep and during the weekends. Also to my parents, Karolina and Alex, who kept encouraging me to publish my work and ideas. Thank you!

Also dedicated to my former ASAP students and the thousands of students I taught over the years—remember the powerful Kay Ryan poem, never *Say Uncle; Make it Happen*!

CONTENTS

TABLES

ABOUT THE CONTRIBUTORS

Dr. DeMethra LaSha Bradley serves as Assistant Dean for Academic and Student Affairs in the College of Education and Social Services at The University of Vermont (UVM). She is also an active member of the NASPA Student Affairs Partnering with Academic Affairs (SAPAA) Knowledge Community, and served as the Promising Practices Awards Committee Chair from 2012 to 2014. Dr. Bradley has authored or co-authored three book chapters and two books on the topics of religious and spiritual differences on college campuses, social class and academic advising. She received a B.A. from the University of California, Santa Barbara and both graduate degrees from The University of Vermont. Dr. Bradley has worked in higher education for 15 years in various roles including: judicial affairs, residential life, fraternity/sorority life, leadership programs, international education, executive operations and Academic Affairs.

demethra.bradley@uvm.edu

Professor Jennie Buoy is from New Jersey, where she earned her B.A. in Spanish at Rowan University and M.A. in Teaching English as a Second Language at The College of New Jersey. She began her career in New Jersey as well teaching English as a Second Language (ESL), Spanish and College Composition. She is currently a Professor of ESL at Arizona Western College on the border; she mostly teaches upper-level academic reading, writing and grammar courses delivered both traditionally and hybrid. She employs various technologies to supplement her instruction while contextualizing language use in terms of authentic situations. She aims to prepare her students for college-level coursework as well as real-world encounters with English. Aside from instruction, Professor Buoy has been chairing the Foundational Instruction Committee, which facilitates the coordination of policies and requirements for developmental education across the college. She also has been working with colleagues to create a home-grown ESL placement test to accurately place incoming ESL students. Additionally, she presented with colleagues at the 2014 NASPA Region II Conference a program titled Curricular Career Development: An Academic and Student Affairs Collaboration and another presentation, Career Development in the ESL Classroom, solo at the 2015 AZTESOL Southwest Mini-Conference.

jennie.buoy@azwestern.edu

Tammy DeFranco is currently the Director of Student Services and Campus Management at the Cape May Campus of Atlantic Cape Community College. She is in the process of working on her dissertation, titled, "Developmental Community College Students Perspective Using a Career Assessment Tool; An Action Research Study" at Atlantic Cape Community College through Capella University. Working for Atlantic Cape Community College has provided Ms. DeFranco with many years of experience assisting students to help them gain confidence, a sense of belonging, direction and achieving academic success through counseling, teaching and developing extracurricular student activities and events. She has had the opportunity to present her work at a NASPA Regional Conference on *Curricular Career Development: An Academic and Student Affairs Collaboration*.

tadefran@atlantic.edu

Susan DePhilippis is an Associate Professor of English as a Second Language (ESL) at Atlantic Cape Community College in Mays Landing, New Jersey. She enjoys infusing an interactive teaching style with various forms of technology for a more engaged student experience and greater language acquisition outcome. Prior to joining the faculty in 1999, she had taught ESL and GED courses, and supervised educational programs at several Federal Bureau of Prisons institutions throughout the United States. She has presented over 30 sessions regarding specific uses of technology in teaching a variety of English skills at local, regional and international conferences primarily associated with TESOL (Teachers of English to Speakers of Other Languages) and the League for Innovation. Susan earned a B.S. in Vocal Music Education from West Chester University, a M.A. in Applied Linguistics (TESOL) from the University of Pennsylvania, and an A.A. Degree in Digital design from Atlantic Cape Community College.

sdephili@atlantic.edu

Erika M. Di Renzo has been a member of the adjunct faculty and an adult educator since 2011, teaching developmental classes for both the English and Social Science departments at Atlantic Cape Community College as well as tutoring in the college's tutoring center. In her teaching position, she interprets and explains what information means and how it can be used from an educational perspective and then applied to a real-world approach; and pinpoints the students' educational needs in order to create purposed and meaningful instruction. Recently, she was selected as a creative content recipient by Atlantic Cape Community College—in this position she will further support the developmental needs of the learners by coaching, mentoring and assisting the learners in improving both their content knowledge as well as overall comprehension skills through the use of data-driven instruction and technology. Prior to her position at Atlantic Cape Community College, she was a Special Education teacher. Also, she serves as an English as a Second Language instructor and an Educational Advocate in the surrounding communities. In these roles, she establishes short and long-range goals and specifies the essential strategies and actions needed to achieve them.

edirenzo@atlantic.edu

Professor Maryann Flemming-McCall is Assistant Professor of Developmental English at Atlantic Cape Community College. She has a B.A. in Literature and Language from Richard Stockton College of New Jersey and an M.A. in English, from the University of Rhode Island. In addition to teaching all levels of developmental English as well as college-level courses, she is currently teaching the Accelerated Learning Program (ALP). This nationally recognized program places first-time students who test into developmental classes directly into college English and a support class, with the goal of retaining them and enhancing their chances for success. She is a member of National Association of Developmental Educators (NADE) and the National Council of Teachers of English (NCTE). She has presented the 2014 Annual National Conference on Acceleration in Developmental Education, the 2012 NADE Conference, and the 2014 NJCCC Best Practices Conference. Prior to joining the faculty at Atlantic Cape, she was Director of Adjunct Support and Development at the college.

mccall@atlantic.edu

Lisa Givens is the Manager for Student Activities and Athletics at Atlantic Cape Community College in Mays Landing, New Jersey. Ms. Givens holds a M.A. in Higher Education, Leadership and Administration from Capella University and a B.A. degree in Business Administration from Franklin University. Her research has primarily focused on the practical application of leadership theories in a community college environment.

lgivens@atlantic.edu

Yevgeniya Granovskaya is a certified Global Career Development Facilitator with over ten years of career-advising experience working with college students, adult learners and job seekers on a diverse community college campus in New York City. Her current research interests include uncovering successful strategies for infusing career development activities into high-impact educational practices, such as first-year experiences, learning communities and service-learning opportunities, as a way to most effectively prepare students for their professional lives after college, as well as to positively affect student engagement, retention and graduation rates. Mrs. Granovskaya holds a B.B.A. in Industrial and Organizational Psychology from Baruch College, CUNY, and an M.S.Ed. in Counseling and Personnel Services from Fordham University, and is a member of American Counseling Association, National Career Development Association and Career Resource Managers Association.

YGranovskaya@lagcc.cuny.edu

Professor Michael Kammer has enjoyed a 17-year career at Atlantic Cape Community College as a Professor of English as a Second Language (ESL). He is a graduate of Rutgers University with a M.A. in English, and earned his certificate of teaching ESL at New School University, which included a capstone project of teaching EFL at New York University in Prague. Since starting at the Atlantic City campus of Atlantic Cape, he has seen the ESL program grow from two full-time faculty to five, with the number of ESL students reaching over 600 a year. He has worked on committees such as the Academic Advising Task Force, and has chaired committees including the Assessment, International Education and Multicultural Awareness, and the Academic Policies and Procedures. Workshops he has presented include "Technology in the Classroom," "Five Great Ways to Use a Smart Phone in the Classroom" and "Assessment of Critical Thinking in the ESL Department." With Dr. Mitchell Levy and other colleagues, he has given several presentations on curricular infusion of career awareness. Since adding career advisement in many of his courses with marked success, Professor Kammer plans on continuing to develop and share this technique, which has encouraged and inspired many college students, giving them a chance to either be reminded or to understand why they are in the classroom, and also giving them a chance to reflect on which career path is right for them.

mkammer@atlantic.edu

Dr. Mitchell A. Levy possesses 33 years of experience in higher education administration, having served as a Vice President, Dean, Executive Director, Program Chairperson, Director and Counselor in both Student Affairs and Academic Affairs. Currently Dr. Levy is the Vice President of Student Affairs and Branch Campus Management at Atlantic Cape Community College in New Jersey. As a faculty member for 24 years he has taught 100+ undergraduate and graduate courses. He was awarded Full Professor (Adjunct) status in the Fordham University Graduate School of Education, and most recently served as Associate Professor (Adjunct) in the Long Island University Graduate school of Education. He has been a member of the National Center for Higher Education Risk Management (NCHERM) Behavioral Mental Health Consultation Team, the National Behavioral Intervention Team Association (NaBITA) Advisory Council, and the New York City Higher Education Task Force on Student Wellness and Anti-Bullying. Dr. Levy has served on the Editorial Review Boards of the *Journal* *of the Professional Counselor, Journal of Behavioral Intervention Teams* and as co-editor of the NASPA Student Affairs Partnering with Academic Affairs (SAPAA) Knowledge Community professional newsletter, *Synergy.*

Dr. Levy has published book chapters, case studies and articles addressing systemic emergency management, student retention and persistence, ADA compliance, multicultural appreciation and best practices in crisis prevention. As a consultant, he has presented 150+ workshops, webinars, and professional development programs regarding emerging issues in higher education. In 2015, Dr. Levy received the NASPA Region II Community College Professional of the Year Award.

See more: www.linkedin.com/in/MLevy

mitchellLevyPhD@aol.com

Janet Marler is the Associate Dean of Academic Support Services at Atlantic Cape Community College in New Jersey. Ms. Marler also teaches literature and composition in the English Department there. Prior to working at Atlantic Cape, Ms. Marler was Manager, Somers Point Branch for the Atlantic County Library System and oversaw the County's bookmobile services. She has been head of reference services for the Ocean City Free Public Library (NJ) and for the James V. Brown Library in Williamsport, PA. Ms. Marler was a reference librarian at Temple University Japan in Tokyo and taught writing at Temple's main and Tokyo campuses. Her publications include articles in the *Williamsport Sun-Gazette, The Press-Enterprise, The Entrepreneurial Edge* and the Pennsylvania Small Business Development Centers newsletter. While working in the online database industry, Ms. Marler wrote and published company newsletters and marketing materials for Telebase Systems and Knowledge Express Data Systems. She also edited and wrote the index for the book, *Fishing the Delaware,* published by Temple University Press. She has written several awarded grants including national-level grants from the American Library Association. She has presented workshops on online searching to the NJ Association of Women Business Owners, the Columbia-Montour Women's Conference, the Columbia County Human Resources Coalition, the Tokyo Association of Professional Librarians and the Economic Development Coalition for Philadelphia and Region. Ms. Marler enjoys the book arts and has taught bookmaking and paper-making workshops at the Noyes Museum. Ms. Marler has an M.S. in Information and Library Studies from Drexel University and a B.A. from Hood College in English.

JMarler@atlantic.edu

Sharon O'Connor, LCSW is a Psychotherapist in private practice in Manhattan. She received her M.S.W. from Hunter College School of Social Work (City University of New York), and has served as a clinician in educational as well as health care settings. Mrs. O'Connor was a co-presenter of *Behavioral Intervention Best Practices for Community Colleges* (Subryan, S., Levy, M.A., O'Connor, S.K.)

at the 2012 NaBITA conference in Bonita Springs, Florida. Other presentations include *Acknowledging LGBTQ Individuals in Opposite-sex Relationships* (2010) at Professional Seminar, Hunter College School of Social Work, and *Discovering Your Preferred Learning Style* (2010) at ASAP Leadership seminar, LaGuardia Community College. O'Connor's previous published works include *Five core considerations for counseling non-traditional students* (Levy, M.A., Polnariev, B.A., O'Connor, S.K., 2012) and *Getting the ducks in a row: Connecting community college students to support services* (Polnariev, B.A., Levy, M.A., O'Connor, S.K., 2012) in Student Affairs E-News. Also published are *Knowing what works for you* (2010) in Elephant in the Room Newsletter at LaGuardia Community College, and *Disparities in the health care experience of lesbian patients* (2010) in the *Journal of Diverse Social Work* at Hunter College.

soconnorlcsw@gmail.com

Judith Otterburn-Martinez is an Associate Professor of English as a Second Language (ESL) at Atlantic Cape Community College. She received her M.A. in Applied Linguistics from Columbia University and her M.A. in Social Anthropology from the Queens University of Belfast, Northern Ireland. She has taught English as a Second Language for 15 years in Mexico, Spain and the United States. She is now tenured at Atlantic Cape Community College. She has presented at the Teaching of English to Speakers of Other Languages (TESOL) International conference, Penn TESOL East, NJ TESOL/NJBE, League of Innovation, NJ Best Practices and NAPSA on a number of topics related to English language teaching, assessment and use of technology in the classroom. She is strongly motivated to navigate her students in learning English in an enjoyable and effective manner so that they may have a better life in this country.

jotterbur@atlantic.edu

Dr. Bernard A. Polnariev has worked assiduously to advance academic quality and student success outcomes in higher education for nearly 20 years—first in the classroom and then in various administrative leadership roles of increasing challenge and responsibility. His work has been grounded in a deep belief in the power of education to advance academic and cultural capital of individuals and communities.

Dr. Polnariev has played a critical role in LaGuardia Community College's 2012 reaccreditation through the Middle States Commission on Higher Education (MSCHE) focusing on the institution's retention efforts and achievements; he is currently working on the 2017 Middle States Periodic Review Report—addressing institutional strategic planning, general education and learning outcomes assessment recommendations. Dr. Polnariev currently serves as the Administrative Executive Officer for Academic Affairs at the same institution—enhancing the institution's alignment of Academic and Student Affairs, strengthening the College's revised advisement model, guiding faculty members in updating curricula and designing new programs grounded in the labor market needs. He previously co-led four cycles of the College's Strategic Planning efforts in collaboration with leaders from all divisions, and also helped transform the learning outcomes assessment infrastructure. Formerly, Dr. Polnariev directed a high-profile community college student success program for almost four years, the Accelerated Study in Associate Programs (ASAP). With his team, they helped attain impressive outcomes including a 51% three-year graduation rate for non-remedial and 55% for remedial-need students (i.e. double the rate for a comparable group); he is on a committee to ensure a three-fold increase of ASAP student enrollment in 2016. Dr. Polnariev spent a decade teaching psychology-related courses, at both the undergraduate and graduate level, in both public and private colleges. He is a huge fan of TED.com talks and is enthralled by research in behavioral economics.

Additionally, from 2009 to 2012, Drs. Levy and Polnariev trained more than 100 faculty members in developmental advisement and goal-clarification activities that can be used with students. Notably, Drs. Levy and Polnariev (with their colleague Laura McGowan) received the 2011 NASPA Student Affairs Partnering with Academic Affairs (SAPAA) Promising Practices Award for the *Art of Advising* faculty professional development seminar series. They continue to serve on the NASPA SAPAA committee helping to support other collaborations across the nation.

See more: www.linkedin.com/in/BPolnariev
bpolnariev@hotmail.com

Dr. Carl Procario-Foley has served on the staff of Iona College's Center for Campus Ministries since 1990. Prior to his years at Iona, Dr. Procario-Foley was employed as a Pastoral Associate at St. Joseph's Church in Chicago, IL where he was one of the founders of Insight, a tutoring and mentoring program that continues to serve children of Chicago's inner city. During his tenure as Director of Campus Ministries at Iona (currently the Office of Mission and Ministry), the department has developed many programs such as the Success After-school Center, the Iona in Mission program, the Iona College Gospel Choir and the many community outreach initiatives that involve Iona students including, among others, its Habitat for Humanity, Best Buddies and Project Sunshine chapters. As an Iona in Mission moderator, Dr. Procario-Foley has traveled with students on over 25 service immersions to serve communities nationally and internationally, as far away as Kenya and as close as the Bronx. He has worked closely with Iona faculty to create service-learning coursework and for the past ten years has served as chairperson of the college's Week of the Peacemaker, an educational week that fosters analysis and reflection on social justice issues. Dr. Procario-Foley earned his Ph.D. in 2011 from Fordham University's Graduate School of Religion and Religious Education. He received his B.A. from St. John's University (Collegeville, MN) and a M.A. in Theological Studies from Catholic Theological Union in Chicago.

cprocario-foley@iona.edu

Dr. Thomas J. Van Cleave, Ed.D. is the Founding Director for the Office of Service and Experiential Learning and Interim Co-Director for Study Abroad at Iona College in New Rochelle, NY. Dr. Van Cleave holds a doctorate in Educational Leadership: Postsecondary Education and a M.A. degree in Postsecondary Educational Leadership and Policy from Portland State University. He also earned a B.A. in Hospitality and Tourism Management from Grand Valley State University. Professionally Dr. Van Cleave works closely with faculty, administrators and community members to incorporate civically engaged pedagogies into the classroom. He has taught graduate courses in postsecondary education and international development and service. His research expertise focuses on faculty perceptions of and pedagogical strategies for the design and implementation of short-term international service-learning experiences.

tvancleave@iona.edu

FOREWORD

In the Twenty-first Century, Student Success Will Depend Upon How Well We Work Together

As leaders in today's higher education climate, we know the value of partnership and its necessity for our institutions' continued survival and service to students. *Academic and Student Affairs in Collaboration: Creating a Culture of Student Success* is a how-to guide for establishing, maintaining and assessing successful partnerships between Student Affairs and Academic Affairs. The editors, Drs. Mitchell A. Levy and Bernard A. Polnariev, are leaders in the realm of Student Affairs and Academic Affairs partnership, having developed a program—*The Art of Advising*—that received the 2011 Promising Practices Award from the National Association of Student Personnel Administrators (NASPA) Student Affairs Partnering with Academic Affairs (SAPAA) Knowledge Community. Both editors have also delivered numerous presentations about this program, focusing on its critical component of Student Affairs partnering with Academic Affairs. Recognizing the need to demystify the process that leads to lasting collaborations between the aforementioned units, Bernard and Mitchell began crafting this guide to address topics of: gaining trust among both units, outlining effective communication strategies and identifying issues of mutual interest and mutual responsibility, alongside examples of successful partnership initiatives.

This book provides answers to so many of the questions that we ask on the road to creating successful partnerships with our Student Affairs or Academic Affairs colleagues. Where do we start and how do we "speak each other's languages?" How can we overcome obstacles when working across units/divisions? What are examples of best practices to sustain these collaborations? How do we support each other? How could this work if there are no fiscal incentives at our disposal? The contributing authors and the editors address these questions and many more in a succinct book equipped with examples of strategic planning, promising practices and next steps.

Having served a two-year term as the Promising Practices Awards Chair for the NASPA SAPAA Knowledge Community, I have read over 75 nominations that seek recognition as a promising practice. All of them showed great effort and the desire to establish long-lasting effective programs for student success. What I found missing from many of the nominations was the establishment of true collaboration which takes time and is more than an invitation to be present at an event as well as the intentional built-in assessment of the initiatives' success beyond anecdotal measures. Through examples from a variety of campus partnerships, the contributing authors provide clear action steps toward true collaboration; they also challenge us to include assessment as part of the planning process, as opposed to it being an after-thought.

This guide can read sequentially or based on the reader's area of collaborative interest. Contributing authors are leaders in a variety of interrelated college matters including experiential learning, curricular career infusion, summer bridge programs, faculty engagement for advisement and orientation programming and strategic planning. After reading this book, I began rethinking the established Student Affairs and Academic Affairs partnerships at my institution as well as how to develop news ones utilizing the strategies and resources mentioned throughout the text. *Academic and Student Affairs in Collaboration: Creating a Culture of Student Success* left me pondering the adage, "if you always do what you've always done, you'll always be what you've always been." Colleagues, we must step outside of the comfort zones of our units and work together in a meaningful way to advance the success of our students!

In Service,
DeMethra LaSha Bradley

2012–2014 *Promising Practices* Chair, NASPA SAPAA Knowledge Community. Co-author of *How to Talk about Hot Topics on Campus: From Polarization to Moral Conversation*, Burlington, Vermont.

1

PROMOTING STUDENT SUCCESS VIA COLLABORATION

Bernard A. Polnariev and Mitchell A. Levy

> Insanity: doing the same thing over and over again and expecting different results.
>
> Albert Einstein (attributed)

Our Philosophy and Approach

The research presented by the contributors throughout this book illustrates the value of intentionally linking Student Affairs success initiatives with the primacy and centrality of the Academic Affairs mission. Fundamentally, we espouse an institutional culture providing a network of holistic support that engages both the "dotted and solid" lines found within organizational charts. As discussed more thoroughly throughout the book, researchers have found the following *five major tenets* help form the backbone of our values for an improved higher education system:

1. *Student success matters!* Student success should be the driving force behind practically all of our professional activities. College leaders ought to "share mutual goals that are well defined and place student success at the center of the work" (Kinzie & Kuh, 2004, p. 4). Forming and sustaining the conditions that foster student success in higher education institutions has never been more important (Kuh, Kinzie, Buckley, Bridges, & Hayek, 2006). Valencia College's President Sanford Shugart poignantly said "student success is the most important mission we have" (as cited by Kimmens, 2014, p. 57).

2. *Student learning matters!* We should conduct outcomes assessment as if learning matters most (Angelo, 1999; see also Gannon-Slater, Ikenberry, Jankowski, & Kuh, 2014). As one of two priorities in need of urgent reform as identified in his revised book on Higher Education in America, Dr. Derek Bok, former

president of Harvard University, stresses that we must "increase not only the quantity of students graduating from college but the amount they learn while they are there" (2015, p. 409). Collaborative approaches to improving learning outcomes are paramount to transforming higher education.

3. *Collaboration across Academic Affairs and Student Affairs boundaries matters!* Such partnership has been documented to increase student integration and engagement within the college community (e.g. Love & Love, 1995; Kezar, 2003; Kuh, 1996; Polnariev, McGowan, & Levy, 2010). Collaboration is essential for any significant organizational reform; faculty "must collaborate within and across departments [and divisions] to systematically build those [valued] outcomes across curricula" (Jenkins, 2014, p. 7). Regrettably, collaboration between faculty and Student Affairs staff is relatively rare (Banta & Kuh, 1998).

4. *Faculty–student interactions matter!* Faculty–student connections are vital for student achievement (Tinto, 2012). Consistent and frequent faculty contact is the most important factor in student involvement and motivation (Chickering & Gamson, 1987). The more *time* faculty give to their students, the more likely are students to graduate (Tinto, 1982). Kezar and Maxey (2014) emphasize that faculty–student interactions are pivotal in promoting student success. They conclude that "all faculty members can foster their students' development through substantive faculty student interaction" (p. 38).

5. *Curricular infusion and systemic approaches matter!* Such an approach is fundamental to efficacious teaching and learning in higher education. Providing students with a "big picture" of the main topics within specific courses and majors, and how they fit together, helps to improve learning outcomes— the aim is for "instructional program coherence" (Jenkins, 2014).

Collaboration and Student Success

From 2009 to 2012, we trained over 100 diverse faculty members in developmental advisement and goal-clarification activities that have been used to foster student success. We took our show on the road—presenting at various national conferences and a few webinars encouraging others to promote student success by forging relationships and collaborations across academic and Student Affairs. In March 2012, we received the "2011 *NASPA Student Affairs Partnering with Academic Affairs* (SAPAA) *Promising Practices Award*" for our *Art of Advising* faculty professional development seminar series. Shortly after winning the award, we began serving on various NASPA[1] (the National Association of Student Personnel Administrators) groups, including the NASPA–SAPAA Promising Practices Award nomination review committee helping to support other cross-divisional collaborations across the nation. Not only is it exciting to endorse such activities, but also witness first-hand the great collaborative initiatives that continue to gain momentum throughout the country. As proposal reviewers, we provide our colleagues with a clear and transparent rubric to help guide them as to what our team (and field) is looking for. Specifically, we currently rate[2] submissions based on the following five dimensions: 1) Integration and Innovation, 2) Partnership, 3) Sustainability, 4) Outcomes and 5) Support. We encourage you to view the definitions of each dimension identified on the SAPAA Promising Practices award rubric[3] and consider applying for the prestigious award.

Before we proceed to our research findings, two key terms are essential to define and operationalize: "collaboration" and "student success." Gray (1989) defines *collaboration* as "a process through which parties who see different aspects of a problem can constructively explore their differences and search for solutions that go beyond their own limited vision of what is possible" (as cited by Myers, 2014, p. 2). Generally, "*student success* represents academic achievement, engagement in educationally purposeful activities, satisfaction, acquisition of desired knowledge, skills, and competencies, persistence, and attainment of educational objectives" (Kuh et al., 2006). We of course support both definitions and perspectives but would also endorse an even broader definition as it would bolster an institution's mission. In moving toward a more systemic approach within higher education, Patrick Terenzini acknowledged that there are multiple forms of college "success" as part of his keynote address at the NACADA[4] *31st Annual Conference on Academic Advising* in 2007. He (2007) identified a handful of *student success* metrics below:

- knowledge acquisition and cognitive development;
- various forms of psycho-social development;
- enhance moral reasoning skills;
- attitudes and values formation, refinement and application;
- education attainment;
- economic and occupational rewards;
- quality of life.

Purpose and Need

One of the greatest imperatives faced by colleges and universities is the need to increase student success while confronting diminishing resources and a continually evolving complexity of student needs. In the preface of their new book addressing college student success, Castleman and his colleagues (2015) argue that "diminishing financial barriers and improving academic preparation require both systemic change and significant ongoing investment" (Castleman, Schwartz, & Baum, 2015, p. vii). In Dr. Thomas Bailey's new book on *Redesigning America's Community Colleges* he and his co-authors similarly stress that "Colleges face a difficult situation: They are being asked to improve their performance without being able to count on additional revenue. And they are doing this in an environment of greater public scrutiny, skepticism, and criticism of college performance" (Bailey, Jaggars, & Jenkins, 2015, p. 2). Furthermore, institutions face rapid technological change, and increased demands for accountability that require college leaders to examine their institutions more deeply, and, possibly, from different perspectives in order to thrive (Garza Mitchell & Maldanado, 2015). Recent legislation disseminated via federal policymakers has called for increased accountability regarding the missions espoused by our institutions of higher education. For purposes of clarity, "accountability," as defined by Dr. Peter Ewell, Vice President at the National Center for Higher Education Management Systems,[5] refers "to the constellation of mechanisms that colleges and universities employ to demonstrate to their external publics that they are responsible stewards of the resources invested in them, that they are soundly managed, and that they produce the kinds of results that they are expected to produce" (Ewell 2005, p. 104).

With an immensely powerful accountability spotlight on American higher education systems, leaders are largely absorbed with enrollment targets, student retention and graduation outcomes. College retention, or as Dr. John M. Braxton and his colleagues (2014) have referred to it, "student departure" represents an enduring problem for higher education at-large, as well as for public policymakers at all levels (Braxton, Doyle, Hartley III, Hirschy, Jones, & McLendon, 2014). The significance of student persistence to the achievement of several markers of college student success, coupled with the adverse impact of attrition on the stability of institutional enrollments, budgets and public perceptions of educational quality, starkly supports the need for strategic actions by college and university constituents in order to increase student retention rates (Braxton et al., 2014). A cursory review of the disturbingly low graduation and retention rates of low socio-economic status and underrepresented student cohorts, among others, indicates many of the traditional models of student success have not worked. Unfortunately, many of our colleagues have confirmed our own observations regarding current practices: utilization of the same traditional approaches, in the same manner, again and again. Based on our research and collective expertise garnered across 45-plus years in higher education, it is evident that college administrators must do more than merely "think outside the box": they need to assume there is no box. Consequently, to foster greater student success, we propose a paradigm shift from traditional approaches to a more holistic and systemic perspective. Specifically, we recommend the infusion of student success initiatives (e.g. addressing increased retention, increased motivation and increased persistence rates) throughout institutional culture.

Why is Collaboration Necessary?

The U.S. Department of Education's Office of Postsecondary Education emphasized that "student success can only be attained through integrated and sustained strategies and programs that are part of an institutional culture" (2012, p. 25).

Throughout our careers in higher education, we have also observed that regardless of how well-intentioned a particular student success initiative, if it operates in isolation (in a "silo"), the likelihood of that program having significant and sustained positive outcomes is greatly reduced, if not eliminated. Too often, we have observed singular student support programs (such as workshops, activities, student success seminars, etc.) designed and implemented without any meaningful link to the vast array of other academic and co-curricular programs on campus. In fact, we regard the belief that a series of disconnected, one-shot programs developed without student input or a link to other programs will have a meaningful impact on student success as a symptom (delusion) of "institutional schizophrenia" (see Levy, Polnariev, & McGowan, 2011). Unfortunately, this has frequently been the "tried and true" approach to promoting student development and success, with less than stellar results.

Undoubtedly, continuing to follow the same path of marginal success or ineffectiveness can be demoralizing for students, staff and faculty alike. In addition, we fervently believe that the students we purport to serve deserve better. Moreover, we contend that our students have the right to expect the best we can offer. It is our contention that a menu of workshops that are sparsely (if at all) attended, based on the long-standing assumptions of educators without student input, with no valid assessment of impact on student learning or perception, is ultimately disrespectful to the students we are obligated to serve. We however applaud those who have moved the dialogue regarding student success outcomes forward so "the past fifteen years have seen accountability become a more important mandate in higher education" (Berger & Lyon, 2005, p. 26). Dr. George Kuh and his colleagues' (2010) book on *Student Success in College* powerfully describes programs, policies and practices that colleges should consider.

Where Does Assessment Fit In?

Assessment of program and institutional goals are of paramount value if done correctly, and for the right reasons. Accreditation notwithstanding, the impetus for assessment should be driven by internal institutional needs, including the use of assessment evidence to support academic program reviews, update curricula, revise learning goals and advance educational effectiveness (Gannon-Slater et al., 2014); the assessment process must align and validate the college's defined mission. As one of several recommendations made by Kuh and his colleagues, they maintain that higher education institutions "must cultivate an institutional culture that values gathering and using student learning outcomes data as integral to fostering student success and increasing institutional effectiveness" (Kuh, Jankowski, Ikenberry, & Kinzie, 2014, p. 35). They further posit that the use of assessment to inform institutional actions in order to continually improve student outcomes—essentially, the "closing of the loop"—remains minimally used across the nation (p. 35). Peter Ewell (1997) boldly notes that assessment "for the most part been attempted piecemeal within and across institutions" (as cited by Angelo, 1999, p. 3). For most institutions, assessment has largely been patchwork across and within divisions for the sake of accreditation instead of a systemic and systematic approach, infused across the curriculum, and for the sake of increased learning and student success.

In one of the formative articles on outcomes assessment, Dr. Thomas Angelo (1999) encourages leaders in academia to more seriously "plan and conduct our assessment projects at every step as if learning matters most—not just the students' learning, but ours, as well—then the distance between means and ends will be reduced and our chances of success increased" (p. 6). Building upon his earlier work, he (1999, pp. 5–6) put forward "*Four Pillars of Transformative Assessment*" worth highlighting:

1. *Build shared trust*: Begin by lowering social and interpersonal barriers to change.
2. *Build shared motivation*: Collectively identify goals worth working toward and problems worth solving—and consider the likely costs and benefits.
3. *Build a shared language*: Develop a collective understanding of new concepts (mental models) needed for transformation.
4. *Build shared guidelines*: Develop a short list of research-based guidelines for using assessment to promote learning.

The Benefits of Collaboration

Although we won't discuss the details further, we encourage you to review Angelo's entire (1999) seminal article. We would argue that these *four pillars* could be used to as "Four Pillars of Transformative *Collaboration*"—between two or more divisions, departments and/or teams. That is, for authentic and viable collaboration to occur for the sake of learning and improving student outcomes, colleagues must develop trust (pillar 1), work toward common goals using a shared language (pillars 2 and 3), and agreed upon metrics to measure and report out on the outcomes (pillar 4).

Collaboration between faculty and staff support higher levels of student engagement (Astin 1993; Pascarella & Terenzini, 2005). When faculty emphasize co-curricular involvement, students reported a higher level of engagement (Umbach & Wawrzynski, 2005). Trudy Banta and George Kuh (1998) posit that quality undergraduate experiences necessitate cooperation by the two college groups that "spend the most time with students: faculty members and student affairs professionals . . . Both groups share an interest in student learning, even as they emphasize different aspects" (p. 42). There is often a disconnect grounded in the perception of roles between Academic Affairs and Student Affairs: faculty do not clearly appreciate the roles that members of Student Affairs play in student learning; Student Affairs practitioners covet to be recognized as educators, similar to faculty members. Victor Arcelus (2011) coherently articulates that "cultural differences between the divisions, as well as the real and perceived differences in the deeply held values and beliefs about students and their education, hamper the pursuit of cross-divisional partnerships" (p. 64). Grounded in his ethnographic dissertation a few years earlier, Arcelus (2011) further argues that "the way people define *educator* can be one of the more significant barriers impeding faculty and student affairs partnerships, and it may be embedded in the cultural norms of both divisions" (p. 65). Hirsh and Burak (2002) state that "Student Affairs and Academic Affairs developed different understandings about the purposes of their work and how it should be measured" (p. 53; as cited by Gully & Mullendore, 2014, p. 661). We've even heard colleagues suggest that "both sides apparently speak different *languages.*"

In *Learning Reconsidered* (2004), Richard Keeling, as the manuscript's editor, advocates that the "holistic process of learning that places the student at the center of the learning experience" (p. 1) demands collaboration. This influential piece further supports the notion that collaboration demands cultural change. In the follow-up report, *Learning Reconsidered 2: A Practical Guide to Implementing a Campus-Wide Focus on the Student Experience* (2006), Keeling encourages a "culture of assessment." He explains that assessment helps teams achieve desired student learning outcomes as it supports institutional goals. One of the most persuasive and yet seemingly simple approaches recently posited for creating sustainable partnerships across both sides of the institution is grounded in the value of developing a *relationship* between faculty and Student Affairs members; such connection is essential for student success. Becki Elkins (who currently serves as both Cornell College's registrar and institutional research director) lucidly states that "we must reach across the divide not with the purposes of getting faculty to collaborate or convincing them of the value of Student Affairs. Rather we must reach out with the intentions of getting to know them, learning about their interests, and seeing students and student learning from their perspectives. As we build relationships, opportunities to engage in conversation about student learning will emerge" (Elkins, 2015, p. 45). A chief "factor that leads to the divide between student and academic affairs is the naturally segmented structure of higher education" (Reif, 2007, p. 94).

Having a Shared Vision

A focus on a common goal of *student learning* has been the central point bringing "both sides of the house" (that is, Academic and Student Affairs divisions) together (Gully & Mullendore, 2014). This fits well with Kuh's (1996) notion of "ethos of learning" (p. 136). Based on survey data, Professor Adriana Kezar (2001) further notes that "learning (35 percent) was by far the most important reason for engaging in collaboration" (p. 43). Well-intentioned, cooperative and coordinated activities from both sides, with partners who have positive attitudes, are necessary for successful outcomes (see Kezar, 2001). Furthermore, Kennedy (2004) found that a positive personal relationship between Chief Officers from both divisions is central to any successful and sustained partnership (as cited by Gully & Mullendore, 2014). Whitt and her colleagues (2008) succinctly note that ". . . partnerships require an understanding of contexts, cultures, and subcultures, and the political landscapes of the institution (and beyond). They require developing and maintaining a shared vision for the purposes of the partnership program and a shared understanding of what is important—and what is not— about student learning" (p. 248). Gully and Mullendore highlight that more work remains to be done documenting such collaboration at both the two-year and four-year college levels.

Remaining elusive, attaining and maintaining authentic reform in higher education is often limited to specific practices that fail to reach the system at-large (Bailey, 2013). In Vincent Tinto's book, *Completing College: Rethinking Institutional Action* (2012), he acknowledges the paramount challenge colleges face in moving their employees to implement promising programs and practices in synergistic ways. Tinto (2012) critiques colleges' complacency and spasmodic interventions. He further posits that "despite years of effort, institutions have yet to develop a coherent framework to guide their thinking about which actions matter most and how they should be organized and successfully implemented . . . Institutions consequently espouse a "laundry list of actions, one disconnected from another . . . [resulting in an] "uncoordinated patchwork" (p. 5).

As higher education researchers strive to successfully address the challenges identified above, there has been increased call for divisions of Academic and Student Affairs to forge partnerships—bridging divisions and creating a cohesive environment in which to improve student outcomes. Creating "effective partnerships between faculty and student affairs professionals is critical to maximizing the educational potential of colleges and universities" (Streit, 1993, p. 40). College leaders must realize the value of collaboration and how it can buttress their strategic priorities and plans. For most of our students, "learning experiences are neither academic nor cocurriculuar; they are college" (Arminio, Roberts, & Bonfiglio, 2009, p. 17). According to the *Student Learning Imperative* (ACPA, 1994), students benefit from numerous and diverse experiences during college. Furthermore, the more students:

> . . . are involved in a variety of activities inside and outside the classroom, the more they gain. Student affairs professionals attempt to make "seamless" what are often perceived by students to be disjointed, unconnected experiences by bridging organizational boundaries and forging collaborative partnerships with faculty and others to enhance student learning (p. 3).

Based on our experiences within both Academic and Student Affairs at a number of institutions, and in consultation with colleagues, it is evident that the design, implementation and assessment of these partnerships continue to prove challenging for a myriad of reasons—even after more than two decades since such a powerful publication (ACPA, 1994). Because culture is collectively formed, it thus requires a collective process in order to effectively change (Martin, 1992 as cited by Kezar, 2003). However, "most campuses are replete with the proverbial academic silos, which inhibit sharing information about student performance as well as promising practices" (Kuh et al., 2015, p. 21).

When we have presented our research nationally illustrating successful Student Affairs and Academic Affairs partnerships, a question that we are always asked is, "How do you break down the silos and get everyone working together on the same page when our culture is not used to this?" Consequently, this book attempts to answer that question via practical, evidence-based presentation of initiatives utilizing successful partnerships between Academic and Student Affairs. Our focus is on the "how-to," providing the reader examples and strategies that they can replicate to tailor best practices at their own institutions and use these approaches to make better informed, data-driven decisions that promote increased persistence, retention, learning outcomes and motivation. In addition, we provide the reader with the necessary tools, resources and assessment templates to foster cultural change. Essentially, readers will learn how to initiate a paradigm shift within their institutional culture, increasing the collaboration between Academic and Student Affairs in support of enhanced student success outcomes.

Why This Book is an Important Step on the Road to Greater Collaboration and Increased Student Success

As higher education becomes an increasingly essential resource for success in an ever-changing society that has become more knowledge- and technology-oriented, student success (as often measured by retention, graduation, job attainment, etc.), is more important than ever (Berger & Lyon, 2005). Given the multiple, and sometimes competing realities—including academic, social and psychological concerns confronted by today's college students—it is imperative that colleges and universities employ a proactive and holistic approach to fostering student success (Gordon & Levy, 2005). Regarding the proliferation of efforts to increase student success in higher education, Alan Seidman (2005) indicates that:

> in spite of these programs and services, retention from first to second year has not improved over time. The data also show that graduation rates have not improved over time. Logic dictates that the addition of programs and services should improve the retention of students, but in reality this seems not to be the case (p. xii).

Tinto (2012) further exclaims that higher education has not made any substantial advances in improving student retention in over 20 years since his theory on student attrition was first introduced. According to Swail, Redd & Perna (2003) in terms of college persistence and achievement, there are three particular forces that account for the entire spectrum of student outcomes: cognitive, social and institutional factors.

How Are We Doing So Far?

The first-year retention rate at community colleges has been low for decades (Barr & Schuetz, 2008). For example, both public and private community colleges average first-to-second year retention rates of 55% (ACT, 2012). Bryan Matthews (2009) noted that: "the first six weeks is the most critical time for a successful transition to the college environment. Based on decades of research, we are quite clear which academic and non-academic factors provide the greatest opportunity for college persistence and completion." Consequently, much attention has been devoted to impacting this "critical time" as defined by Matthews (2009), again with disappointing results. Unfortunately, student attrition, especially at community colleges, is one of the most significant problems facing our nation (ACT, 2012). Dropout is perhaps the greatest problem facing institutions of higher education (McCubbin, 2003; Braxton et al., 2014). Two key common metrics of *student success* include retention and graduation.

Berger and Lyon (2005) assert that "retention efforts are well established on virtually every campus in the nation, retention is used as a key indicator of institutional effectiveness" (p. 25). There are literally thousands of research studies on this key topic, and the field has even developed its own academic journal in the late 1990s, the *Journal of College Student Retention: Research, Theory & Practice*— devoted solely to this issue. Nevertheless, achieving positive outcomes regarding student success remains elusive. Although the data has not changed much over the past 50 years, two recent broad data examples reveal the degree to which retention and graduation has indeed challenged us. One of clearest and most powerful distinctions made in the literature comes from Dr. Linda Serra Hagedorn (2005), who said that "institutions retain students and students persist" (p. 92). For the purposes of their investigation, ACT[6] defines *retention rate*, as the "percent of first-time/full-time students who first enrolled in fall 2013 and were also enrolled in fall 2014 at the same institution" (2015, p. 2). According to the latest ACT (2015) findings:

- Only 54.7% of students at public two-year colleges, and 63.4% at private two-year colleges continue on to their sophomore year (see ACT, 2015, Table 1, p. 3).
- Among four-year colleges, retention rates averaged from 64.2% at public colleges to 70.2% at private colleges (see ACT, 2015, Table 1, p. 3).
- Among four-year colleges, retention rates were lowest among schools that offered only bachelor's degrees, higher among schools that offered bachelors

and master's degrees, and the highest among those which also offered doctorates (ACT, 2015).

Additionally, as we investigate the rates at which students *actually* complete their degrees across different types of institutions, more differences become apparent. For the purposes of this discussion, ACT defines "persistence to degree" as "completion in three years for associate degree; five years for BA/BS" (ACT, 2015, p. 7):

- The graduation rates among students at private two-year colleges was 40.2%—this was approximately double the rate of those of students from public two-year colleges which was 21.9% (ACT, 2015, Table 5, p. 7).
- The disparity in public vs. private college graduate rates continues to be apparent among students earning four-year degrees as well. Degree completion rates for four-year students attending public colleges was significantly lower at 36.4% as compared to their peers who attended private four-year colleges—57.2% graduated with a BA/BS within five years (ACT, 2015, Table 5, p. 7).

A Few Thoughts and Questions

- What happened to the staggering number of students who were not retained?
- What happened to those who didn't even have a chance to graduate?
- Why are these "success" outcomes acceptable to the public? To the city, state and federal systems which provide these institutions with further funding? Where is the accountability (and sanity)?

These data are certainly only a part of our story—part-time and transfer students, for example, are not included in data-set provided by these national agencies. Low graduation rates remain a persistent concern across higher education, but especially at community colleges (Barr & Schuetz, 2008). In *Answers in the Toolbox* (2004), Clifford Adelman emphatically states that "degree completion is the true bottom line for college administrators, state legislators, parents, and most importantly, students—not retention to the second year, not persistence without a degree, but completion" (p. 1). Increasing student degree attainment is essential to the economic health of the United States. The *American Graduation Initiative* was established by President Barack Obama as a national priority—the goal of the program is for our nation to add 5 million more graduates to the workforce in this decade to remain competitive in the global marketplace (Obama, 2009). In order to meet this lofty target, higher education institutions must significantly advance degree completion rates that have been fairly stable for decades, achieve equity in achievement gaps between minority groups and decrease overall student time-to-degree. Our nation's challenge is indeed great because by 2018, an estimated 63% of jobs will require some postsecondary education (Carnevale, Smith, & Stohl, 2010). Carnevale and his team further posit that "by 2018, the postsecondary system will have produced 3 million fewer college graduates than demanded by the labor market" (p. 16) A focus on connecting curricula to careers and appropriate learning outcomes will prove vital in meeting America's challenge. As such, intervening promptly to retain students beyond the first year is the "most efficient way to boost graduation rates" (Levitz, Noel, & Richter, 1999, p. 37). Cassazza and Silverman (2013) make a case that "support systems must align with particular student populations and institutional missions" (p. 8). They persuasively advance that at the very least, academic support must be intentional and systematic.

How Can We Think About This Differently?

To address these concerns, we have incorporated a non-traditional perspective within our work with colleagues to further promote student success. It is our contention that to truly impact students in a meaningful way, we must construct a *culture of success*, in which all facets of the institution are committed to student goal attainment. In essence, this is our higher education version of "it takes a village." A model that has significantly informed our work is the retention formula developed by Seidman (2005):

$$RET = E_{ID} + (E + I + C)_{IV}$$

In other words, Seidman (2005) states *Retention (RET)* is based on *Early Identification of Challenges* (E_{ID}) in addition to *Early, Intensive and Continuous Interventions* $(E + I + C)_{IV}$. we have found Seidman's focus on early intervention combined with a holistic and longitudinal model of support extremely valuable. These factors have been critical in guiding our efforts in promoting student success. Specifically, we have observed that meaningful attempts at promoting student success must be grounded in proactive, comprehensive and institution-wide interventions, not isolated within "silos." In essence, only an institutional culture truly committed to student success can actually achieve it. Bray articulated 30 years ago that "the single most important factor in advising at-risk students is helping them feel they are cared for by institutions" (Bray, 1985 as cited by Heisserer & Parette, 2002, p. 6). We believe students who feel that they belong and are valued as individuals are more likely to take advantage of the resources the institution provides for their learning. When ethics of membership and care characterize a college, students are more likely to perceive that the institution is concerned about their welfare and committed to their success (Kuh, Kinzie, Schuh, & Whitt, 2010).

Consequently, we have found that one valuable approach in developing a culture of success is an increased and genuine collaboration between the divisions of Academic and Student Affairs. McCoy and Gardner (2012) maintain that "departmental support of interdisciplinary work is key to successful collaboration" (p. 47). In their seminal work, Pascarella and Terenzini (2005) argue that "what happens to students after they enroll at a college or university is more important than the structural characteristics of the institution they attend" (p. 642). They also highlight that:

> Students' in- and out-of-class experiences are interconnected components of complex processes shaping student change and development (associated with) classroom experiences and pedagogies, coursework, institutional environments and cultures, and an array of out-of-class activities (p. 629).

Confirmation of This Book's Importance

Researchers have documented the benefits of collaboration between Academic Affairs and Student Affairs, such as increased student integration and engagement in the college community (Kezar, 2003; Love & Love, 1995). Hagedorn (2005) states "students' beliefs are affected by the interaction between the student and different components of the institution similar to interaction between employees and corporations." However, creating partnerships between Academic and Student Affairs have frequently proven problematic for various reasons. A significant challenge to the development of a holistic, truly success-oriented institutional culture has been the prescribed roles of many faculty. Kuh (2009) skillfully articulated that:

> ... this shift toward a student- or learner-centered philosophy is a long way from being fully realized in most colleges and universities. For example, in state-assisted colleges, where the heavy emphasis on undergraduate instruction is often coupled with aspirations to move up in the prestige pecking order, teaching loads remain heavy even as expectations for scholarly productivity increase. In addition, many faculty members often feel conflicted between devoting time to research (to which many were socialized to value over teaching in graduate school) and the daily demands of teaching and student advising. At some types of institutions, such as community colleges, faculty members have heavy teaching loads and many students in their classes who require compensatory assistance to succeed academically (p. 66).

The primary negative characteristic linked to student attrition was inadequate academic advising (Tinto, 1987; Wycoff, 1999; Habley, 2004; Pascarella & Terenzini, 2005). Intrusive academic advising, along with other rigorous interventions, seem to have a positive influence on measures of student success (Fowler & Boylan, 2010). In part due to the growth of scarce resources, the

National Science Foundation (NSF) and the National Institutes for Health (NIH) for example, have called for more interdisciplinary scholarship (McCoy & Gardner, 2012). Clearly, as many in higher education are faced with "doing more with less" (Levy, 2010, cited in Dembicki, 2010), the need to collaborate and pool resources via a cross-divisional perspective becomes even more imperative. Having had the opportunity to develop, implement and assess holistic and collaborative approaches to student success, we have been able to witness the significant impact of such a paradigm shift within institutional culture. For example, readers will learn how one institution presented faculty with an opportunity to participate in a new campus-wide advising initiative and achieved a 100% increase in participation (from fall 2008 with 48 faculty; to fall 2009 with 84; and to fall 2010 with 96 faculty) within a two-year period and with *no resistance*. We found faculty wanted to support student success when given the opportunity coupled with the appropriate support mechanisms.

When we have presented similar data at numerous professional conferences across the nation, we are frequently asked, "How much did you have to pay the faculty to participate?" People are shocked when we provide them with the answer: "Zero!" Often, the next question asked was, "How bloody was the fighting with the faculty union over this?" Again, workshop participants are stunned when we explain that we received no resistance at all. We were quite encouraged when our data revealed that 94% of the 1500-plus students who interacted with the faculty at these various advising programs reported that they *benefited the way they hoped to* and 95% said *they were motivated to take next steps to achieve their goals.*

Readers will learn how we informed an institutional paradigm shift to achieve these results and how to replicate this approach at their institutions. In addition, readers will learn how to use student data regarding learning outcomes and proposed next steps to inform enhanced programming. Not only do we believe that a holistic, collaborative approach is the most effective way to promote student empowerment and success, the quantitative and qualitative data we present validate the infinite possibilities of such an approach. It is our sincere hope that readers of this book will be motivated and better prepared to carry the torch by working to increase cross-divisional partnerships at their institutions in support of student success.

How This Book Can Help You and Your Students

As previously stated, our intention is to present our colleagues with a resource that demonstrates how to design, implement and evaluate a vast array of collaborative programs promoting student success. Our main objective is to provide the reader with a number of "takeaways" regarding:

1.   Increase readers' knowledge of current research regarding use of cross-divisional collaboration to create and enhance a culture of *success across the institution.*

2. Demonstrate how readers can reproduce collaborative best practices with respect to the following initiatives:

    a) curricular infusion of key success and retention information;
    b) curricular infusion of career development pathways;
    c) service-learning and community volunteerism;
    d) faculty engagement in developmental advising;
    e) faculty engagement in assessment-based orientation programming;
    f) holistic approaches to developing and assessing successful "bridge" programs for at-risk and developmental students;
    g) strategic planning informed by a collaborative paradigm;
    h) the utilization of assessment feedback loops to inform all success initiatives.

3. Provide structure for the development and utilization of assessment templates that will guide program evaluation, revision and enhancement.
4. Support readers in initiating a paradigm shift within their institution toward enhanced collaboration, more effective communication, increased accountability and increased data-driven decision making.

Our book is a passionate and evidence-based approach toward appreciating collaborative efforts for achieving student success. It is comprised of expert testimonies and examples from various higher education areas organized into three main interconnected sections focused on Academic and Student Affairs collaboration with an overarching goal toward the student success imperative: I—*Curricular Infusion* (of career development pathways for both English as a Second Language (ESL) and college-ready students, and service-learning); II—*Faculty Engagement* and *Targeted Student Programs* (addressing developmental advising, assessment-based orientation programming, bridge programs for at-risk students, and academic support services); and III—*Creating Collaborative Synergy*. The last section in the book vis-à-vis Strategic Planning helps readers to more conceptually and systemically connect goals and activities discussed from the previous two sections in order to maximize student success. We also provide a summary of our concluding thoughts and suggestions to move collaborative efforts of college programming at your institutions forward.

To advance cross-divisional partnerships, leaders from both Academic and Student Affairs "need to cultivate a synergistic relationship between academic and student affairs that goes beyond a potentially successful collaborative project. Faculty and staff should relentlessly pursue campus dialogue that fosters deep institution-wide commitment to a shared approach for student learning" (Arcelus, 2011, p. 72). As pointed out in an excellent book on shared governance, there is clearly a need for enhanced institutional mechanisms affording more effective and collaborative opportunities to make better institutional decisions which support student success (Bowen & Tobin, 2015). It is our hope that the readers of this book will use the shared information to continue to have dialogues beyond the silos and across divisions. We will be extremely proud and grateful if this book contributes to a new "cultural norm" of increased collaboration with student success as the central tenet driving institutional decisions.

Notes

1. NASPA now refers to Student Affairs Administrators in Higher Education: https://en.wikipedia.org/wiki/NASPA_-_Student_Affairs_Administrators_in_Higher_Education (accessed December 1, 2015).
2. The NASPA–SAPAA Promising Practices team will review and re-evaluate the award rubric for 2017 so that it more effectively addresses our broader goals. This direction will help us elevate the organization and award submitters to a higher standard of excellence.
3. NASPA–SAPAA Promising Practices award (2016) rubric: www.naspa.org/about/awards/knowledge-communities/promising-practices-award2 (accessed December 1, 2015).
4. As taken from its website, NACADA promotes and supports quality academic advising in institutions of higher education to enhance the educational development of students: www.nacada.ksu.edu/ (accessed December 1, 2015).
5. National Center for Higher Education Management Systems (NCHEMS), a research and development center founded to improve the management effectiveness of colleges and universities. Learn more about NCHEMS: www.nchems.org/(accessed December 1, 2015).
6. ACT's mission is to help people achieve education and workplace success: www.act.org/aboutact/overview.html (accessed December 1, 2015).

References

ACT. (2012). National collegiate retention and persistence to degree rates. Retrieved on December 1, 2015 from: www.act.org/research/policymakers/pdf/retain_2012.pdf.

Adelman, C. (2004). Answers in the toolbox. Retrieved on December 1, 2015 from: www.ed.gov/pubs/Toolbox/index.html.

American College Personnel Association (ACPA). (1994). The student learning imperative: Implications for student affairs. Retrieved on December 1, 2015 from: www.myacpa.org/sites/default/files/ACPA%27s%20Student%20Learning%20Imperative.pdf.

Angelo, T. A. (1999). Doing assessment as if learning matters most. *AAHE Bulletin, 51*(9), 3–6.

Arcelus, V. J. (2011). If Student Affairs-Academic Affairs Collaboration is Such a Good Idea, Why Are There So Few Examples of These Partnerships in American Higher Education? In P. M. Magolda, & M. B. Baxter Magolda (Eds.) *Contested issues in student affairs: Diverse perspectives and respectful dialogue* (Chapter 4: pp. 61–74). Sterling, VA: Stylus.

Arminio, J., Roberts, D. C., & Bonfiglio, R. (2009). The professionalization of student learning practice: An ethos of scholarship. *About Campus, 14*(1), 16–20.

Astin, A. (1993). *What matters in college? Four critical years revisited.* San Francisco, CA: Jossey-Bass.

Bailey, T. (2013). Foreword. In V. Smith Morest (Ed.) *Community college student success: From boardrooms to classrooms* (pp. xiii–xvi). ACE Series on Community Colleges. London: Rowman & Littlefield Publishers.

Bailey, T. R., Jaggars, S. S., & Jenkins, D. (2015). *Redesigning America's community colleges: A clearer path to student success*. Cambridge, MA: Harvard University Press.

Banta, T. W., & Kuh, G. D. (1998). A missing link in assessment: Collaboration between Academic and Student Affairs Professionals. *Change, 30*(2), 40–46.

Barr, J., & Schuetz, P. (2008). Overview of foundational issues. Are Community Colleges Underprepared for Underprepared Students? *New Directions for Community Colleges, 144*, 7–16.

Berger, J. B., & Lyon, S. C. (2005). Past to present: A historical look at retention. In A. Seidman (Ed.), *College student retention* (pp. 1–29). Westport, CT: Praeger Publishers.

Bok, D. (2015). *Higher education in America*. Princeton, NJ: Princeton University Press.

Bowen, W. G., & Tobin, E. M. (2015). *Locus of authority: The evolution of faculty roles in the governance of higher education*. Princeton, NJ: Princeton University Press.

Braxton, J. M., Doyle, W. R., Hartley III, H. V., Hirschy, A. S., Jones, W. A., & McLendon, M. K. (2014). *Rethinking college student retention*. San Francisco, CA: John Wiley & Sons.

Carnevale, A. P., Smith, N., & Strohl, J. (2010). *Help wanted: Projections of job and education requirements through 2018*. Indianapolis, IN: Lumina Foundation.

Casazza, M. E., & Silverman, S. L. (2013). Meaningful access and support: The path to college completion. Council of Learning Assistance and Developmental Associations (CLADEA). Retrieved on December 1, 2015 from: http://aladenet.org/uploads/3/2/3/8/3238519/cladea_white_paper_final.pdf.

Castleman, B. L., Schwartz, S., & Baum, S. (2015). *Decision making for student success: Behavioral insights to improve college access and persistence*. New York: Routledge.

Chickering A. W., & Gamson, Z. F. (1987). Seven principles for good practice in undergraduate education. *AAHE Bulletin, 39*, 3–7. Retrieved on December 10, 2011 from: http://files.eric.ed.gov/fulltext/ED282491.pdf.

Dembicki, M. (2010, June 25). Counselors see more severity, complexity among student cases. *The Community College Times*. Retrieved from: www.ccdaily.com/Pages/Campus-Issues/Counselors-see-more-severity-complexity-among-student-cases.aspx.

Elkins, B. (2015). Looking back and ahead: What we must learn from 30 years of student affairs assessment. *New Directions for Student Services, 151*, 39–48.

Ewell, P. T. (2005). Can assessment serve accountability? It depends on the question. In J. C. Burke (Ed.) *Achieving accountability in higher education: Balancing public, academic, and market demands* (pp. 104–124). San Francisco, CA: John Wiley & Sons.

Fowler, P. R., & Boylan, H. R. (2010). Increasing student success and retention: A multidimensional approach. *Journal of Developmental Education, 34*(2), 2–10.

Gannon-Slater, N., Ikenberry, S., Jankowski, N., & Kuh, G. (2014). Institutional assessment practices across accreditation regions. Retrieved on December 1, 2015 from: www.learningoutcomeassessment.org/documents/Accreditation%20report.pdf.

Garza Mitchell, R, L., & Maldanado, C. (2015). Strategic planning for new presidents: Developing an entrance plan. *Community College Journal of Research and Practice, 39*, 113–121.

Gordon, L., & Levy, M. (2005). Career Transitions. In J. S. Taylor & G. S. Wilson, G.S. (Eds.) *Comprehensive perspectives in applied sports psychology: From researcher and consultant to coach and athlete* (pp. 249–266). Champaign, IL: Human Kinetics Press.

Gully, N. Y., & Mullendore, R. H. (2014). Student affairs and academic affairs collaborations in the community college setting. *Community College Journal of Research and Practice, 38*(7), 661–673.

Habely, W. R. (2004). *The status of academic advising: Findings from the ACT Sixth National Survey.* National Academic Advising Association.

Hagedorn, L. S. (2005). How to define retention. College student retention formula for student success, 90–105. Retrieved on December 1, 2015 from: http://files.eric.ed.gov/fulltext/ED493674.pdf.

Heisserer, D., & Parette, P., (2002), Advising at-risk students in college and university settings. *College Student Journal, 36*(1), 1–12.

Jenkins, D. (2014). Redesigning community colleges for student success: Overview of the guided pathways approach.

Keeling, R. (Ed.). (2004). *Learning reconsidered: A campus-wide focus on the student experience.* Washington, DC: American College Personnel Association and National Association of School Personnel Administrators. Retrieved on December 1, 2015 from: www.naspa.org/images/uploads/main/Learning_Reconsidered_Report.pdf.

Keeling, R. P. (Ed.) (2006). *Learning reconsidered 2: A practical guide to implementing a campus-wide focus on the student experience.* Washington, DC: American College Personnel Association, Association of College and Housing Officers—International, Association of College Unions—International, National Academic Advising Association, National Association of Campus Activities, National Association of Student Personnel Administrators, & National Intramural—Recreational Sports Association.

Kezar, A. (2001). Documenting the landscape: Results of a national study on academic and student affairs collaborations. *New Directions for Higher Education, 116,* 39–51.

Kezar, A. (2003). Achieving student success: Strategies for creating partnerships between academic and student affairs. *Innovative Higher Education, 28*(2), 137–156.

Kezar, A., & Maxey, D. (2014, fall). Faculty matter: So why doesn't everyone think so? *Thought & Action,* 29–44.

Kimmens, R. M. (2014). *Presidential leadership practices of high-performing community colleges* (Doctoral dissertation, Northern Arizona University).

Kinzie, J., & Kuh, G. D. (2004). Going deep: Learning from campuses that share responsibility for student success. *About Campus, 9*(5), 2–8.

Kuh, G. D. (1996). Guiding principles for creating seamless learning environments for undergraduates. *Journal of College Student Development, 37*(2), 135–148.

Kuh, G. D. (2009). Understanding campus environments. In G. McClellan and J. Stringer (Eds.) *Handbook on student affairs administration* (3rd ed.) (Chapter 4: pp. 59–80). San Francisco, CA: Jossey-Bass.

Kuh, G. D., Ikenberry, S. O., Jankowski, N., Reese Cain, T., Ewell, P., Hutchings, P., & Kinzie, J. (2015). *Using evidence of student learning to improve higher education.* San Francisco: Jossey-Bass.

Kuh, G. D., Jankowski, N., Ikenberry, S. O., & Kinzie, J. (2014). Knowing what students know and can do: The current state of student learning outcomes assessment in US colleges and universities. Urbana, IL: University of Illinois and Indiana University, National Institute for Learning Outcomes Assessment (NILOA). Retrieved on December 1, 2015 from: http://utsa.edu/students/sanews/2014/issue05/files/2013SurveyReportFinal.pdf.

Kuh, G. D., Kinzie, J., Buckley, J. A., Bridges, B. K., & Hayek, J. C. (2006). What matters to student success: A review of the literature commissioned report for the national symposium on postsecondary student success: Spearheading a dialog on student success. Washington, DC: National Postsecondary Education Cooperative. Retrieved on December 1, 2015 from: http://nces.ed.gov/npec/pdf/kuh_team_report.pdf.

Kuh, G. D., Kinzie, J., Schuh, J. H., & Whitt, E. J. (2010). *Student success in college: Creating conditions that matter.* San Francisco, CA: John Wiley & Sons.

Levitz, R. S., Noel, L., & Richter, B. J. (1999). Strategic moves for retention success. In G.H. Gaither (Ed.), *Promising practices in recruitment remediation, and retention* (pp. 31–50). (New Directions for higher Education, 108). San Francisco, CA: Jossey-Bass.

Levy, M. A., Polnariev, B. A., & McGowan, L. (2011, August). The integration of reality-based programming to address "schizophrenic" support services. Student Affairs News (SAN) website: www.studentaffairsnews.com (retrieved December 1, 2015).

Love, P. G., & Love, A. G. (1995). Enhancing student learning: Intellectual, social, and emotional integration. ERIC Clearinghouse on Higher Education Washington DC. Retrieved on December 1, 2015 from: http://eric.ed.gov/?id=ED400741.

Matthews, B. (2009, November, 2). Retention Matters. *Inside Higher Ed.* Retrieved on December 1, 2015 from: www.insidehighered.com/views/2009/11/02/matthews# sthash.pngb3LMo.dpbs.

McCoy, S. K., & Gardner, S. K. (2012). Interdisciplinary collaboration on campus: Five questions. *Change: The Magazine of Higher Learning, 44*(6), 44–49.

McCubbin, I. (2003). An examination of criticisms made of Tinto's 1975 student integration model of attrition. Retrieved on December 1, 2015 from: www.psy.gla. ac.uk/steve/located/icubb.pdf.

Myers, S. (2014). *Enhancing collaboration by examining faculty and student affairs professionals through an intercultural lens.* Washington, DC: ACPA.

Obama, B. (2009, July 14). Excerpts of the President's remarks in Warren, Michigan and fact sheet on the American Graudation Initiative. Warren, Michigan. Retrieved December 1, 2015 from: www.whitehouse.gov/the-press-office/excerpts presidents-remarks-warren-michigan-and-fact-sheet-american-graduation-init.

Office of Postsecondary Education. (2012). Evidence meets practice: Institutional strategies to increase college completion. Alexandria, VA: U.S. Department of Education. Retrieved on December 1, 2015 from: www.edpubs.gov/document/ed005 371p.pdf.

Pascarella, E. T., & Terenzini, P. T. (2005). *How college affects students: A third decade of research.* San Francisco, CA: Jossey-Bass.

Polnariev, B. A., McGowan, L., & Levy, M. A. (2010). *Reframing faculty resistance to academic advising.* National Academic Advising Association (NACADA) 2010 Annual Conference. October 6, 2010.

Reif, G. (2015). Higher education's missing link: Examining the gap between academic and student affairs and implications for the student experience. *The Vermont Connection, 28*(1), 90–99.

Seidman, A. (Ed.). (2005). *College student retention: formula for student success.* Westport, CT: ACE/Praeger.

Streit, C. (1993). Between a rock and a hard place: Barriers to collaboration between Academic and Student Affairs. *Journal of Higher Education Management, 9*, 39–45.

Swail, S. W., Redd, K. E., & Perna, L. W. (2003). ASHE-ERIC higher education report: 30. Retrieved on December 1, 2015 from: www.educationalpolicy.org/pdf/Swail_ Retention_Book.pdf.

Terenzini, P. T. (2007, October 18). *From myopic to systemic thinking.* NACADA 31st Annual Conference on Academic Advising, in Baltimore, MD.

Tinto, V. (1982). Limits of theory and practice in student attrition. *Journal of Higher Education, 53*, 687–700.

Tinto, V. (1987). *Leaving college: Rethinking the causes and cures of student attrition.* Chicago, IL: University of Chicago Press.

Tinto, V. (2012). *Completing college: Rethinking institutional action.* Chicago, IL: *University of Chicago Press.*

Umbach, P. D., & Wawrzynski, M. R. (2005). Faculty do matter: The role of college faculty in student learning and engagement. *Research in Higher Education, 46*(2), 153–184.

Whitt, E. J., Nesheim, B. E., Guentzel, M. J., Kellogg, A. H., McDonald, W. M., & Wells, C. A. (2008). "Principles of good practice" for academic and student affairs partnership programs. *Journal of College Student Development, 49*(3), 235–249.

Wycoff, S. C. (1999). The academic advising process in higher education: History, research, and improvement. *Recruitment & Retention in Higher Education, 13,* 1–3.

SECTION I
Curricular Infusion

2

CURRICULAR INFUSION OF STUDENT SUCCESS STRATEGIES

Sharon O'Connor, Mitchell A. Levy and Bernard A. Polnariev

Why Does This Matter?

The first year of college can be an overwhelming time of change for many students. Some students are leaving the familiar world of high school while others are returning from years raising families or participating in the work force (Tinto, as cited in Gardner, 2013). Many students continue these responsibilities concurrently with their education. Every student arrives with his or her own set of unique strengths and challenges. It is imperative that Student Affairs staff and faculty members increase their understanding of the challenges faced by students and the barriers that they present to students' academic success and ultimate goal achievement to more effectively assist them through this often difficult time of transition. Toblowsky, Mamrick, and Cox (2005) have stated that a freshman-year seminar can provide for an easier transition to campus life by assisting students in focusing on career and academic goals. As we illustrated with solid data from American College Testing (ACT) in Chapter 1, retaining and graduating students has proven quite challenging!

The initial period of transition to higher education is a time when students may feel isolated and disconnected from what was previously familiar. Particularly for students living away from home for the first time, feelings of homesickness can present challenges for adjustment to the college environment. Students experiencing increased feelings of homesickness have been found to have reduced feelings of self-efficacy when compared to peers experiencing lower levels of homesickness (Smith, 2007). Among female students in particular, feelings of homesickness have been associated with increased "fear of failure" as well as greater test anxiety (p. 3). Students experiencing homesickness have lower "quality of attention," and are less likely to engage in behaviors which contribute to success including preparation for exams and seeking out help from teachers and peers (p. 3).

Although homesickness may not present as frequently as a factor among community college students, these students face a unique set of challenges that can impact persistence and success during their first year. Academically, community college students are often less likely to have the foundation of preparation more common among four-year students. Nearly half of community college students "end-up" in remedial classes which not only costs money (they often do not have), and takes significant time to complete (which is often perceived as a burden), but offers no credit toward graduation (Rath, Rock, & Laferriere, 2013). In addition to being academically underprepared, community college students may experience challenges related to "social skills, study habits, and time management strategies, necessary to succeed in college" (Rath et al., 2013, p. 3).

Community college students are also more likely than their peers who attend four-year colleges to work while attending school. Well over half (60%) of students attending community college "work 20 hours a week, and 25% work 35 hours a week" (Rath et al., 2013, p. 3). Community college students are more likely to be more financially independent and, thus, more financially vulnerable. These students are also more likely to have childcare or other family responsibilities outside of school, which can lead to students feeling overwhelmed and pulled in many directions (Rath et al., 2013, p. 3).

College students are vulnerable to attrition "during the initial six weeks of the first semester" (Reid, 2009, p. 20; see Braxton, Doyle, Hartley III, Hirschy, Jones, & McLendon, 2014). It is during this initial transition to higher education that students may find that they are academically underprepared, anxious about being among a new group of peers or overwhelmed by the increased diversity encountered at college (Reid, 2009). As students often have difficulty during this initial period of transition, it is this time when integration into the community of the institution is most important (Tinto, as cited in Gardner, 2013). This time of transition presents the challenge/opportunity for the student to forge new connections, as well as an opportunity for the college to engage the student by creating opportunities to facilitate these new connections. If students are able to become engaged in the community and feel connected to their peers and faculty, they are more likely to continue in their educational pursuits (Gardner, 2013).

Among the efforts of schools to promote integration and increase student retention, the first-year seminar course has been widely implemented. A 2011 study by Clark and Cundiff identified that students who engaged in first-year seminar courses were more likely to continue their educations (as cited in Tampke & Raifu, 2013). Although these courses vary from one institution to another, and even from one instructor to another, they have some relatively common elements. First-year experience courses may integrate concepts such as study skills, time management and promote understanding among students of what is expected of them academically within the college setting. As these elements are deftly infused into the first-year experience curriculum, students' feelings of self-efficacy may increase as they gain the skills to manage the challenges of higher education, and the demands of college become less nebulous (Porter & Swing, 2006). "Academically," Goodman and Pascarella (2006) express, "students who participate in first-year seminars have more positive perceptions of themselves as learners. These students achieve higher grades in college" (p. 27). Students with greater self-esteem and increased positive self-perception are also more likely to demonstrate improved coping during times of stress, as well as stronger belief that they can overcome challenges (Eisenbarth, 2012).

How a student feels about his or her own ability to learn and grasp new material is crucial as these beliefs can turn into self-fulfilling prophecies. We want to encourage students to learn in academic areas that may be out of their comfort zones by reducing fear of failure. If we can help students understand that challenges, failures and setbacks can be natural elements of the learning process, students may be more likely to explore new academic territory and be more resilient to the challenges ahead. According to Mangels, Butterfield, Lamb, Good, & Dweck (2006), students who "believe intelligence is a fixed entity," are more "vulnerable to negative feedback and likely to disengage from challenging learning opportunities . . . In contrast, students who believe intelligence is malleable" (Mangels et al., 2006, p. 75) are more resilient when failures happen.

Porter and Swing (2006) also suggest that along with academic information, integration of health and wellness information into the curriculum has a positive effect on first-year students. They posit that inclusion of this information may help newly independent students relieve anxiety or answer questions they may have about their own health concerns, but can also aid in fostering a connectedness to staff as the inclusion of a health and wellness element may convey an inherent care and concern for the students (Porter & Swing, 2006). This holistic approach can help students adopt healthier habits for self-care, as well as feel a tangible support from faculty and staff, equipping students to manage an otherwise stressful time (Porter & Swing, 2006).

In addition to providing a foundation of connection to faculty and staff members, the first-year seminar offers students a chance to connect with other new students in their academic peer groups. In schools where cohorts or "learning communities" have been implemented, groups of students may remain together after completing first-year experience courses for many of their subsequent courses throughout the remainder of their programs (Tampke & Raifu, 2013). Bailey and his colleagues (2015) state that "mandatory student success courses, well-designed web-based information, and explicit career counseling help students explore their options and choose a college-level program of study as quickly as possible" (p. 17). As we continue this chapter, we will explore best practices for implementation of first-year seminars to maximize positive outcomes on retention and overall student success.

Promising Practices

One implementation of curricular infusion, which has had a significant impact on student success research, is the evolution of student success or freshman seminar courses. A review of the literature addressing student retention, persistence, engagement and success, among other variables, illustrates how integral these initiatives have been to current student development practices (see Cook & Lewis, 2007; Keup & Petschauer, 2011). This section will identify the value and importance of developing courses (or seminars) which do not focus on didactic presentation of academic content, rather, there is a curricular focus on the academic "survival skills" necessary to increase the likelihood of retention, persistence and ultimate goal attainment (transfer or graduation).

Freshman seminar courses typically address topics identified as "academic or study skills," often including introduction to time management, effective note-taking (e.g. Cornell method), and how to read text-books with increased comprehension and retention (e.g. SQ4R method). However, in addition to academic skills development, student success seminars often address non-academic issues, which often have been identified as "psycho-educational" and more recently fall within the category of "non-cognitive factors" (Goodman & Pascarella, 2006). These topics often include communication skills (e.g. assertive communication), substance abuse prevention, date and acquaintance rape, financial management, forming healthy interpersonal relationships, prevention of STDs and HIV, multi-cultural awareness and diversity appreciation, and more recent emerging issues (anti-bullying). Given the increasing number of students who report having personal issues when entering college, many administrators view the opportunity to educate students regarding these topics as essential (see Gallagher's 2009 National Survey of Counseling Directors findings; see also the interview of Dr. Levy conducted by Dembicki, 2010). Quite simply, as the number and severity of student psycho-social issues increases, a programmatic structure allowing for standardized and mandated discussion of these topics is often viewed as essential for promoting positive student development (Dembicki, 2010).

If one of the primary objectives of student success programs is to help students transition successfully into institutional culture, then it is imperative that diverse facets within that culture collaborate to create a "network of care" (O'Connor, Polnariev, & Levy, 2012). For example, at many institutions, the division of Academic Affairs is often responsible for the administration of these courses within the traditional academic schedule. However, Student Affairs professionals often teach these courses, and more importantly, provide the necessary training regarding those psycho-educational topics that require a sensitivity to, and awareness of, student development issues (O'Connor et al., 2012; Sue, Arredondo, and McDavis, 1992). In essence, at many institutions, students participate in an academic seminar whose curriculum introduces them to social, psychological and personal topics that are often addressed by professional counselors and mental health clinicians.

Case Example—Accelerated Study in Associated Programs (ASAP)

A powerful example:

> This program has changed my life. In less than two years, the ASAP program has provided resources and support which have eliminated all obstacles to my educational success and personal fulfillment . . . ASAP . . . has re-affirmed my belief in community learning; we all benefit from our collective success. My story of success is just one of many that can be told, nevertheless, they all have one common theme; we are part of a program that believed more in us than we believed in ourselves . . . this program has allowed its students to seek new educational "horizons." I will forever be in debt to the hard work and diligence of LaGuardia's ASAP staff for providing me the opportunity to be more than I even thought I could be.
>
> LaGuardia ASAP cohort 1 alumni
> (received via email on March 11, 2009)

CUNY's *Accelerated Study in Associated Programs* (or ASAP)[1] has indeed transformed many lives. It is an example of a successful college bridge program which has demonstrated impressive outcomes with respect to curricular infusion, advisement, remediation, retention and graduation, which was directed by one of the authors (Dr. Polnariev) for almost four years at LaGuardia Community College in NYC. ASAP's primary goal is to graduate a minimum of 50% of their students within three years (truly ASAP)—a grand undertaking given the less than inspiring national completion rates at urban community colleges (see outcomes from Chapter 2; other ASAP key outcomes are discussed in Chapter 7). Sue Scrivener, a senior MDRC associate, noted that it's "designed to address multiple potential barriers to student success and ASAP provides structure and support for up to three years" (Scrivener, Weiss, Ratledge, Rudd, Sommo, & Fresques, 2015, p. 28). ASAP's defining components include intrusive advisement grounded in a case-load model (managed by full-time dedicated advisors), abundant tutoring (provided by part-time staff and coordinated by a full-time advisor; see Jaafar, Toce, & Polnariev, 2016 to learn more about LaGuardia's Community College's math and also ASAP tutoring impact), linked ASAP courses (including a first-year ASAP seminar), and several pivotal financial incentives (including free textbooks, school travel funds and tuition to those who qualify).

In a recent press release as part of his powerful proposal for a free community college model, President Obama (2015) stated that:

> colleges must also adopt promising and evidence-based institutional reforms to improve student outcomes, such as the effective Accelerated Study in Associate Programs (ASAP) programs at the City University of New York

(CUNY) which waive tuition, help students pay for books and transit costs, and provide academic advising and supportive scheduling programs to better meet the needs of participating students, resulting in greater gains in college persistence and degree completion.

ASAP has gained national attention for their outstanding results that have been evaluated by both CUNY and also MDRC[2] as part of a five-year random-assignment study. MDRC researchers stated that ASAP's effects seem to be "unparalleled in large-scale experimental evaluations of programs in higher education" (Scrivener and Weiss, 2013, p. 2). For background purposes, CUNY ASAP has supported over 6,300 students since 2007 (seven cohorts at the time of this writing), with over two-thirds of the students receiving some financial aid, approximately three-quarters being identified as "minorities" (specifically either Black and/or Hispanic). Furthermore, one of the authors (Dr. Polnariev) serves on the LaGuardia Community College ASAP expansion committee, which has planned to significantly scale the program—supporting approximately 200 freshmen in 2007 to almost 2,000 new students by fall 2016 (which is approximately 40 per cent of the college's incoming student body). CUNY ASAP will support the success of over 13,000 new students across the CUNY system starting in fall 2016 (see Scrivener et al., 2015; also see Colangelo & Chapman, 2015).

Research findings consistently buttress the positive impact that first-year seminars have on both student academic and social integration (e.g. Cho & Karp, 2013; Cuseo, 2005; Tinto, 1993). For example, from 2008 through 2011, ASAP advisors facilitated weekly seminars in collaboration with the ASAP career and employment specialist. Guests included faculty from various majors, college leaders such as vice presidents from both Academic Affairs and Student Affairs, and also *EKOarts*[3] (a group of psycho-educational and motivational performers). LaGuardia's ASAP seminar was developed to meet build social capital for non-traditional freshman while introducing them to the college and ASAP policies and resources, providing group advisement, linking majors and career topics and connecting them to faculty partners.

In addition to providing social support, the ASAP Leadership seminar was developed to further help students by teaching necessary "soft skills" that are essential for success, including problem-solving skills, study skills and stress and time management. Rutschow and her MDRC colleagues (2012) led an evaluation of a success course targeting students with remedial education needs. They found that the success course had an encouraging impact on students' self-reported interdependence, self-awareness, emotional intelligence and engagement in college among students with low levels of these attributes (Rutschow, Cullinan, & Welbeck, 2012). The ASAP seminar was yet another platform for ASAP advisors and students to connect with faculty from the limited number of ASAP-supported majors. The ASAP team collaborated with faculty members to provide success expectations, connect program coursework and majors to related careers, and at its very root, help student develop relationships with faculty who will educate them as they progress through their majors. As a snapshot example, there were 154 students between ASAP cohorts 2 and 3 (i.e. students who joined the program in fall 2009 and spring 2010, respectively) who were enrolled in the ASAP seminar during the spring 2010 semester; 64% (n = 99 out of 154 students) were officially registered for the 0-credit, 1-hour, 12-week ASAP Leadership seminar. Using a summative assessment student survey (from 89 spring 2010 seminar respondents) several valuable ASAP Leadership seminar findings include:

- 87% found the overall seminar "very useful" or "useful";
- 84% have a better understanding of the resources available on campus;
- 77% reported being "very satisfied" or "satisfied" with the *Building Self-Confidence* and *Stress Reduction/Management* workshops (led by *EKOarts*);
- 86% agreed that they made stronger career and major connections with the faculty presenters (based on three faculty class presentations);
- 89% "learned a lot" or "somewhat" from the *Employing Interdependence, Accepting Personal Responsibility and Developing Emotional Intelligence* workshops (led by the ASAP academic advisors).

Although the above seminar survey results were generally encouraging, the ASAP team met several times thereafter to reflect and discuss improving the outcomes. The team consequently revised the workshops that both ASAP advisors and *EKOarts* led in fall 2010 based on the spring 2010 quantitative and qualitative outcomes. Specifically, advisor-led lesson plans were updated to be more interactive and connected to how the information will be useful for job and career placement—this was based on feedback from several students in the comments section on how to improve the seminar (*we listened!-* B. Polnariev). Advisor-led survey results (from 60 fall 2010 seminar respondents) showed slight positive gains:

- 89% found the overall seminar "very useful" or "useful"—a gain of 2 percentage points;
- 84% have a better understanding of the available campus resources—no gain;
- 89% reported being "very satisfied" or "satisfied" with the *Building Self-Confidence* and *Stress Reduction/Management* workshops (led by *EKOarts*)—a gain of 12 percentage points;
- 90% agreed that they made stronger career and major connections with the faculty presenters (based on three faculty class presentations) a gain of 4 percentage points;
- 93% "learned a lot" or "somewhat" from the *Employing Interdependence, Accepting Personal Responsibility and Developing Emotional Intelligence* workshops (led by the ASAP academic advisors).

Of course the staff were proud of the various gains in positive student seminar responses from spring to fall 2010. And of course there are many confounding variables that could have positively impacted seminar survey outcomes. Our point is not the outcomes per se, but rather that a focus on and dedication to collaboration across the institution, with an agenda of continuous improvement of support services, can help improve student success outcomes. A more in-depth overview of ASAP's features are discussed in their appropriate context throughout the book (see Chapter 6 regarding faculty participation with advisement and Chapter 7 on faculty engagement with orientation programming).

Additional Case Examples

Based on our experience as directors and teachers of student success programs and seminars, we provide the following list of common best practices that are easily replicable at *any* institution:

1. Coordinate meaningful engagement between course curriculum and institutional resource offices. For example, as Director of the Suffolk County Community College CSP summer bridge initiative, Dr. Levy had students visit Math and Writing Labs as part of their success seminar curriculum and scheduled individual meetings for each student with the lab coordinators. This allowed the lab coordinators to create a unique file for each student, identifying their strengths and weaknesses to ensure they received the necessary assistance when seeking tutoring services. The goal for this intervention was to help the students who all had placed into two or three developmental courses to feel more comfortable seeking help from the tutoring labs and increase the likelihood of resource utilization (O'Connor et al., 2012).

2. Utilize course curriculum to introduce psycho-educational programming in collaboration with the goals of Student Affairs. For example, when working in Student Affairs, we have observed the increase of students seeking support services (e.g. counseling, advising,, and tutoring) after having participated in a course-mandated workshop in support of the curriculum. Basically, having students participate in curricular-mandated workshops addressing a difficult or embarrassing topic can often lead to those students seeking individual support later, and in private.

3. Revise course curriculum to address diverse needs of various student cohorts. At one community college, Dr. Levy supervised the offering of freshman success courses via bilingual pedagogy. Utilizing a text which had been translated into Spanish, in addition to other translated course materials, ESL–Spanish students were afforded the opportunity to develop academic and wellness skills while improving language skills, as opposed to waiting for these students to become more fluent in English before providing them with the college-success curriculum.

Moving Forward

As a next step, we recommend establishing a curriculum for first-year experience courses that offer a comprehensive spectrum of infused information to help students navigate through their first year of college and beyond. The foundation of the freshman seminar should include:

- Information related to basic services at the college: support that is available and how to access these resources. However, the course must also address obstacles to help-seeking (O'Connor et al., 2012) to increase the likelihood of student utilization of support services. As Director of the Suffolk County Community College CSP program, Dr. Levy and program staff asked the participants (new students in two or more developmental courses) what would keep them from seeking assistance on campus. Multicultural concerns and issues related to "academic shame" (embarassment regarding prior academic performance and/or placement into developmental courses) were addressed to help students feel more comfortable seeking support (O'Connor et al., 2012).
- Strategies to promote academic success: basic time management, scheduling, study skills, "knowing what works for you" (O'Connor, 2010), when to seek tutoring and how to find it. Also, how to effectively use tutoring. Assess why students are not using tutoring and develop programs to help "bridge the gap" between introduction of academic support and non-utilization. Dr. Levy and colleagues have collected data regarding the correlation between academic achievement and participation in tutoring. This data is then presented by student leaders and peer educators to freshmen, illustrating the "norms" of success on campus (O'Connor et al., 2012).
- Life skills: balancing outside responsibilities with academic requirements.
- Health and wellness: stress management, knowing when to seek help for mental health concerns, healthy eating, exercise, sleep and relaxation. Use of proactive prevention strategies regarding stress management and wellness such as workshops, seminars, peer education and curriculum-infused reflection.
- Connect to where "students are." Levy and his colleagues developed the Life Skills Goal Assessment to determine the level of prior career planning of freshman at one community college. The instrument was infused into freshman seminar, asking students to identify how much research and exploration they had done prior to choosing a college major. Based on their scores (level of prior career planning) students were invited to specific career workshops designated for their specific level of prior career planning and research.
- Utilize community building and service-learning (see Chapter 5). For example, Levy and colleagues infused a community service project into a summer bridge program to enhance team building and community among at-risk students.

Another key recommendation is to facilitate connection among students through opportunities for socialization related to mutual interests, as well as academic collaboration. Indeed, a well-designed freshman seminar, incorporating a holistic and collaborative curricular perspective, will likely be vital to promoting student success and goal attainment.

Notes

1. As of 2014, ASAP was offered at six CUNY Community College's: BMCC, BCC, Hostos, Kingsborough, LaGuardia, and Queensborough. Plans to expand ASAP into comprehensive CUNY colleges such as CSI and Medgar Evers are underway.
2. MDRC is a non-profit, non-partisan education and social policy research organization: www.mdrc.org/ (accessed December 1, 2015).
3. Learn more about *EKOarts* approach and amazing work: http://ekoarts.org/ (accessed December 1, 2015).

References

Bailey, T. R., Jaggars, S. S., & Jenkins, D. (2015). *Redesigning America's community colleges: A clearer path to student success.* Cambridge, MA: Harvard University Press.

Braxton, J. M., Doyle, W. R., Hartley III, H. V., Hirschy, A. S., Jones, W. A., & McLendon, M. K. (2014). *Rethinking college student retention.* San Francisco, CA: John Wiley & Sons.

Cho, S.-W., & Karp, M. M. (2013). Student success courses in the community college: Early enrollment and educational outcomes. *Community College Review, 41,* 86–103.

Colangelo, L., & Chapman, B. (2015, October, 16). CUNY unveils $42M plan to boost graduation rates. *New York Daily News.* Retrieved on December 1, 2015 from: www.nydailynews.com/new-york/exclusive-cuny-42m-plan-boost-grad-rates-article-1.2399 541.

Cook, J. H., & Lewis, C. A. (2007). *The divine comity: Student and academic affairs collaboration.* Washington, DC: National Association of Student Personnel Administrators (NASPA).

Cuseo, J. (2005). Decided, undecided, and in transition: Implications for academic advisement, career counseling, and student retention. *Improving the first year of college: Research and practice, 27–48.* Retrieved on December 1, 2015 from: www.shawnee.edu/retention/media/Decided-Undecided-and-in-transition.pdf.

Dembicki, M. (2010, June 25). Counselors see more severity, complexity among student cases. *The Community College Times.* Retrieved on December 1, 2015 from: www.ccdaily.com/Pages/Campus-Issues/Counselors-see-more-severity-complexity-among-student-cases.aspx.

Eisenbarth, C. (2012). Does self-esteem moderate the relations among perceived stress, coping, and depression? *College Student Journal, 46*(1), 149–157.

Gallagher, R. P. (2009). National survey of counseling center directors 2009. Retrieved on December 1, 2015 from: www.collegecounseling.org/pdf/nsccd_final_v1.pdf.

Gardner, A. F. (2013). Predicting community college success by participation in a first-year experience course. Western Carolina University. Retrieved on December 1, 2015 from: http://libres.uncg.edu/ir/wcu/f/Gardner2013.pdf.

Goodman, K., & Pascarella, E. T. (2006). First-year seminars increase persistence and retention: A summary of the evidence from How College Affects Students. AAC&U.

Retrieved on December 1, 2015 from: http://aacu-secure.nisgroup.com/peerreview/pr-su06/documents/prsu06_research.pdf.

Jaafar, R., Toce, A., & Polnariev, B.A. (2016). A Multidimensional Approach to Overcoming Challenges in Leading Community College Math Tutoring Success. *Community College Journal of Research and Practice, 40 (6)*, 534-549.

Keup, J. R., & Petschauer, J. (2011). Designing and administering the course (Vol. 1). In *The first-year seminar: Designing, implementing, and assessing courses to support student learning & success* (Series). Columbia, SC: University of South Carolina, National Resource Center for the First-Year Experience and Students in Transition.

Mangels, J. A., Butterfield, B., Lamb, J., Good, C., & Dweck, C. S. (2006). *Why do beliefs about intelligence influence student success? A social cognitive neuroscience model*. Oxford University Press. Retrieved on December 1, 2015 from: https://web.stanford.edu/dept/psychology/cgi-bin/drupalm/system/files/cdwecklearning%20success.pdf.

Obama, B. (2015, January). Fact sheet—White House unveils America's college promise proposal: Tuition-free community college for responsible students. Retrieved on December 1, 2015 from: www.whitehouse.gov/the-press-office/2015/01/09/fact-sheet-white-house-unveils-america-s-college-promise-proposal-tuitio.

O'Connor, S., Polnariev, B. A., & Levy, M. A. (2012). Five core considerations for counseling non-traditional students. Student Affairs News (SAN) website. Retrieved on December 1, 2015 from: www.studentaffairsnews.com.

O'Connor, S., Polnariev, B. A., & Levy, M. A. (2012, March). Five core considerations for counseling non-traditional students. Student Affairs News (eSAN). Retrieved on December 1, 2015 from: www.studentaffairsnews.com.

Porter, S. R., & Swing, R. L. (2006). Understanding how first-year seminars affect persistence. *Research in Higher Education, 47*(1), 89–109. Retrieved on December 1, 2015 from: www.stephenporter.org/papers/fyspersist.pdf.

Rath, B., Rock, K., & Laferriere, A. (2013). Pathways through college: Strategies for improving community college success. Our Piece of the Pie. Retrieved on December 1, 2015 from: www.opp.org/docs/PathwaysCollegeStrategies_StudentSuccess.pdf.

Reid, K. R. M. (2009). A multiple case study of college first-year seminars. University of Nevada. Retrieved on December 1, 2015 from: http://digitalscholarship.unlv.edu/cgi/viewcontent.cgi?article=1063&context=thesesdissertations.

Rutschow, E. Z., Cullinan, D., & Welbeck, R. (2012). *Keeping students on course: An impact study of a student success course at Guilford Technical Community College*. New York: MDRC.

Scrivener, S., & Weiss, M. J. (2013). More graduates two-year results from an evaluation of Accelerated Study in Associate Programs (ASAP) for developmental education students. MDRC policy brief. Retrieved September 10, 2014 from: www.mdrc.org/sites/default/files/More_Graduates.pdf.

Scrivener, S., Weiss, M. J., Ratledge, A., Rudd, T. Sommo, C., & Fresques, H. (2015). Doubling graduation rates three-year effects of CUNY's Accelerated Study in Associate Programs (ASAP) for developmental education students. Retrieved on December 1, 2015 from: www.mdrc.org/sites/default/files/doubling_graduation_rates_fr.pdf.

Smith, G. A. (2007). Effects of self-efficacy and self-esteem on homesickness and college adjustment. Dickinson College. Retrieved on December 1, 2015 from: http://0-files.eric.ed.gov.opac.msmc.edu/fulltext/ED497507.pdf.

Sue, D. W., Arredondo, P., & McDavis, R. J. (1992). Multicultural counseling competencies and standards: A call to the profession. *Journal of Counseling and Development, 70*(4), 477–486.

Tampke, D. R., & Raifu, D. (2013). Improving academic success for undecided students: A first-year seminar learning community approach. *Learning Communities Research & Practice, 1*(2). Retrieved on December 1, 2015 from: http://washingtoncenter.evergreen.edu/cgi/viewcontent.cgi?article=1028&context=lcrpjournal.

Tinto, V. (1993). *Leaving college: Rethinking the causes and cures of student attrition* (2nd Edn). Chicago, IL: University of Chicago Press.

Toblowsky, B. F., Mamrick, M., & Cox, B. E. (2005). The 2003 national survey of first-year seminars: Continuing innovations in the collegiate curriculum. Columbia, SC: National Resource Center for the First Year Experience.

3

CURRICULAR INFUSION OF CAREER DEVELOPMENT

Yevgeniya Granovskaya and Lisa Givens with Jennie Buoy, Tammy DeFranco, Susan DePhilippis, Erika M. Di Renzo, Michael Kammer, Judith Otterburn-Martinez, Maryann Flemming-McCall and Mitchell A. Levy[1]

Why Does This Matter?

> The world in which today's students will make choices and compose lives is one of disruptions rather than certainty, and of interdependence rather than insularity. To succeed in a chaotic environment, graduates will need to be intellectually resilient, cross-culturally and scientifically literate, technologically adept, ethically anchored, and fully prepared for a future of continuous and cross-disciplinary learning.
>
> Association of American Colleges & Universities 2007,[2] p. 15

It is estimated that an average American can expect to change jobs ten or more times before the age of 40 (AAC&U, 2007). Technological advancements and economic globalization, among other factors, render some jobs obsolete, while creating new career opportunities faster than ever before. With increasing job market volatility, return on investment (ROI) has become the "hot topic" when discussing the value and effectiveness of higher education in the current social and economic landscape. Higher education stakeholders—including students, their family members, employers and government agencies—want to see data and measurable dividends, such as lucrative career options, as well as a qualified, globally competitive labor force, as ROI with respect to college tuition, hiring of a recent graduate and funding allocations to colleges and universities. The pressure to quantify the value of specific college majors, academic scholarship and skill acquisition presents both a challenge and an opportunity for universities to address the needs of various stakeholders and defend the importance of higher education in talent development. Additionally, colleges and universities hold the responsibility to continuously evaluate the effectiveness of current educational practices and adapt to the changing social and economic outlook, in order to best prepare their students to skillfully master career management challenges and create opportunities in pursuit of professional success. Such preparation is not possible without infusing career and professional development concepts, as well as employment-related competencies, into all levels of curricula and for all college majors. Additionally, Banta and Kuh (1998) indicate that we cannot evaluate the complete impact of a college education by focusing only on performance in the classroom, as both curricular and extracurricular experiences impact the student.

The American Association of Community Colleges (AACC), in its "Reclaiming the American Dream" report, sent an urgent challenge to the nation's community colleges to reinvent themselves in order to reverse the increasing trend of income inequality contributing to the decline of the middle class (2012). It called for a shift to the culture of collaboration, assessment, student success and learning, in order to increase student credential completion rates, create clear educational and career pathways, close the American skills gap and prepare students for existing and future career opportunities aligned with labor market needs.

Millar (1995) defines *career infusion* as "introduction of career concepts and strategies into the regular curriculum in order to instill relevance and quality to the subject matter at school." It is important to acknowledge the widely accepted view that "liberal education" is by definition "non-vocational," which contributes to the perceived separation in the roles and missions of Academic and Student Affairs (AAC&U, 2007, p. 3). This view also perpetuates the idea that career-related instruction takes away from academic rigor and narrows the focus of college curricula to that of short-term vocational trainings. The "either/or" approach to student educational and professional preparation is as antiquated as it is counterproductive to the mission of higher education in the new millennium. The role of career and professional development centers is shifting from providing graduates with job placements to helping students develop realistic job search expectations and skills in order to effectively market themselves for years to come after graduation (Blau & Snell, 2013). Institutions need to foster students' sense of ownership of their educational preparation and professional advancement, especially since researchers have reported students' inflated perception of preparedness in sought-after workplace skills, compared to employer observations of their performance (Hart Research Associates, 2015). Career infusion and the related approach of curriculum integration can help bridge the gap between the perceived disparities in the achievement of academic and career competencies, and be utilized to complement, integrate and enrich student learning in general education and major-specific courses across disciplines.

Chernus & Fowler (2010) define *curriculum integration* as "an instructional approach that incorporates key content from two or more disciplines; has well-defined educational objectives (such as academic, industry and workforce-readiness standards) and uses authentic applied problems (problem-based learning) to engage and challenge students" (p. 2). The purpose of curricular integration, similar to that of career infusion, is to "strengthen the academic base of [students'] work-related skills while providing context and motivation for academic learning" (p. 2).

Based on the aforementioned research, we believe the practice of infusing career concepts into the academic curriculum can serve as the foundation of collaborative efforts between Academic and Student Affairs, linking the academic departments with offices of career and professional development, leadership and service-learning and student life, among many others. As an example of such collaboration, Banta and Kuh (1998) discuss the student development transcript (SDT) designed at the Sumter campus of the University of South Carolina to supplement students' academic transcripts and document their involvement in co-curricular learning opportunities. Every department submits a list of planned activities to a cross-divisional SDT Committee that matches these activities to key competencies and learning outcomes outlined by the college's mission (Banta & Kuh, 1998). Students are then able to earn credits for participation in approved activities, and track as well as share their co-curricular accomplishments with prospective employers, funders and other universities to which they may want to transfer (Banta & Kuh, 1998). Faculty members can also take a more proactive approach to infusing their lesson plans and syllabi with career and professional development-related activities, and, together with Student Affairs staff, identify disconnected students to encourage them to participate in appropriate co-curricular activities (Banta & Kuh, 1998).

According to Chrislip and Larson (1994), effective collaborative efforts are rooted in overtly stated common goals and expectations and involve joint implementation and investment in a project; they necessitate relationship building as an essential starting point in such efforts, especially since Student and Academic Affairs professionals often have divergent priorities, allegiances and perceptions of success (as cited in Foxx, 2013). In addition to building on the common goals of student development and success, as well as reducing redundancies and gaps in services, the collaborative efforts around SDT implementation can contribute to an increased faculty appreciation of Student Affairs programs by linking them to university's academic mission (Banta & Kuh, 1998). To make parallel such collaborative efforts with AACC's recommendations for reimagined community colleges, "student support services [should] be aligned with student's needs and schedules and . . . integrated into redesigned courses and curriculum pathways. Teaching strategies [should] promote active learning and extensive student-student and student-faculty interaction. Assessment of learning outcomes [should] be embedded in key courses to ensure the quality of credentials awarded" (2012, p. 25).

The Center for Community College Student Engagement (CCCSE) identifies 13 "high-impact" practices: academic goal-setting and planning, orientation, accelerated or fast-tracked developmental education, first-year experience, student success course, learning community, experiential learning beyond the classroom, tutoring, supplemental instruction, assessment and placement, registration before classes begin, class attendance, alert and intervention (2013, p. 6). Institutions committed to high-quality implementation of these practices, especially at high levels of intensity (multiple practices within structured group experiences) and scalability (requiring student participation) report seeing "notable differences in [student's level of] engagement" (CCCSE, 2013, p. 3). The AAC&U also identifies ten "high-impact" educational practices (some overlapping with those presented by CCCSE): first-year seminars and experiences, common intellectual experiences, learning communities, writing-intensive courses, collaborative assignments and projects, undergraduate research, diversity/global learning, service-learning/community-based learning, internships, and capstone courses and projects (AAC&U, 2007, p. 9).

These practices certainly lend themselves well to the integration of career development concepts, are intentional by design, emphasize active learning and allow for learning to be applied to new, complex and unstructured problems across disciplines. According to Kuh (2008), participation in such educational activities "correlates with higher levels of student performance," deepens students' learning, awareness of their own values and understanding of themselves and the world around them (p. 27). CCCSE echoes AACC's recommendation of making high-impact practices scalable and inescapable for students by building them into highly structured career pathways that streamline the course selection process, have multiple entry points, offer stackable credentials, teach skills in the context of students' areas of study and "[emphasize] outcomes, seamless transitions, college success strategies, relevance, coherence, and embedded support" to facilitate credential completion, successful transfer and gainful employment (2014, p. 34).

Blau and Snell (2013) cite a number of studies linking student engagement in career and professional development-related activities with college persistence and post-graduation employment success. These researchers also found that too few students utilize the resources available at Career and Professional Development Centers on their campuses. Infusing career development concepts into high-impact educational practices and embedding them into curricular and co-curricular requirements for all majors may offer a solution to the challenge faced by many colleges and universities in making engaging and impactful learning accessible to all students, rather than just a select few. In addition, Frost, Strom, Downey, Schultz and Holland (2010) identify several research studies linking divisional collaborations to creating effective supports for student learning outcomes, contributing to a more personal student learning environment, and creating an institutional culture with a shared mission and accountability for student success. Researchers identify Professional Development Engagement (PDE) as an externally focused component of student engagement that includes "activities designed to help the student persist and successfully transition from college to work" (Blau & Snell, 2013, p. 690).

Tinto (2002) asserts that to retain and actively engage students in learning, institutions need to restructure the learning environment, so they do not continue to "take courses as detached, individual units, one course separated from another in both content and peer group, one set of understandings unrelated in any intentional fashion to the content learned in other courses" (p. 3). Tinto (2002) further suggests that since classroom is the primary and often the only place where learning, faculty and peer interactions take place, a collaborative approach to curriculum development and implementation between Academic and Student Affairs is key to creating an engaging, enriching and supportive learning environment. Such collaborations can address academic and student development requirements—as well as the needs of industries, employers and communities that students will soon join.

Multiple studies are in agreement that leadership, problem-solving and decision-making abilities, written and oral communication skills, critical thinking, teamwork skills and the ability to apply knowledge in real-world situations make the short list of attributes sought after by employers (Bertelsen & Goodboy, 2009; Hart Research Associates, 2015; NACE, 2015). Leaders from AAC&U concur that these intellectual and practical skills—along with knowledge of human cultures and the physical and natural world, personal and social responsibility and integrative learning—make up the essential learning outcomes required to prepare students for success in the twenty-first century (AAC&U, 2007, p. 3). Robinson, Burns and Gaw (1996) emphasize the need to communicate the importance of involvement in co-curricular and leadership development activities to students in order to facilitate maturation of students' personal and professional identities, as well as their bankability in the job market. Clearly, student attainment of these essential skills and competencies can continue to be difficult without intentionally infusing career development and professionalism concepts into curricula through collaborations between Academic and Student Affairs.

Briggeman and Norwood (2011) suggest that employers use a number of "signals," such as grades, involvement in internships, extracurricular activities, leadership roles, prior employment, etc., to infer whether applicants possess the desired attributes. Although the majority of curricular and co-curricular programs aspire to develop most of the above-mentioned skills, albeit at various levels of depth, importance and intentionality, employer surveys reveal that college graduates are perceived as lacking in leadership skills, critical thinking and analytical skills, along with other essential learning outcomes (Bertelsen & Goodboy, 2009; Hart Research Associates, 2015). Based on their experiences with recent two- and four-year college graduates, industry experts recommend institutions of higher learning welcome and seek out input and partnerships with the industry, encourage students to obtain work experience before graduation, provide career exploration and job search readiness preparation and assist students in strengthening project management skills by replicating workplace conditions in the classroom (CUNY, 2012).

Further, the AAC&U warns about the dangers of a publicly perpetuated view of a college diploma as a "piece of paper" or "a ticket to be stamped," instead of recognizing the value of cross-disciplinary knowledge and skills, relevant to students' career goals, which the diploma should represent (AAC&U, 2007, p. 8). Borgard (2009) states that many students and faculty members think about individual courses as "content absorption" experiences that exist in isolation from the rest of college curriculum and professional aspirations, thus missing the opportunity to reflect on the practical, work-related skills developed over the course of each semester. Students need more training in recognition and presentation of their skills to potential employers, as well as practice in applying their skills and professional behaviors to real-life situations. Briggeman and Norwood (2011) found that although employers use a multitude of factors, such as internships, grades, extracurricular activities and leadership positions, as signals to determine a student's level of skill and fit for a position, "developing good interviewing skills is one of the most important skills to acquire in college" since many employers give the most weight to a student's interview performance in making hiring decisions (p. 26). Therefore, to facilitate a successful college-to-work transition, it is imperative not only to assist students in the development of academic and professional skills, but also to prepare and coach them on how to properly showcase those attributes to market themselves effectively during the job search process.

In a paper on Strategic Advising (2013), the Community College Research Center states:

> For many community college students—a significant portion of whom are the first in their family to attend college—these tasks (completing financial aid applications, choosing a major, registering for the "right" courses, transferring) appear to be insurmountable hurdles. The sheer number of choices students face can lead them to stumble. Students may waste time and money on unnecessary courses; they may miss a financial aid deadline. These stumbles can contribute to a sense they do not "belong" in college (p. 1).

For many students who place into developmental or remedial courses when first beginning college, this sense of "not belonging" can have extremely deleterious consequences. Developmental skills students are confronted with having to wait to take the courses in the major that interests them. It has been our observation (M. Levy, B. Polnariev) that too often, students who are forced to wait to "take" what they are interested in often do not feel like "real college students" and too easily leave school. Contextualized basic skills instruction helps address this crucial motivational variable (exploration of career interests) and provide students with the opportunity to pursue their career interests as soon as they enroll in college (Bryk & Treisman, 2010). Washington's Integrated Basic Education and Skills Training (I-BEST) has become a national model for helping students who test into the lowest levels of remediation earn job-related credentials. Early data demonstrates that I-BEST students are more likely to earn a job-related credential than similar students not enrolled in the program. Consequently, it is imperative that developmental skills students begin the process of career planning and research as early in their careers as possible while simultaneously improving their reading, writing and math skills. As the Community College Research Center (2013) states:

> Ideally, academic and career advising is a multiphase process that occurs over a prolonged period of time. College advisors integrate academic and career counseling by guiding students through an exploration of their strengths, skills and interests. Finally, advisors work with students to develop an academic plan that will help them progress toward the professional goals they have identified (p. 1).

It is vital that students who are "waiting" to progress into their chosen area of interest have the opportunity to make informed decisions regarding their chosen career path and explore their interests while they are attempting to move forward academically. The curricular infusion of career development into developmental skills courses provides an excellent opportunity for these students to reflect on their interests and passions even before they are fully embedded in their majors. Additionally, it allows students the opportunity to confirm that they have chosen the "correct" major for themselves based on informed decision making.

In addition to the challenges confronted by college students for whom English is the first language regarding effective career planning, ESL students face an additional challenge with respect to developing interviewing and job search skills, given their need to improve their ability to communicate with English-speaking employers. Many ESL students come to community colleges with professional degrees from foreign universities but must develop the communication skills necessary to demonstrate proficiency with respect to certification and licensing exams. Despite these challenges, Conway (2010) states "research has shown that immigrants and their children who are pursuing the American dream are enrolled in higher education programs to a greater extent than native born Americans" (p. 210). Additionally, Conway (2010) presents data indicating immigrants are 20% more likely to begin higher education at a community college than natives, and two-thirds of these enrolled immigrants state the intention of completing a four-year program" (p. 210). Consequently, curricular infusion of career development can play a significant role in helping ESL students work toward their professional aspirations while simultaneously improving their communication skills. (Section 3a of this chapter will introduce a number of innovative interventions to enhance developmental skills and ESL student engagement in career planning via curricular infusion.)

Purposeful, skillful and overt infusion of career development-related concepts into the design of curricular and co-curricular activities can contribute to student learning and achievement of the above-mentioned learning outcomes. Additionally, heightening students' awareness of connections between their classroom learning and the workplace demands should motivate them to take ownership and become more intentional in their learning. For example, a successful performance on a job interview requires a student to apply research, critical thinking, reflection and communication and analytical skills, among others, to a real-world situation. Academic competencies developed in class come to life and possess both the practical application and motivational power that is essential for students' career advancement. Such intersections in learning competencies form a rich environment for developing ideas regarding the curricular infusion of careers and for Academic and Student Affairs collaborations.

There are a number of challenges inherent in applying a collaborative approach to infusing career-related concepts into the curriculum by Academic and Student Affairs. As mentioned previously, one challenge is the widely accepted perception that career education is "vocational" and therefore separate from the mission of Academic Affairs (AAC&U, 2007, p. 3). Related obstacles to collaboration, as summarized by Frost et al. (2010) include "cultural distinctions in administration, faculty, and services staff; the historical separation between curricular and co-curricular instruction; the perceived second-class status of student affairs in relation to the academic mission; and differing views on student learning" (p. 38). Grubb and Associates (1999) indicate that "collaboration is counter to the prevailing norm of autonomy and isolation that characterizes the experience of most community college faculty" (as cited in Goldfien & Badway, 2013). Therefore, institutional recognition of a holistic approach to student development as the shared mission and priority for Academic and Student Affairs professionals alike is essential to laying the groundwork for successful curriculum integration of career (Frost et al., 2010). Additionally, as Huber, Hutchings and Gale (2005) point out, it is also essential:

> [To implement] connection-making as an important learning outcome in its own right, [and] not simply a hoped-for consequence of the mix of experiences that constitute undergraduate education colleges and universities need to review and revise faculty reward systems and role definitions to recognize interdisciplinary and applied scholarship, not to mention the extra efforts involved in designing, teaching, and assessing courses aimed at

integrative learning, and [addressing] the persistent gaps between programs in the professions and the liberal arts and sciences, the curriculum and the co-curriculum, and campus and community life (p. 5–6).

Although Academic and Student Affairs professionals may lack the understanding or professional training in each other's content areas, collaborative projects present an opportunity for cross-divisional professional development, information sharing and collegiality to foster the culture of mutual appreciation for each area's contributions to student development (Chernus & Fowler, 2010; Robinson et al., 1996). The need to create and implement a consistent structure for assessing learning outcomes from career-related interventions during students' matriculation will present additional challenges. Curricula and learning assessment rubrics may need to be reviewed and revised to ensure that career and professional development concepts are intentionally and organically included. (Section 3a includes use of a Career Maturity Rubric (Levy, Robinson and Romanello, 2009) used to investigate developmental change via assessment of writing in an ESL course. Additionally, section 3b includes utilization of a cover letter rubric to investigate developmental change via assessment of writing in a college-level English course.)

Although there is significant empirical evidence connecting student engagement and student success, Blau and Snell (2013) point to the need to further test and study the sub-construct of PDE and its specific impact on student success. Further research in this area should contribute to an increase in the perceived and empirically tested value of career infusion as an effective student success strategy which, in turn, should increase faculty buy-in and willingness to collaborate with Student Affairs professionals on PDE interventions. Moreover, with mounting pressures from the government and the public to measure the value of a college degree, such as President Obama's College Scorecard initiative,[3] institutions face the need to expand the definition of student success beyond graduation and persistence rates to include measures of utility of students' learning in their lives post-graduation (AACU, 2007, p. 10). Since the career and professional development process is dynamic and ongoing, applying career infusion to curricula throughout students' college experience and across majors will allow institutions to continuously expose all students to activities facilitative of professional growth and workplace readiness.

The following subsections present examples of career development activities infused into course curricula that have contributed to increases in student learning, awareness and motivation. These best practices are aligned with AAC&U recommendations and provide examples of "active, hands-on, collaborative, and inquiry-based forms of teaching and learning [that make] full use of new educational technologies . . . to ensure that all students have rich opportunities to fully achieve the intended learning outcomes" (AAC&U, 2007, p. 11).

Promising Practices in Developmental and ESL Courses

Professor Judith Otterburn-Martinez

Teaching the English language to prospective college students drives me to constantly look for ways my students can use the targeted language structures being studied in an interesting and useful way to promote their academic success. By infusing career development into my intermediate and advanced-level ESL classes, the students not only learn more about the American academic culture and choosing a career path but also improve the language skills that they will need to be successful in that career. The success that I have had with this project has been two-fold—one was in partnering with my college's Student Affairs area, and the second was in creating level-appropriate projects to encourage and interest students in the topic.

A major hurdle for immigrants studying in a new country is trying to lower their affective filter. If students feel uncomfortable, they will not be able to learn as successfully compared with those who feel at ease. Immigrants have a double challenge because they often do not know the American educational system and they are not fully proficient in English. As a faculty member partnering with the Student Affairs and Career Services, the students learn that there are other personnel besides their ESL instructor at the college who are there to help them and want them to succeed. That is a very strong message to a population that is often meek and feels at a disadvantage. Specifically, when the vice president of Student Affairs has come to meet them personally, they feel honored as valued members of the college community. From a linguistic perspective, hearing a career presentation and participating in a career "value auction" activity, the students are actively listening and taking notes, which is an important academic skill. This engagement has also fostered an environment of collaboration as students are asked to discuss and work together as a unit; again a skill needed for success in American college. The students not only take away valuable information about the services that the college provides, but also websites and resources to guide them in making their career choice and planning.

Once the students have met the representative from Career Services or vice president of Student Affairs, we start a career infusion project that I created to coincide with the goals and outcomes of the course. The skills that students practice are reading, writing and speaking while incorporating targeted grammar and vocabulary within the assignment. In any ESL classroom there is wide diversity of knowledge and prior education. Generally, I will ask students before the planned session with Career Services to write about their career goals, education and work experience. This information allows me to be more prepared to help my students individually and group them appropriately for the activity with Career Services. After the session, the students discuss in small groups what they learned and something they want to know more about; then they *freewrite*.[4] I find that students are able to write more fluently after they have already discussed the topic.

Before any topic is discussed in an ESL class, introduction of vocabulary is generally the beginning point. I present to the class the vocabulary that is specific to this topic, such as: *career, certificate, degree, A.A., B.A., M.A., field, major, minor* etc. In exploring the meaning of each word, we also practice how it is used in spoken and written English. Then, as the students' progress through the project, they will be repetitively using these targeted vocabulary words to become a permanent part of their vocabulary.

For the students to explore a specific career or compare a few, they are given a few reliable resources to conduct level-appropriate research. I generally start with the *Occupational Outlook Handbook* and then refer them to the college catalog. Once they have gathered enough information and made an informed decision, I assign a project. Regardless if I assign an oral presentation or a formal written composition, the process of researching, organizing information and presenting it in a clear and coherent manner is the same. If I am focusing on writing, then I will typically choose a descriptive or process essay or paragraph. Using these different forms of compositions, the students have to explain all pertinent information or how they plan to reach this career goal. If I assign an oral presentation, I expect the students to explain the career goal, why they have chosen the goal and how they expect to reach this goal. To present, the students use Windows Microsoft's *Power Point* or *Glogster*.[5]

No matter what the result of their finished project, I have found that students come away more focused and more prepared to start their academic careers in the United Sates and better prepared to succeed academically. Since I have started doing this work, students are grateful and more motivated to continue studying as they know it will bring them closer to a better future.

Professor Michael Kammer

Soon after the casinos opened their doors in the late 1970s, Atlantic City, New Jersey attracted many immigrants who were seeking to take advantage of the job opportunities. With the closing of several casinos, however, many immigrants are either struggling to find other jobs or moving to other cities. As Atlantic City tries to reinvent itself, so too are the immigrants who have remained. For many, coming to Atlantic Cape Community College has been the key to this reinvention. It is now more important than ever for these students to carefully consider their career paths as they pursue their academic goals toward future success. Despite the uniqueness of this region, the challenges of defining a career path are shared by many students around the country. Especially during difficult economic times, it is worthwhile for faculty members to consider infusing curriculum with career advising in order to guide students in the right direction.

When building career advisement into the classroom experience, the following three points should be considered:

1. *Seek the support of the administration of the institution.* The president and provost should be made aware of your endeavors. Since it is in the interests of the president to showcase new ideas that are working well to the Board of Trustees, offer to present some of the initial successes at a board meeting. Also, the support of your institution's Student Services director will naturally lead to a collaborative environment with the counselors, advisors and tutors.

2. *This partnership with Student Affairs provides students with greater assistance outside the classroom.* What is started in the classroom can be continued and enhanced in the office of a career counselor. Faculty should become familiar with the resources that academic counselors can provide students. Initiatives such as writing-across-the-curriculum, pairing of courses and service-learning extend learning between and outside the classrooms. The partnering of Student Affairs and faculty will work to inspire and empower students to better take ownership of their career goals and path.

3. *When bringing academic advising into the classroom, no major changes are needed.* Most professors would argue that the course curriculum could not hold "an ounce more" of material or activities. However, I have found that all that is needed are some minor curricular adjustments and substitutions to provide career goal-oriented activities that would be well worth the sacrificed content material. Career advising works well in ESL and Developmental Writing courses, but it could also easily be used in a wider array of courses.

These three aspects of infusing career advising—the solicitation of cooperation from administration, partnering with student support services and understanding the simplicity of substituting activities rather than major curricular renovations—will help ease the infusion of career advising into the classroom. Following are some activities to consider, most of which are adaptable to the specific course in which they are used.

Activities

Values Auction:[6] This is one of the most entertaining and valuable student success activities. This activity encourages students to think about the values they place on their education and/or on having a career they are passionate about. I have successfully incorporated this activity into my ESL courses at Atlantic Cape Community College. The Values Auction activity was introduced by Atlantic Cape's Vice President of Student Affairs Dr. Mitchell Levy. One material to prepare ahead of time is a group of six auction paddles. Each paddle is made with two 4" x 6" pieces of paper taped to the top end of a paint can stirrer and marked with numbers one through six. The first step of this activity is to break the class into four to six groups. Group size varies depending on the size of the class, but try to have roughly the equal number of participants in each group. Ask the students: Why are you in college? How would you like to be different when you graduate? Then ask students to provide answers to the two questions and make a list of 15–20 "values" on the blackboard. Some values may need to be modified or combined to avoid duplication of ideas. The next step is to explain the rules to the groups:

1.   Each group has $5,000 in its imaginary bank account to spend, but will forfeit its values if it spends over that amount.
2.   Each value will be auctioned, and bidding is made in increments of $100.
3.   It does not matter how many values a group buys, but that it gets the value or values it believes to be most important.

As each value is bought, write down the group number and the amount paid in order to keep track of the groups' spending. You will find that the students will become rather animated as they vie for the values of their choice. When all values are auctioned, capture the moment by taking a picture of the board before you erase it. Here is an example of a list of 20 student *values* from one of my classes (in order that the class identified the items), followed by the group (or table) number and how much was bid for each value:

- being example for children: 3—$1,500;
- getting a job: 3—$100;
- getting a career: 3—$1,900;
- better money: 5—$3,500;
- better lifestyle: 4—$2,300;
- have more opportunities: 3—$2,800;
- a chance to try a new field: 2—$500;
- get respect: 1—$2,000;
- gateway for universities: 2—$500;
- improve your speaking: 2—$1,000;
- changes how you think: 5—$900;
- proving to others you can do it: 2—$700;
- proving to yourself you can do it: 1—$800;
- better communication for services: 2—$800;
- better social communication: 4—$700;
- getting more knowledge: 4—$600;
- deal with children better: 5—$600;
- help your children with homework: 4—$600;
- better teach your children: 1—$1,000;
- reaching your goals: 1—$1,000.

It is interesting to note that we have conducted the same activity with faculty and staff, finding the values of education or career that staff generate can be quite *different* from what students generate. We then discuss the potential disconnect between programs developed by the faculty and staff as opposed to student goals and values, and how this can impede program effectiveness and student success. Later in the semester, after the other activities are completed, I show the picture of the values that the class bid for, which brings on smiles of the memory, but also glimmers of understanding that maybe some of the values have become less or more important because of the other activities since then.

The Occupational Outlook Handbook[7] *and work sheet:* This is an excellent website for students to explore various careers. At the end of the chapter is the link to the *Occupational Outlook Handbook.* The handbook organizes careers into occupational groups such as "Arts and Design" and "Healthcare." After choosing an occupational group and then an occupation within that group, the user will see that the occupation page divides the information into seven tabs: "Summary," "What They Do," "Work Environment," "How to Become One," "Pay," "Job Outlook," "Similar Occupations" and "More Info." I usually use a computer lab hour to allow students to explore the online handbook while filling out a worksheet that asks the students to pick one or two of the occupations most interesting to them and then answer specific questions. The questions necessitate the students go to the different tabs for the information, thereby giving the students the opportunity to explore the handbook to its full capacity.

Career presentation: Because the students are presenting their career of interest, motivation is high and their presentations are well done. I do a quick tutorial on using *PowerPoint* to get the students started on preparing for their presentations. The more technologically gifted students help the less-experienced classmates. Afterward, I always get feedback from the students that they enjoyed doing this activity. I use a simple rubric with the following criteria to evaluate the presentation:

- fluent speech and frequent eye contact;
- choice of a career was appropriate and interesting;
- *PowerPoint* was interesting and audience-friendly;
- key words used on the slides;
- easy to understand.

Interview: Students are provided a list of typical interview questions that they practice to prepare for the in-class interview. Without fail, I have at least one student each semester that said this activity increased confidence for a "real" interview. During the role-play, students take turns being the interviewer and the interviewee. These are the questions I use:

1. Why should we hire you?
2. When I contact your last supervisor and ask which area of your work needs the most improvement, what will I learn?

3. Describe the best boss you have ever reported to.
4. What was your biggest mistake at work and how did you handle it?

Visit from the career counselor. This is where a partnership with student support services can help. A good pre-visit activity is having the class brainstorm a list of questions they could ask the counselor. Here is the list generated by a recent class:

1. Should I have an advisor help me with my academic career?
2. Sometimes I don't know what I want to be. Can you evaluate me on what career would be good for me? For example, can I tell you what I like and what you think would be good for me?
3. I love writing and reading. How can I find a career that would use those skills and desires?
4. As someone who has a lot of experience advising, what should I avoid doing to prevent wasting time and money studying?
5. What resources do you have that could help me?
6. How can I find out about careers; for example, training requirements or wages?
7. I am confused between two careers. What could I do?
8. How can I find career matches for my values? For example, if one of my values is making a positive difference in the world, how could I find a career where that value is important?

The advisor came in prepared with a handout of links to career-oriented websites and self-discovery career instruments. He demonstrated a few websites and answered questions that the students posed. Because of the introduction and interaction with the counselor, more of my students signed up with him for one-on-one career counseling sessions.

Pre-writing and post-writing with rubric. I usually do the pre-writing as the first activity, explaining to the students to do the best they can, and that they would receive the first draft back for a chance to do a second draft after all of the other activities are completed. They get the same writing prompt for both drafts:

Purpose: The purpose of this writing is to get you thinking about your plans for your career. Follow the outline below:

1st paragraph: Why is choosing a career difficult/important to do? How difficult has it been for you? What career would you like to be working in? Why? What interests and talents have led you to this choice? How do your values affect the choice? How important is it for you to follow this career path?

2nd paragraph: Describe what it is about you that would make you the right person for that career choice (interests, talents, values)?

3rd paragraph: Description of the career's environment, related fields and job market.

4th paragraph: Description of the academic path needed to train for the career.

5th paragraph: What steps do you need to take to reach your career goals? What qualities do you need to achieve your goal?

Using a Career Maturity Rubric developed by Levy, Robinson and Romanello (2009), the first and second drafts are scored together so that the improvements are easily seen in the second draft. Not only do the students write with more confidence and see their progress, but I have found that they develop their paragraphs with more detailed explanations. The purpose of using the detailed writing prompt listed above in the Advanced II ESL class is to guide them in writing an essay with organized paragraphs. In my last Advanced II ESL class of 18 students, over 94% of students improved in career maturity by at least one level on the rubric.

Here are some inspiring quotes from my students' essays:

- "To me, it will mean a lot to be able to work in what I like, and I know this will be really good for me and my family."
- "I like this career because of my influence to help people and by making myself useful to the community I'm living in and I'll be comfortable in it."
- "I know that I don't like to study so much but now I have to develop that quality in me, so I can do better to get that profession."
- "Nursing is a good career for me because I like to work with people. I'm responsible, and patient."
- "I know it's not easy for me to achieve this dream. But I'm working on it now."

Our students have very busy lives with many competing responsibilities whether they are recent high school graduates taking 15 credits or stay-at-home parents finding time for one class. By infusing career development into the course curriculum, students are given a chance to either be reminded or to understand why they are in their classes, and they are given time to reflect on which career path is right for them without having to compete with other responsibilities outside the classroom.

Professor Susan DePhilippis

In a capstone ESL reading and writing course, career infusion works well with a comparative essay writing assignment. After introducing the career topic and writing assignment parameters, I lead students through the pre-writing, writing and post-assignment life application process described Table 3.1.

In the pre-writing phase, I prioritize orienting ESL students to content-specific vocabulary and more precise definitions of words in an American cultural context, e.g. job vs. career, college degrees vs. certificate programs, credentials and quali-fications. Second, if at all possible, students go immediately to a computer lab or other Internet-access device to complete the Holland Code Quiz after the Values Auction in collaboration with Student Affairs (described by M. Kammer above), seizing on the momentum and focus it has generated. The quiz has vivid vocabulary, particularly adjectives. Professors can also incorporate these words into ongoing vocabulary journaling assignments. Third, using an online dictionary or application, most students complete the Holland Quiz in 20–30 minutes. Immediately thereafter, a customized list of careers is generated, compatible with the answers given about their personalities, skills and preferences.

In the writing phase, I emphasize learning activities related to English language learning and essay writing. Students gather career information from credible websites and write reflectively of their own work experiences, skills, credentials and career aspirations. As they complete more research and writing, students iden-tify an emerging, dominant focus (or theme) around which to select and organize the main and supporting ideas they choose to include in their comparative essay. Mini-lessons of citation, quoting, comparative wording/grammar, essay elements, etc. occur throughout this phase, and additional ones as teachable moments arise, e.g. subject–verb agreement, parallel structure, thesis statement writing, etc.

In the post-assignment phase, students take an action step for themselves based on what they have learned from this assignment through which the professor continues to teach English skills. Students prepare for and meet with a content-specific professor in their career field and/or a college counselor about career, major and/or transfer (to a four-year school) issues. Ultimately, students complete this project with a comparative essay per course goals, an awareness of and interaction with broader college services and professionals, and a specific action point for their career aspirations that often sustains their motivation for continued education.

ESL Comparative Essay Assignment

Goals: To develop learners' abilities . . .

1. To locate, evaluate and effectively use information to explain concepts and vocabulary found when reading academic texts and needed when writing.
2. To cite the words and ideas of others using various techniques accepted in American college essay writing.
3. To express and edit their comparative ideas in standard written American English with fluency, clarity, coherence and grammatical control.
4. To organize and revise their comparative ideas in a unified, coherent essay of at least five paragraphs.
5. To identify and evaluate individual career goals and needed academic requirements for wanted careers to meet their personal definition of successfully living in an American English-speaking community.

TABLE 3.1 Flow Chart Syllabus

Goals	Learning Activities in Presentation Order		Mode
Intro/ Overview	Overview and Pre-writing	Overview of unit with students; list class expectations; discuss questions raised	By teacher class discussion
5		Participate in class Values Auction	Small group competition
1, 5		Complete Holland Code Quiz: www.roguecc.edu/Counseling/Holland Codes/test.asp	Individual online
1, 3, 5	Essay writing Assignment	Reflective writing 1–15 minute freewrite: reaction to Values Auction and Holland Code Quiz results; the set of life circumstances affecting current career choice/goals	Individual on paper
1–5		Review Essay Rubric and Assignment/ Q&A; read & review sample essays with rubric	Class and small group discussion
1–5		Research interests; narrow career choices to two: www.bls.gov/ooh/	Individual online
1, 3, 5		Reflective writing 2–15 minute freewrite: What steps (action plan) can/should be taken now with this added information?	Individual on paper
1, 3, 4		Review both free writings and finished research; identify one personal theme (essay focus)	Individual on paper★
1–5		Choose a quote reflecting theme/focus	Individual on paper
1–5		Write introduction and conclusion paragraphs referencing rubric	Individual on paper★
1–5		Decide on and write detail paragraph topic and supporting sentences referencing rubric	Individual on paper
1–5, Mostly 3		Complete first draft of essay referencing rubric	Individual on paper★
1–5, Mostly 4		Complete final draft of essay referencing rubric	Individual on paper

continued . . .

TABLE 3.1 Continued

Goals	Learning Activities in Presentation Order		Mode
1, 3, 5	Post-Assignment Life Application	Prepare specific action plan for career and/or list of career questions for counseling staff and/or professor meetings	Individual on paper★
1, 5		Have follow-up appointment with counseling staff and/or professors of selected majors	Individual in person
1, 4, 5		Revise personal career action plan after meeting with counseling staff and/or professor	Individual on paper★
Teacher Review		Assess/evaluate unit	By teacher for next use

Note: ★ Small group or partner discussion; peer review; class discussion of questions raised thereafter.
Source: Susan DePhilippis

Professor Erika M. Di Renzo

> Once you know better, you do better.
>
> Maya Angelou

I believe higher education must *align meaningful curricular infusion to the pursuit of future career goals.* In my role as an English adjunct and tutor, it is important to understand the complex nature of contemporary learners; therefore, it is essential to create career development initiatives through the use of infusing dynamic instructional strategies providing industry-relevant information and tools, increasing student "buy-in" and success. Higher education and lifelong learning are interconnected and highly valuable in learners' pursuits of securing thriving career pathways. Consequently, when career curriculum is embedded in the campus-wide community, learners become vested stakeholders.

In my Developmental English, I decided to have the learners engage in a whole group discussion about personal interests and identify future career goals. In the beginning of the semester, the whole class is taken on a campus tour whereby I explain the functions of each department/personnel. The learners create their own campus map, which will be used for this specific writing engagement. The learners will use this map as a graphic organizer; this is done in an effort to cause learners to evaluate purpose, identity, behaviors, competence and values, as well as create a cooperative learning environment via the writing process to help them develop meaningful pathways to their personal career passions. On the classroom board I begin compiling a list of future careers—nursing, teaching, police work, and human and social services are identified as career points of interest. From there, I ask the learners, "So what do you need to do to get there?" The answers vary from on-the-job training to real-world simulations and mentoring.

Next, the learners are asked, "Who will help you get there?" Further, the learners are prompted to brainstorm individually ten questions to ask a mentor. The learners come back together in small groups and begin to share their individual thoughts and ideas. During this class I have the learners read an article entitled, "Five Questions Every Mentee Should Ask." This article is given as a handout, presented on the whiteboard or Smart Board, and posted on the course's digital library. This allows the learners to utilize the many facets of multiple intelligences while allowing them to revisit this material as needed for reinforcement. Ultimately, all of these pedagogical practices make this a manageable task as they have been exposed to teacher-initiated discussion, peer discussion and, now, individual reflection.

Subsequently, an outline is given for writing an Illustration and example essay. This essay outline is done by hand in class. The outline requires them to identify what resources in the campus community will enable their academic successes to help lead to career crossroads. The learners provide the following answers: Academic Advisement, Tutoring and the Career Center. By the next class, the list has to be narrowed down to five questions that are vital to achieving their personal career endeavors with the assistance of a mentor. The college's computer lab is reserved for the career exploration session. Upon entering class, the learners are given a handout that provides them with useful career exploration websites, e.g. the *Occupational Outlook Handbook*, Career One Stop, The Riley Guide, What Can I Do with a Major In?, Career Cornerstones Center and the Holland Quiz. This equips the students with a full range of resources to research and "reflect on" potential likes and dislikes, take into consideration past as well as current achievements, review past and present job trends and access the value of the involvement of a mentor.

As a result of this career-writing exercise the learners begin to see their strongest collection of natural talents take shape by bringing all of this to the forefront as they are developing a keen awareness for what draws them toward their future career path. On a side note, we take part in a discussion to further enhance their career performances, such as participation in clubs, organizations and volunteerism on and off the campus. In the end, the final product is an Illustrative and example essay that has become both a blueprint and intervention tool. Ultimately, this career development exercise is results-oriented, showcases new and existing skills and provides resources through self-and guided discoveries for career planning in the learning community.

Promising Practices in College-level Courses

Professor Maryann Flemming-McCall

The "two-year" college is anything but that for many students. According to Atlantic Cape Community College Institutional Profile (2013), only 5% of first-time/full-time students enrolled in fall 2009 graduated in two years. Academic underpreparedness is of course a factor for why many of these students enter the institution without the necessary academic skills and habits essential to succeed at college-level work. As a result, many of them initially place into the developmental sequence. As the Institutional Profile (2013) shows, in fall 2012, at Atlantic Cape, 64.1% of first-time, full-time students were enrolled in remedial classes, 55.2% in algebra and 45.1% in English, combining reading/writing. This delay of their ability to enroll in college-level courses and pursue their original plans with respect to the time needed to graduate and/or transfer can result in frustration, financial difficulties and, ultimately, dropping out.

Unfortunately, the underprepared students have a lot of company in their long trek to graduation. A common characteristic shared by developmental and college-ready students alike is often a lack of clear goals and direction. Students who enter Atlantic Cape with definite and informed ideas of their desired career paths—for example, two successful programs at Atlantic Cape are nursing and paralegal—tend to be those who are retained and succeed. Unfortunately, a majority of the students do not have an identified area of interest and basically have no clear sense of direction, or perhaps worse, have unrealistic career expectations and spend time and money trying to reach unattainable goals. Career exploration and planning provides a good opportunity for these students. Identifying goals early and mapping out a path to reach those goals are essential to keeping students on track and moving toward completion. Career activities expose students to the necessary tools, engage them in the process and introduce them to accessible support via Student Affairs personnel and faculty. Enrollment in an English class can make them a "captive audience" and career exploration via the course curriculum provides resources and materials that make the process of enhancing reading and writing skills more germane to the students' needs.

Career exploration was introduced to students in college-level English who were enrolled in Atlantic Cape's Accelerated Learning Program (ALP). This program gives students who test into the higher level of developmental reading and writing the opportunity to bypass enrollment in developmental English. Students who place into ENGL080 (developmental), Reading and Writing II, are instead enrolled in ENGL101, College Composition and a co-requisite support class that incorporates academic support, introduction to the college's support services and personnel and educational planning and advising. Career planning is a natural fit for the ALP classroom. A primary focus is orienting the students to the college and academic life, and student success and retention is part of the daily discussion. Two key components of the program are as follows: first, one instructor teaches both the ENGL101 section and the support class, so students and instructor are together for six hours per week, which engenders more awareness of individual student needs; and second, the class meets one session per week in the computer lab, facilitating the online components of career exploration. Additionally, the career activities directly support the ALP learning outcomes and objectives. Student will:

1.   practice computer and information literacy skills;
2.   become familiar with the college culture;
3.   make use of available and appropriate resources;
4.   take advantage of websites that enrich the student's academic skills;
5.   choose a program path for the next two years, study the schedule of classes and make effective decisions for scheduling an academic semester.

At Atlantic Cape Community College, Vice President of Student Affairs Dr. Mitchell Levy came to the classes to lead the Values Auction activity. This in itself was notable to the students who usually only see Dr. Levy for behavioral issues or participation in extracurricular activities. It signaled to them, and was reiterated by Dr. Levy, that career planning and their success was important to the institution. At first, the students participated reluctantly. Before long, a fierce competition ensued among groups that were competing to achieve the goals they had prioritized. It was interesting to observe students who had not spoken to each other all semester bantering back and forth. The activity energized the students, who were then asked to write a reflection response. This follow-up assignment required identifying careers of interest by taking the Holland Code Quiz and then writing a compare/contrast essay of two careers of interest, using information from the *Occupational Outlook Handbook* that was also introduced by Dr. Levy. Since the assignment was personally relevant for each of them, the end product and the feedback from the students were overall positive.[8]

For both of the English classes, the activities and assignments achieved important steps in support of student retention. They provided a framework for goal-setting and exploration and the opportunity to discuss academic advising in preparation for advisement for the following semester. In addition, information literacy components were addressed as students were required to locate, evaluate and use information. Students became aware of college resources and Student Affairs personnel available to help them as they pursue their goals. At the same time, the Student Affairs personnel involved in facilitating the activities grew more cognizant of the nature and needs of the student body, which enhanced their ability to support them. Additionally, once their interests were identified, the students could be directed to appropriate faculty to discuss their fields of interest, identify potential pathways and connect to those professors who can guide them on that path. Connections between instructors and students, between Student Affairs and students and appropriate faculty members are all integral to career exploration in the English classroom. However, the discussion of hopes, dreams, goals and motivations also fostered greater interconnections among the students, and as research indicates, the more human connection students have at the institution, the stronger their connection will be to the institution, making their chances of achieving their goals more likely.

Professor Jennie Buoy and Adjunct Professor/Director of the Cape May Campus Tammy DeFranco

Tammy: Atlantic Cape Community College students enrolled in a college-level English course were introduced to the basics of creating a cover letter that will help them when seeking a career. When creating the first draft of the cover letter, students did not have any guidance, support or use of a rubric to help them organize their cover letter. This was done purposefully to create a baseline regarding their ability to create an effective cover letter. The first draft of the cover letters was collected and scored using a cover letter rubric that was obtained via the Internet. The cover letters were then returned to the students with the rubric to review and determine where they needed improvement.

After the cover letters were returned to the students, the instructor introduced a team of staff members from Academic Affairs (tutoring) and Student Affairs (Vice President of Student Affairs Dr. Mitchell Levy and the Director of the Cape May campus, Tammy De Franco). The team was then divided to meet with small groups of students and review their cover letters and to explain the rubric to them so when they revised their first draft the student could compare their first draft cover letter to the final cover letter. Students improved significantly on their second and final cover letters thanks to the help of the supportive college resources and knowing how to use a rubric scale to help improve their writing. This also allowed students to become better acquainted with my area, Student Affairs, and make personal connections with campus tutors.

Jennie: In my College Composition I course, I decided to incorporate cover letter-writing in accordance with the course learning objectives—reading and analyzing a written work for main and supporting points; writing in an organized, logical manner; and making editorial and other revisions. In order to establish an accurate baseline, the students were prompted to, "imagine your dream job and write a cover letter for that position," where scant additional directions were given. This pre-test resulted in a mean score of 9.3 on a cover letter rubric, developed by Illinois State University Career Center (www.careercenter@IllinoisState.edu), with a scale ranging from 6 (lowest level of effectiveness) to 18 (highest level of effectiveness) (2012). The intervention took form as a cover letter workshop delivered by two Student Affairs administrators, the course instructor and staff from the campus tutoring center (Academic Affairs). The students analyzed a cover letter sample in terms of how effective the writer communicated her main points (i.e. why she was qualified for that position) and how well she supported her assertions (i.e. how well she persuaded the employer to offer her an interview and/or hire her). The presenters then proceeded to illustrate how to compose an effective cover letter, including correct formatting and essential elements. They strongly emphasized the necessity of constructing a well-organized piece that clearly explains a central idea and reflects a defined purpose (i.e. how the applicant demonstrates the necessary and desired qualifications and properly supports the controlling idea with examples, explanations, etc.).

After the presentation, the students received their evaluated pre-intervention cover letters with constructive comments; they were also able to conference one-on-one with the cover letter evaluators (faculty members, Student Affairs staff or tutors) for more personalized assistance. To determine the effectiveness of the intervention, a survey was administered. In addition, the participants were given the same prompt as the pre-test; they could utilize any of the tools at their disposal, such as a cover letter example and the checklist provided during the workshop. This post-test yielded a promising average of 14.6/18 (scale 6–18). The average improvement of 5.3 points (41% increase) post-intervention vs. pre-intervention demonstrated the effectiveness of the workshop and the magnitude of the knowledge acquired by the students. As an instructor, this evidence of growth truly inspires one to continue similar valuable activities and assignments. In the post-workshop survey, all the students stated they benefited from the workshop. Equally important, they listed various steps that they were motivated to take toward developing their careers, such as researching more careers, exploring volunteering and/or club options and speaking with a counselor. They also itemized their newly acquired knowledge derived from the workshop: "Researching job postings and fields" and "How to better structure my cover letter." The most informative comments expressed how their composition and cover letter skills apply to their future career paths.

Additionally, in an exit survey of the College Composition I course, the students were asked to identify how they would utilize the knowledge and skills gained from the class. Several students specifically mentioned the cover letter assignment as a valuable aspect of the course, as shown by some of their comments: "I will feel more confident in applying for positions with my professional-looking cover letters" and "I really liked the cover letter assignment because it is something I will need . . . one day." Upon reflection, the success of this project leads me to consider additional course-related career development activities. For example, the instructor could require other writing assignments, such as a research paper in which the students either explore their desired career or contrast two potential careers. The students could also interview an employee in their future field, observe that work environment and compose a reflective piece based on this experience. Accordingly, the most valuable skills an instructor can incorporate into a classroom reinforce real-world applications. Course infusion of related activities and assignments can not only prepare students for their success beyond the classroom but can also potentially motivate them to be successful in the course and for the remainder of their academic career—provided that they recognize the importance that their academic career holds in their overall success.

Moving Forward

As indicated throughout this chapter, there are innumerable possibilities with respect to incorporating career planning into the curriculum of Developmental, ESL and college-level courses. Faculty who are comfortable and willing to be creative afford their students the opportunity to simultaneously develop their academic skills (e.g. language proficiency) while doing so within the context of academic and career planning. Given the importance of non-cognitive factors in promoting student success (resiliency, persistence, retention), it is imperative to provide students whose academic skills are not yet college-level with the opportunity to engage their reasons for attending college. This is especially important for first-generation college students who are engaging an academic culture that may be unfamiliar and inconsistent with norms of their communities.

Consequently, one important next step is increased integration of career development within course curriculum in a longitudinal manner. For example, given that many students participate in multiple levels of developmental and/or ESL education, we recommend that career development interventions be developed in a logical "sequence," with the curricular infusion within course level #1 leading to curricular infusion into course level #2. A longitudinal model that links curricular experiences across multiple developmental courses would both: a) reinforce the career assessment and exploration introduced to students in their first-level courses; and b) allow students to continue the process of career decision making. In essence, students can add to their academic and career portfolios as they proceed through critical junctures (Dickmeyer and Michalowski, 2012).

A second next step is utilization of advanced assessment to investigate student learning outcomes and non-cognitive factors (self-expectancy, help-seeking, confidence). Within this chapter, Professors Kammer, DePhilippis, Otterburn-Martinez and Buoy identified how increases in student knowledge and motivation post-career intervention were measured. We recommend further examination of how increases in career knowledge, maturity (see Career Maturity Rubric developed by Levy et al., 2009) and goal-clarification have an impact on student self-expectancy and confidence. In addition, we strongly recommend assessment of the impact of career interventions beyond the immediate semester in which they were implemented—in essence, what is the long-term impact on student resiliency and the success of infused career interventions?

As described in this chapter, Professors Buoy, DeFranco and Flemming-McCall utilized a variety of creative pedagogical techniques to engage their college-level students in career exploration and professional development-related activities. A thought-provoking consideration is the confluence of experiences that have shaped their work. For example, Tammy DeFranco is trained as a counselor, serves as a campus director and Student Affairs administrator, and is an adjunct instructor. It is clear that her experiences provide her with a unique perspective when infusing career development and student success "messages" into course curricula.

Consequently, another next step we recommend is consideration of how to effectively train faculty to incorporate career-planning resources into their pedagogy. A number of faculty members we have collaborated with have commented on the positive impact of their involvement in this research. Many have stated that their involvement in the curricular infusion research has caused them to "rethink" their courses and how to engage their students. In the *Art of Advising* professional development seminar (Polnariev, Levy & McGowan, 2010), faculty were provided the opportunity to learn how to utilize relational, conceptual and informational factors (NACADA, 2012) to engage in effective developmental advising. When asked if this seminar provided them with information that would help them engage with students, the faculty participants had a mean response of 4.63 on a Likert scale in which 1 = strongly disagree and 5 = strongly agree. Consequently, we support continued exploration of the impact that curricular infusion has not only on student development, but also on the professional development of faculty and staff, consistent with the notion that developmental advising (as in forming a developmental relationship) is an interactive, mutually beneficial relationship (Frost, 1991; NACADA, 2012).

Primary is the value of faculty having an increased understanding of "how career development actually works." As educators, it has been our experience that too often students and staff alike have incorrect assumptions regarding career development, especially with respect to career assessment. We have all too often heard students and staff ask counselors to use a "test that can tell students what they should do." Clearly, as the authors will attest, it is incumbent upon educators to explain the difference between *interest assessments* that invite students to self-identify values, interests and perceived skills as opposed to a "test" (which does not exist), which will emphatically tell someone what to do with his or her life. For faculty members to effectively and appropriately incorporate career development into their curricula, they need at least a basic understanding of career development and assessment principles. This can easily be accomplished via professional development workshops and presentations by Student Affairs staff. We endorse a review of the National Academic Advising Association (NACADA) website for information and resources regarding the role that career development plays in "developmental advising."

Another important next step is increased linkage across critical junctures of a student's experience at *critical junctures* (Dickmeyer & Michalowski, 2012) based on the assessment of the level of career preparation. For example, for those students who begin at the college level, we advocate for linkages within program curricula that is germane for their current level of career development. The career development interventions that take place as students begin their program of study (major) ideally should prepare them for career development activities in the next level of program courses—in essence, utilizing a longitudinal and developmental approach. Student Affairs professionals can collaborate with faculty within a program to identify the developmental stages of career development, appropriate interventions for each stage and ways various courses within program curricula can incorporate specific interventions. An example of this is recognition that not all students will need the same level of career intervention even if they are "at the same level" with respect to the curriculum. Dr. Levy once coordinated the development of The Life Goals Planning Instrument at a community college to assess the level of career planning and research each freshman had completed prior to attending college. The instrument was disseminated within a mandatory freshman seminar course, including versions translated into Spanish for ESL students. The faculty members collected and returned the instrument to the counseling department, which scored the instrument (total score based on forced choice responses). The instruments and feedback were returned to students, explaining that based on their level of prior career planning and inquiry, they were invited to specific workshops for students at their level of preparation (High, Moderate and Beginning). Clearly, the impetus for this intervention was to not assume that all developmental or all college-level students were "in the same place" with respect to their knowledge of and experience with career planning. Additionally, this allowed the freshman seminar faculty to more clearly identify the individual needs of their students to more effectively facilitate their successful transition into college. This initiative contributed to a 4 percentage point increase in retention among new students within a two-year period.

The consensus among the faculty and staff that contributed to the work illustrated in this chapter is infusing career planning into the curriculum via cross-divisional collaboration: a) can be easily replicated; b) benefits students, faculty and staff; and c) helps to promote a holistic institutional culture of student success.

Notes

1. Editors' note: The research contained in this chapter was recognized with the 2016 NASPA Student Affairs Partnering with Academic Affairs Knowledge Community *Promising Practices Award*.
2. Association of American College's & Universities (AAC&U). AAC&U is the leading national association concerned with the quality, vitality and public standing of undergraduate liberal education. Learn more: www.aacu.org/ (accessed December 1, 2015).
3. Explore the national scorecard by degree, location or institution size: https://collegescorecard.ed.gov/ (accessed December 1, 2015).
4. *Freewriting's* purpose is to get ideas from one's head onto paper. The term means to write freely without inhibition of grammar, spelling, punctuation etc. Learn more: https://en.wikipedia.org/wiki/Free_writing (accessed December 1, 2015).

5. Learn more about *gloster*: www.glogster.com/#one (accessed December 1, 2015).
6. You can see a clip of the activity performed by Drs. Mitchell Levy and Bernard Polnariev at a 2009 LaGuardia Community College Student Leadership summit: www.youtube. com/watch?v=hqY6JDP7wpk (accessed December 1, 2015).
7. Explore the Occupational Handbook: www.bls.gov (accessed December 1, 2015).
8. Editors' note: Assessment data collected from 350+ students across ESL, developmental and college-level courses indicate that 95% of students stated "they learned something new" when participating in the in-class career activities. In addition, 95% of students stated "they were motivated to take next steps to achieve their goals."

References

American Association of Community Colleges (AACC). (2012). *Reclaiming the American dream: Community colleges and the nation's future.* Washington, DC: American Association of Community Colleges.

Association of American Colleges and Universities (AAC&U). (2007). *College learning for the new global century: A report from the National Leadership Council for Liberal Education and America's Promise.* Washington, DC: Association of American Colleges and Universities. Retrieved on December 1, 2015 from: www.aacu.org/sites/default/files/files/LEAP/ GlobalCentury_final.pdf.

Atlantic Cape Community College. (2013). Atlantic Cape Community College Institutional Profile. Retrieved on December 1, 2015 from: www.state.nj.us/higher education/IP/IP2013/full_reports/Atlantic%202013.pdf.

Banta, T. W., & Kuh, G. D. (1998). A missing link in assessment. *Change, 30*(2), 40–46.

Bertelsen, D. A., & Goodboy, A. K. (2009). Curriculum planning: Trends in communication studies, workplace competencies, and current programs at 4-year colleges and universities. *Communication Education, 58*(2), 262–275.

Blau, G., & Snell, C. M. (2013). Understanding undergraduate professional development engagement and its impact. *College Student Journal, 47*(4), 689–702.

Borgard, J. H. (2009). Toward a pragmatic philosophy of academic advising. *NACADA Journal, 29*(1), 43–46.

Briggeman, B. C., & Norwood, F. B. (2011). Employer assessment of the college graduate: What advisors need to know. *Journal of Natural Resources & Life Sciences Education, 40,* 19–28.

Bryk, A. S., & Treisman, U. (2010, April 18). Make mathematics a gateway not a gate-keeper. *The Chronicle of Higher Education.* Retrieved on December 1, 2015 from: http:// chronicle.com/article//65056.

Center for Community College Student Engagement (CCCSE). (2013). *A matter of degrees: Engaging practices, engaging students (high-impact practices for community college student engagement).* Austin, TX: The University of Texas at Austin, Community College Leadership Program.

Chernus, K., & Fowler, D. (2010). Integrating curriculum: Lessons for adult education from career and technical education. Report for National Institute for Literacy. Washington, DC. Retrieved on December 1, 2015 from: https://lincs.ed.gov/publications/pdf/ IntergratingCurriculum2010.pdf.

City University of New York (CUNY). (2012). *Jobs for New York's future: Report of City University of New York Jobs Task Force 2012.* New York, NY.

Community College Research Center. (2013). Designing a system for strategic advising. Teachers College, Columbia University. Retrieved on December 1, 2015 from: http://ccrc.tc.columbia.edu/media/k2/attachments/designing-a-system-for-strategic-advising.pdf.

Conway, K. M. (2010). Educational aspirations in an urban community college: Differences between immigrant and native student groups. *Community College Review, 37*(3), 209–242.

Cover Letter Rubric. (2012). Illinois State University Career Center. Retrieved on December 1, 2015 from: www.careercenter@IllinoisState.edu.

Dickmeyer, N., & Michalowski, S. (2012, June). *The relationship between student time allocation decisions and outcomes: An interactive simulation model.* Paper presented at the 52nd Annual Forum of the Association for Institutional Research, New Orleans, LA. Illinois State University Career Center.

Foxx, K. W. (2013). Student Affairs partnering with Academic Affairs (SAPAA): Three critical issues to consider when partnering with Academic Affairs. *Synergy: Newsletter for NASPA SAPAA Knowledge Community.* Retrieved on December 1, 2015 from: www.naspa.org/images/uploads/kcs/SAPAA_Synergy_2013_October.pdf.

Frost, S. H. (1991). Academic advising for student success: A system of shared (ASHE-ERIC Higher Education Report No. 3). Washington, DC: The George Washington University, School of Education and Human Development.

Frost, R. A., Strom, S. L., Downey, J., Schultz, D. D., & Holland, T. A. (2010). Enhancing student learning with academic and student affairs collaboration. *The Community College Enterprise, 16*(1), 37–51. Retrieved on December 1, 2015 from: http://iws.collin.edu/dweasenforth/Calderwood/CCE%20Sp2010_Frost%20et%20al.pdf.

Goldfien, A. C., & Badway, N. N. (2014). Engaging faculty for innovative STEM Bridge programs. *Community College Journal of Research and Practice, 38*, 122–130.

Hart Research Associates. (2015). Falling short? College learning and career success: Selected findings from online surveys of employers and college students conducted on behalf of the Association of American Colleges & Universities. Retrieved on December 1, 2015 from: www.aacu.org/leap/public-opinion-research/2015-survey-results.

Huber, M. T., Hutchings, P., & Gale, R. (2005). Integrative learning for liberal education. *Peer Review, 7*(4), 4–7.

Kuh, G. D. (2008). Why integration and engagement are essential to effective educational practice in the twenty-first century. *Peer Review, 10*(4), 27–28.

Levy, M. A., et al. (1997). The Life Goals Assessment Instrument. Instrument utilized in all Freshman Orientation (FO-102) courses, Passaic County Community College. Paterson, NJ.

Levy, M. A., Robinson, D., & Romanello, M. (2009). *Career Maturity Rubric.* Instrument developed for use in LaGuardia Community College FPA course.

Millar, G. (1995). Helping schools with career infusion. Retrieved on December 1, 2015 from: www.counseling.org/resources/library/ERIC%20Digests/95-057.pdf.

National Academic Advising Association (NACADA). (2012). Definition of developmental advising. Retrieved on December 1, 2015 from: www.nacada.ksu.edu.

National Association of Colleges and Employers (NACE). (2014). Job outlook 2015. Retrieved on December 1, 2015 from: www.naceweb.org/surveys/job-outlook.aspx.

Polnariev, B. A., Levy, M., & McGowan, L. (2010, March). Reframing faculty resistance to academic advising. Program ID—149. Half-Day Pre-Conference Workshop, NASPA Annual Conference. Chicago, IL.

Robinson, D. G., Burns, C. F., & Gaw, K. F. (1996). Orientation programs: a foundation for student learning and success. *New Directions for Student Services*, *75*, 55–68.

Tinto, V. (2002, April). Taking student retention seriously. Speech presented at the annual meeting of the American Association of Collegiate Registrars and Admission Officers, Minneapolis, MN. Retrieved on December 1, 2015 from: http://survey. csuprojects.org/gedocuments/taking-student-retention-seriously—rethinking-the-first-year-of-college.

4

CURRICULAR INFUSION OF SERVICE-LEARNING

Carl Procario-Foley and Thomas J. Van Cleave

First, it is helpful to ask: *why promote service-learning?*

Why Does This Matter?

Over the past 20 years, the scholarship of civic engagement and service-learning has grown both in amount and rigor, and has helped to show empirically the benefits of service-learning to divisions of Student Affairs and Academic Affairs. These findings have helped solidify this high-impact pedagogical practice as an integral part of a postsecondary educational experience. While not an exhaustive list, numerous scholars have identified many positive outcomes from students who have participated in service-learning or civic engagement experiences, including:

- Academic or intellectual skills:
  See Astin & Sax, 1998; Astin, Vogelgesang, Ikeda, & Yee, 2000; Cress, Burack, Giles, Elkins, & Stevens, 2010; Deeley, 2010; Eyler & Giles, 1999; Eyler, Giles, & Braxton, 1997; Gallini & Moely, 2003; Hart & King, 2007; Hudson, 1996; Mpofu, 2007; Vogelgesang & Astin, 2000.
- Retention:
  See Astin et al., 2000; Cress, et al., 2010; Gallini & Moely, 2003; Hatcher, Bringle, & Muthiah, 2004; Jacoby, 2015; Vogelgesang, Ikeda, Gilmartin, & Keup, 2002.
- Intercultural skills:
  See Amerson, 2009; Borden, 2007; Jay, 2008; Marullo, 1998.
- Leadership development:
  See Astin & Sax, 1998; Astin et al., 2000; Cress, Yamashita, Duarte, & Burns, 2010; Jay, 2008; Marullo, 1998; Sax & Astin, 1997.

- Critical thinking:
  See Cress, 2004; Nokes, Nickitas, Keida, & Neville, 2005.
- Personal transformation:
  See Deeley, 2010; Kiely, 2005.
- Civic involvement:
  See Jay, 2008; Keeter, Zukin, Andolina, & Jenkins, 2002; McCrillis, 2013; Morgan & Streb, 2001; Nokes et al., 2005; Wang & Jackson, 2005.
- Knowledge about political and civic issues:
  See Colby, Beaumont, Ehrlich, & Corngold, 2007; Eyler et al., 1997; Kellogg, 1999; Marullo, 1998; Sedlak, Donehy, Panthofer, & Anaya, 2003.
- Self-efficacy:
  See Astin et al., 2000; Brody & Wright, 2004; Marullo, 1998; Nokes et al., 2005; Rockquemore & Schaffer, 2000.

Student Affairs professionals will be especially interested in the literature above that shows how service-learning fosters retention, intercultural skills, civic involvement and leadership development; service-learning grounds students in the missions of their institutions and motivates them to contribute to local communities. Academic units will particularly value the ways service-learning enhances critical thinking, knowledge about political and civic issues and self-efficacy. Through meaningful service-learning placements and analysis, students can hone their analytical and problem-solving skills while adding to their own depth of knowledge about the day-to-day social and environmental issues their neighbors face.

Simply put, service-learning benefits communities, engages students in their institutions and social environments, fosters purposeful learning and research and can contribute positively to student success and retention (Astin et al., 2000; Cress, et al., 2010; Jacoby, 2015; Simonet, 2008; Vogelgesang & Astin, 2000). "Service-learning is one of the high-impact educational practices that have been widely tested and shown to be beneficial to students from many backgrounds" (Jacoby, 2015, p. 11). Cress and colleagues (2010) further note, "designed and well-executed [service-learning and community engagement] efforts result in increased student learning, retention, and graduation rates. In short, [it] works" (p. 6).

Overall, service-learning courses or co-curricular service experiences can challenge students to engage with others: peers, faculty/staff and community-based agencies. Such engagement can cultivate positive relationships and resourcefulness among all parties. Community needs can be addressed in constructive and creative ways allowing for benefits for all stakeholders, students, faculty/staff and community members. But how might service-learning begin and be sustained at an institution? Let us consider this scenario below that readers may find applicable to their very own institutions.

From one of the largest U.S. cities with a sprawling metropolitan area, a professor takes a commuter train each day to a nearby historic town which has suffered from economic blight in its city center since the 1960s. Just beyond this depressed downtown area, affluent homes, a country club and upscale apartments envelop the nucleus of the city. As a sociologist this professor relishes his daily walk from the train station to the university where he teaches courses on ethnic and cultural diversity. He first walks by homeless people sitting on train station benches only to turn the corner to the fresh aroma of El Salvadoran *pouposas* while passing by abandoned storefronts, large churches, and within 15 minutes he arrives on campus. During this trek, it is not uncommon for him to see discarded drugs on the side of what can be the very uneven pavement. When in the distance he sees generous front lawns and decorated driveway entrances, he knows he is close to his campus, which serves as a buffer between two worlds, a struggling city center and wealthy enclaves of exclusion. He would welcome the opportunity to understand better some of the relationships between the ethnic groups and economic classes that occupy this diverse city.

Simultaneously, in the basement of one of the city churches, a community outreach worker organizes an after-school tutoring and mentoring program for children. In an attempt to provide one-on-one attention for the children she relies on some retired church members and some high school National Honors students who are required to complete service hours for membership. She would love to expand the computer education classes she offers but needs more dedicated volunteers. Also, since the earthquake of 2012 there is a growing Haitian population in the neighborhood and many of these recent immigrants report violence and harassment at school. She would like to solicit the support of some people who know Creole and can assist her in some door-to-door outreach. Additionally, on campus an assistant director of student life is charged with the strategic goal of expanding the involvement of academically at-risk students in extracurricular activities and promoting resilience. He hears the same thing again and again. Students have to run to work, commuters have a very small window of time for involvement, but many students seek a deeper involvement in something. From "where he sits" in Student Affairs, he ponders many different options for student involvement. Some of these college students do speak Creole and Spanish but this student life professional does not know about the needs of the nearby after-school center nor has he met the junior professor of sociology whose teaching has an excellent reputation.

It might be said that this professor, community outreach worker and Student Affairs assistant could be compared to ships passing in the night. There is much opportunity for cross-divisional collaboration, response to community need, robust learning and active engagement that retains students and transforms communities. But will this happen? Unfortunately, this scenario is too frequent in higher education circles. Though the community engagement and service-learning movements have made tremendous strides in the past 25 years, there are still far too many missed opportunities. In this scenario alone, a listing of potential service-learning courses connected to this after-school community initiative might include: urban studies, ethnic relations, computer programming, public relations, conflict resolution and modern language studies. That's just the beginning! Before we get too far ahead of ourselves with this scenario, it is useful to take a step back and consider:

- What is service-learning?
- What are its challenges?
- What are its opportunities? and
- What are its best practices?

Promising Practices

Community engagement is understood as any and all forms of "collaboration between institutions of higher education and their larger communities . . . for the mutually beneficial exchange of knowledge and resources in a context of partnership and reciprocity" (New England Resource Center for Higher Education, 2015, para. 11). Community engagement can be academic, co-curricular, faculty based or originate from institutional administration. Examples of community engagement include faculty or student research that benefits a community, faculty or expert pro bono consulting for non-profit organizations (NFO), reduced facility rental fees for NFOs, extracurricular volunteer experiences and service-learning.

The term "service-learning" has historically been a common way used to describe an institution's vision and implementation of a community-engaged *pedagogy*, meaning as an integrated component of a student's graded coursework. While there is ongoing debate regarding the term service-learning and the inherent implications of the embedded power and privilege of the concept of "service" (Butin, 2006), service-learning is still considered common terminology at institutions nationwide.

For us and members of our institution, Iona College, the term "service-learning" as opposed to "community-engaged learning" or "community-based learning" felt the most appropriate considering our school's historical and foundational roots in "service" work and taking into account the longevity that "service-learning" has had within the educational literature. The hyphen in service-learning is just as important as the two words it connects as it "symbolizes reflection and depicts the symbiotic relationship between service and learning" (Jacoby, 2015, p. 2). At Iona, it is almost considered a misspelling to omit the hyphen. But just because we decided to adopt the term service-learning (and the hyphen), it did not mean we then had one cookie cutter definition exactly the same as other institutions. As Plater (2004) reminded members of the field, there are, and should be many different definitions of the phrase considering each institution's own unique identity.

There are a myriad of excellent definitions of service-learning (see Bringle, Clayton, & Hatcher, 2013; Cress, 2013; Jacoby, 1996, 2015); however, while they have similarities, "each [definition] may emphasize a slightly different orientation to or aspect of the pedagogy" (Bringle et al., 2013, p. 337). For example, at some institutions the term service-learning could be an umbrella term for any experience that is supposed to be learned from, be reflected upon and somehow benefits the community (e.g. one-time volunteering at a soup kitchen). Though other institutions limit the term to being used solely with service experiences that contribute to a student's grade in a class. This is not to say that it is "better" or "worse" to have or not have the service as a part of an academic experience, but does highlight that these are two different concepts: concept (a) is an umbrella term under which many versions may be housed (see Jacoby, 1996, 2015); (b) is more restricted and only refers to a more specific and contained academic pedagogy (see Bringle et al., 2013; Cress 2013).

At Iona College, the group tasked with institutionalizing an academic service pedagogy decided that in order for an experience to be considered service-learning, it needed to meet specific criteria including being a graded part of an academic course. In the end, the group's decision addressed a myriad of issues. The first is of quality control, which may sound like a strange consideration for an academic pedagogy. However, by narrowing what is considered service-learning (academic experiences and not co-curricular), we are able to better ensure that when we are assessing our service-learning programs, that we are comparing programs and experiences that are as similar as possible, even though academic disciplines may differ. The second is a matter of clarity, to help faculty and students understand who on campus provided primary support for different types of service experiences.

Therefore, at Iona College, service-learning is understood as a credit-bearing academic experience describing a unique and specialized collaborative course design strategy that combines: a) an academic content area; b) fulfilling a community identified need through a reciprocal relationship; and c) intentional reflection strategies in order to enrich the learning experience, explore civic responsibility and strengthen communities (Bringle et al., 2013; Bringle & Hatcher, 1996; Cress, 2013; Duke University, 2013; Jacoby, 1996, 2015; National Youth Leadership Council, 2013).

Academic Content

In a service-learning course, students acquire knowledge and develop skills based on academically rigorous content through scholarly literature, faculty lectures, independent research, group activities and a variety of other educative experiences that often are connected to Student Affairs initiatives. These knowledge and skill sets are then paired with and applied to what a community partner group (public and non-profit agencies; civic, charitable and governmental organizations) has identified as a need for the community it serves. Courses with a service-learning component can be offered in *any* academic discipline, focus on *any* applicable academic topic, and be facilitated by *any* faculty regardless of rank, position or years of experience. What is essential is that the service component of the service-learning course be connected to specific learning outcomes outlined in a course syllabus. As with any other assignment or text, each pedagogical strategy needs to be a mechanism for achieving a learning outcome. Just as a faculty member would not assign an article to read that did not inform the academic topic being explored, a service experience should never be assigned without a curricular justification.

Fulfilling a Community Identified Need

In service-learning pedagogy, community partners are central co-instructors in the educative process. Community partners work with institutions, often Student Affairs, and individual faculty members to design and implement service activities that enable students to apply newly developed knowledge and skill sets in a way that provides meaningful outcomes for the community partner and its members. It is not the intention of our institution that individual faculty members or students design service projects without the direct involvement and collaboration of community organizations or community members. Service-learning pedagogy emphasizes that community voice, knowledge and identity play a formative role in defining what service initiatives are implemented.

In an effective service-learning dynamic, the key word that describes institutions' relationships with community partners is "reciprocal." This means the institution is committed to never taking more from a community partner than is given, or to give more to that community partner than is learned from the experience (Reitenauer, 2013). In order to do this, we believe that all service-based initiatives must honor the values, perspectives, identities and knowledge sets of community partners. In part, this means that as an institution our community partners identify the need that our faculty and students will partner in serving. It is not the role of the college to decide in isolation what a community needs or how these needs will be met.

Intentional Reflection

Intentional reflection is a cornerstone of service-learning pedagogy (Collier & Williams, 2013; Jacoby, 2015). Scholarship on experiential and service-learning pedagogies consistently asserts that reflection is one of the most impactful mechanisms that equips students to make meaning out of their experience. "Reflection serves as a bridge for the back-and-forth connecting between what [students] learn in class and what [they] are experiencing in the community" (p. 95). This is not to say that without intentional reflection students can't or won't make meaning out of an experience, but that with these strategies, the potential is substantively increased. Reflection provides the opportunity for students to integrate not only what they see during a service experience, but also to hypothesize what they think it may mean. It is on this platform where these hypothesizes can be tested, challenged and sometimes revised.

For example, for many faculty members who choose to have students work with a vulnerable population, such as individuals experiencing homelessness, they are confronted with students returning from their service sites saying something to the effect of:

- "Why don't they just go to school and get an education [like me] so that they weren't poor anymore?"
- "Why don't they just get a job?"
- "How is it fair that I have to work so hard for everything I have, but they are just take free stuff and don't have to work for anything?"

While these reactions are not what service-learning faculty hope to hear after a service experience, they are not entirely unheard of or even uncommon considering that for many students this may have been the first time they were in close contact with a person who was experiencing homelessness. In order for service-learning to achieve many of its intended goals, these reactions need to have a platform to be expressed so that they can be understood from a different perspective. However, unless that platform (such as reflection) is provided, these reactions may just be the final lesson learned from the experience. It is for this reason that every academic service-learning course at our institution includes a graded reflection component that seeks to equip learners to move beyond surface level understandings of complex social issues and facilitates deep critical thinking, academic learning and engaged citizenship. This speaks to the importance of linking service-learning experiences within the curriculum.

What Service-learning is NOT

There are innumerable definitions of the term "service-learning" which emphasize the importance of institutions defining the pedagogical practice in light of specific institutional characteristics. In addition to a common vision for what service-learning is, it is similarly important to identify what service-learning is not. According to the Service-Learning Toolkit created by the Faculty Senate of The State University of New York (2009), service-learning is *not*:

a. an episodic volunteer program;
b. an add-on to an existing school or college curriculum;
c. logging a set number of community service hours in order to graduate;
d. compensatory service assigned as a form of punishment by the courts or by school administrators;
e. one-sided: benefiting only students or only the community (p. 5).

Goals for Service-learning Students

The overarching student learning outcome as a result of utilizing service-learning pedagogy is that students will begin to, or further develop the knowledge, skills and values necessary to meaningfully and substantially contribute to addressing global, national and local human and ecological needs. Specifically, service-learning at our institution seeks to equip students to be agents of change through four dimensions of learning and development, including interpersonal, intrapersonal, intercultural and academic (adapted from Van Cleave, 2013 with permission) (Table 4.1).

TABLE 4.1 Student Learning Outcomes Through Service-Learning at Iona College (adapted with permission from Van Cleave, 2013)

Dimension of Learning and Development	Student Learning Outcome "After a service-learning course, students should be equipped to . . ."
Overarching Goal	. . . develop the knowledge, skills and values necessary to meaningfully and substantially contribute to addressing global, national and local human and ecological needs.
Interpersonal	. . . interact effectively and respectfully with diverse classmates and community members toward a common goal that addresses a human/ecological need.
Intrapersonal	. . . apply reflective, analytical and evaluative skills necessary to understand how their own cultural perspectives, past experiences and individual identities impact how they understand human/ecological needs.
	. . . understand how actions or inactions can eliminate or perpetuate human/ecological needs.
	. . . see themselves as individuals with the potential to significantly and meaningfully contribute to reducing and eliminating human/ecological needs.
Intercultural	. . . identify, articulate and honor the significance that culture and context have as they relate to eliminating or reducing human/ecological needs.
Academic	. . . to use data (historical, qualitative, quantitative or other) in order to explore and understand root causes of human/ecological need.
	. . . understand and apply academic skills and knowledge in ways that meaningfully address a human/ecological need.
Professional	. . . recognize how their own professional skills can contribute to addressing human/ecological needs.

Determining that a course will use a significant amount of service-learning pedagogy is an essential part of the institutionalization process. This readily visible indicator is listed on the Needs Clarification registration webpage that clearly shows students' courses utilize service-learning as a prominent pedagogy. This designation strategy is directly in line with what have been established as principles of best practice for the field of service-learning and civic engagement (Carnegie Foundation, 2013). The service-learnning designation assigned in-course registration software systems help to streamline and implement holistic assessment strategies, track impact on community, ensure reciprocity, gauge student learning, support faculty scholarly pursuits and articulate program growth, among many other benefits.

Guidelines and expectations for an Iona College course earning the service-learning designation (including new and re-designation) include the following expectations:

- at least 30% of the graded content of the course is informed by the service-learning experience;
- student reflections on the service component of the course are graded and accounted for in the total points for the course;
- the service is not optional, extra credit or other "not's" as outlined by the SUNY Faculty Senate (2009, p. 5);
- fulfills institutional service-learning expectations of reciprocity and academic rigor;
- follows course syllabus guidelines (see IPFW, 2015);
- instructor has performed a risk management assessment in consultation with the service-learning office or Student Affairs departments (see GVSU, 2011);
- there is a mechanism for disseminating the work of the service-learning course to the greater college community.

Notably, as definitions of service-learning differ from institution to institution, so do the guidelines and expectations. For example, Iona College is unique in not requiring a specific number of service hours needed to earn the designation. The reason for this lies in the belief that service integration with the curriculum is essential and that hours served do not relate to depth of learning. However, a caveat to this is that students must serve a reasonable number of hours in order to adequately inform 30% of the graded course content. For example, if a faculty proposes that one two-hour visit to a soup kitchen can inform a substantive portion of the assessed material for the course, the faculty member would have to justify to what extent they believe this could reasonably occur or if more direct experience with the community would be more beneficial to student learning and integration of the experience with the academic topic.

It is important to note that *not* every course with aspects of service-learning needs to pursue the service-learning designation, only those wishing to be designated as service-learning using service-learning as a prominent pedagogy. Faculty who are interested but may not want to fully pursue the designation are encouraged to "start small," and work up to the designation as it is appropriate for individual courses. If a course has a service experience that is reciprocal, academically rigorous and intentionally reflective, that should be considered a "service-learning experience." If in total the sum of the graded course material adds up to 30%, the course should be considered a "service-learning course."

Moving Forward

This discussion began with a sociologist, a community outreach worker and an assistant director of student life. The sociologist observes the community needs every day in his commute to and from work; the community outreach worker is struggling to manage a tutoring/mentoring program in the face of formidable challenges of literacy, immigration and ethnic tensions; and the student life administrator seeks to engage students more deeply in the institution so as to promote volunteer service, retention and resiliency. Regardless of these variables, academic service-learning can be applied successfully if it is responsive to the community needs, grounded in academic content and committed to intentional reflection. It needs to be a well-planned pedagogy and not a well-intentioned add-on. Here are some recommended steps for newer institutions developing academic service-learning.

Step I: Form a Cross-divisional Partnership

Some institutions have designated academic service-learning officers who can bring together all parties involved in service-learning. Many institutions do not have this luxury. In order to assure reciprocity and not impose the institution's agenda on the community, it is essential that all stakeholders in service-learning (academic department, student life/volunteer service office and community-based agency) be involved from the start in the collaboration. From the perspective of the community-based agency this partnership can help promote realistic expectations so that the agency does not expect involvement from the academic institution that it cannot produce.

Sometimes faculty members may not see the necessity of collaborating with a student life/volunteerism office and, in some cases, this may not have to be a priority. There are often clear advantages for such collaboration. First, it will be important to distinguish academic service-learning from volunteerism efforts. The students need to know the different expectations of each community engagement experience. Also, for many community-based agencies, there may be placements or projects suited best for one-time volunteers (e.g. environmental clean-up/ painting project/assistance with a fund-raiser) and others geared better for ongoing academic service-learning (e.g. client-based mentoring/tutoring/developing a website/creating a promotional materials). Second, for the sake of clarity of communication, it is important for academic institutions to establish clear liaisons with community-based agencies so as to avoid misunderstandings and confusion. Finally, volunteerism offices can be excellent resources for faculty who need assistance in handling the many logistics of service-learning. These could include: 1) transportation of students to and from sites; 2) program funding to develop projects; and 3) administrative support. These three functions can help to alleviate fear on behalf of the faculty that the logistics or other aspects of the service experience are too complicated or time-consuming to make the effort worthwhile. It is important to note that volunteerism offices do not always know what factors might be preventing a faculty member back from teaching a service-learning course. In our own experience, a campus-wide survey highlighted that logistics were a significant concern for faculty and appeared to be a detractor from engaging the pedagogy. Therefore, both Academic Affairs and Student Affairs offices engaged in service made special efforts to advertise and promote the extent to which various constituents could support faculty in areas that they expressed concern.

Step II: Secure Institutional Mandate

It is ideal that commitment to academic service-learning should flow from an institution's mission statement and strategic plan while enjoying broad support from the highest level of administration. Furco and Holland (2004) note that the "chief academic officer has a critical role in leading the campus toward a consensus on the level of commitment to service-learning, as well as articulating the role of service-learning in advancing progress on specific core goals and objectives" (p. 33). They are, in fact, pivotal in the institutionalization process (curricular and co-curricular) and their support "through rhetoric and action . . . affirms the value of [civic engagement] as an institutional strategy and as a hallmark of campus-community relationships" (p. 33).

One of the most "serious pitfalls in the institutionalization of service-learning is the establishment of service-learning as an independent, separate program" (Furco & Holland, 2004, p. 35). And while service-learning often begins in diverse areas such as career development, faculty departments, student activities, advancement/community relations or campus ministry, for it to be institutionalized, it cannot be viewed as "a discrete 'program' but as a means to accomplish other important goals of the campus" (p. 35), as articulated by the institutional leaders. If service-learning is understood only as an activity of this specific area, it will likely not be embraced, let alone flourish at the institution and will be viewed as something that is someone else's responsibility. Therefore, creating and sustaining collaborative institutional and community partnerships must be clearly articulated and regularly assessed both in quality and quantity to ensure that it remains a priority-infused service-learning pedagogy throughout the institution. Without this mandate, service-learning programs may not receive the needed funding, attention and legitimacy needed in order to move the pedagogy from the margin of the institution to becoming a hallmark and central experience.

Step III: Prepare for Challenges

Institutions that are serious about service-learning will inevitably encounter challenges. The first concerns workload. Neither an "add-on" nor a means to satisfy service hours, authentic service-learning demands creativity, hands-on support and academic rigor. Faculty, administrators and students must know this before they undertake this pedagogy. Faculty are lead people in cultivating relationships with community partners. Does it always have to be faculty? Can it be Student Affairs professionals in this role? All interested parties need to collaborate on goals, trouble shoot when needed and maintain ongoing communication. Faculty must be present at community agencies as often as they can and thus demonstrate to students the essential dimension to this work. Without such faculty engagement, service-learning could easily lose its creative edge and overall effectiveness.

A second challenge follows from the first and that concerns compensation and rewards. In order to grow and develop service-learning, it needs to be justly compensated and rewarded. The development of a new service-learning course especially takes a considerable amount of time and can be a strain on the normal teaching load expectations. A reduced teaching load or additional compensation should be considered for faculty willing to develop these courses. Also rank and tenure committees should consider favorably the development of service-learning pedagogy as a meritorious component of a tenure application.

Third, some naysayers to service-learning will argue that the logistics make it too difficult. In other words, student academic and work schedules are too time-consuming to make it possible for them to complete service-learning. Additionally, transportation to and from community agencies poses very real challenges. Both time and transportation constraints can be predicaments that need to be carefully considered from the very beginning stages. On-campus projects (after-school centers, clinics, senior continuing education) that serve the community are ideal in addressing the transportation issue. In recognition of the time demands of service-learning, some institutions add a "fourth credit" option, comparable to a "lab hour" that is expected of students. Because of the time service-learning requires, faculty may need to adjust their reading and writing assignments in the course so as to allow for challenges. These logistical issues cannot be ignored and may require creative planning and additional funding to address them satisfactorily.

Step IV: Educate the Stakeholders

Now 25-years-old at some institutions, academic service-learning has arrived into its "young adult" years and thus, as a field, can boast of its seers and well-versed practitioners. It has survived the critique of being a "fad" and, at many institutions, service-learning is positioned for a long future. That said, there is a wealth of resources on service-learning. To grow service-learning, institutions need to invest in these resources through workshops, conferences and library acquisitions. Membership in Campus Compact can avail faculty of excellent workshops at low costs; also member institutions can benefit from a Campus Compact professional who will visit the campus, help assess the needs of the institution and assist in the development of a plan to expand service-learning.

Conclusion

This chapter has discussed service-learning definitions, strategies and learning goals. It has provided examples of how service-learning can respond to community and student needs through collaborative and strategic partnerships both within the institution and with the community. Suffice it to say, service-learning is an integral pedagogy in the twenty-first century academy for many reasons, including benefits for students, faculty and communities. In other words, service-learning and other civically engaged pedagogies have the "potential to create a win-win-win situation for the university, students, and community" (Vernon & Ward, as cited in Bushouse, 2005, p. 32): Students are likely retained and graduate at higher rates while developing essential skills and values for long-term engaged citizenship (Cress et al., 2010; Jacoby, 2015); faculty members are more likely to remain up-to-date in their fields and find new sources of satisfaction in their fields (Beere, Votruba, & Wells, 2011); and community needs can be fulfilled in ways that could be difficult to meet without the partnership (Bushouse, 2005).

It is important to end by noting that not all service-learning programs or projects are the same, and that many of the accolades for this pedagogy and the impact that it has are based on well-defined projects, well-supported programs and well-trained faculty members. Service-learning is not a "set it up, and forget it" style of teaching. Instead, it takes careful collaborative facilitation, consistent monitoring, open communication and room to learn from mistakes. Service-learning is not an easy pedagogy, but it is important and can be effective for all parties involved.

References

Amerson, R. (2009). The influence on international service-learning on cultural competence in baccalaureate nursing graduates and their subsequent nursing practice (Ph.D. Dissertation). Clemson University, Clemson, SC.

Astin, A. W., & Sax, L. J. (1998). How undergraduates are affected by service participation. *Journal of College Student Development*, *39*(3), 251–263.

Astin, A. W., Vogelgesang, L. J., Ikeda, E. K., & Yee, J. A. (2000). How service learning affects students. University of California, Los Angeles. Retrieved on December 1, 2015 from: http://heri.ucla.edu/pdfs/hslas/hslas.pdf.

Beere, C. A., Votruba, J. C., & Wells, G. W. (2011). *Becoming an engaged campus: A practical guide for institutionalizing public engagement*. San Francisco, CA: Jossey-Bass.

Borden, A. W. (2007). The impact of service-learning on ethnocentrism *in intercultural communication course*. Journal of Experiential Education, *30*(2), 171–183.

Bringle, R. G., Clayton, P. H., & Hatcher, J. A. (2013). Research on service learning: An introduction. In P. Clayton, R. G. Bringle, & J. Hatcher A. (Eds.) *Research on service learning: Conceptual frameworks and assessment* (Vol. 2B, pp. 335–358). Sterling, VA: Stylus.

Bringle, R. G., & Hatcher, J. A. (1996). Implementing service learning in higher education. *Journal of Higher Education, 67*(2), 221–239.

Brody, S. M., & Wright, S. C. (2004). Expanding the self through service-learning. *Michigan Journal of Community Service Learning, 77*(1), 14–24.

Bushouse, B. K. (2005). Community nonprofit organizations and service-learning: Resource constraints to building partnerships with universities. *Michigan Journal of Community Service Learning, 12*, 32–40.

Butin, D. W. (2006). The limits of service-learning in higher education. *The Review of Higher Education, 29*(4), 473–498.

Carnegie Foundation. (2013). Carnegie Classifications | Community Engagement Classification. Retrieved on May 16, 2013, from: http://classifications.carnegiefoundation.org/descriptions/community_engagement.php.

Colby, A., Beaumont, E., Ehrlich, T., & Corngold, J. (2007). *Educating for democracy: Preparing undergraduates for responsible political engagement*. San Francisco, CA: Jossey-Bass—Carnegie Foundation for the Advancement of Teaching.

Collier, P. J., & Williams, D. R. (2013). Reflection in action: The learning-doing relationship. In *Learning through serving: A student guidebook for service-learning and civic engagement across academic disciplines and cultural communities* (2nd ed.). Sterling, VA: Stylus.

Cress, C. M. (2004). Critical thinking development in service-learning activities: Pedagogical implications for critical being and action. *Inquiry: Critical Thinking Across the Disciplines, 23*, 87–93.

Cress, C. M. (2013). What are service-learning and civic engagement? In C. M. Cress, P. J. Collier, & V. L. Reitenauer (Eds.) *Learning through serving: A student guidebook for service-learning and civic engagement across academic disciplines and cultural communities* (2nd ed., pp. 9–18). Sterling, VA: Stylus.

Cress, C. M., Burack, C., Giles, D. E., Elkins, J., & Stevens, M. C. (2010). A promising connection: Increasing college access and success through civic engagement. Boston: Campus Compact. Retrieved on December 1, 2015 from: http://www.compact.org/wp-content/uploads/2009/01/A-Promising-Connection-corrected.pdf.

Cress, C. M., Yamashita, M., Duarte, R., & Burns, H. (2010). A transnational comparison of service-learning as a tool for leadership development. *International Journal of Organizational Analysis, 18*(2), 228–244.

Deeley, S. J. (2010). Service-learning: Thinking outside the box. *Active Learning in Higher Education, 11*(1), 43–53.

Duke University. (2013). What is service-learning? Retrieved on December 1, 2015 from: http://servicelearning.duke.edu/about/what-is.

Eyler, J., & Giles, D. E. (1999). *Where's the learning in service-learning?* San Francisco, CA: Jossey-Bass.

Eyler, J., Giles, D. E., & Braxton, J. (1997). The impact of service-learning on college students. *Michigan Journal of Community Service Learning, 4*(1), 5–15.

Furco, A., & Holland, B. A. (2004). Institutionalizing service-learning in higher education: Issues and strategies for chief academic officers. In M. Langseth & W. M. Plater (Eds.) *Public work and the academy* (pp. 23–40). Bolton, MA: Anker.

Gallini, S. M., & Moely, B. E. (2003). Service-learning and engagement, academic challenge, and retention. *Michigan Journal of Community Service Learning, 10*(1), 5–14.

Grand Valley State University (GVSU). (2011). Risk Management. Retrieved on December 1, 2015 from: www.gvsu.edu/servicelearning/risk-management-24.htm.

Hart, S. M., & King, K. R. (2007). Service learning and literacy tutoring: Academic impact on pre-service teachers. *Teaching and Teacher Education, 23*, 323–338.

Hatcher, J. A., Bringle, R. G., & Muthiah, R. (2004). Designing effective reflection: What matters to service learning? *Michigan Journal of Community Service Learning, 11*, 38–46.

Hudson, W. E. (1996). Combining community service and the study of American public policy. *Michigan Journal of Community Service Learning, 3*(1), 82–91.

Indiana University–Purdue University Fort Wayne (IPFW). (2015). Service learning: Syllabus guidelines. Retrieved on December 1, 2015 from: www.ipfw.edu/offices/sl/faculty-resources/guidelines.html.

Jacoby, B. (1996). Service-learning in today's higher education. In B. Jacoby (Ed.) *Service-learning in higher education* (pp. 3–25). San Francisco, CA: Jossey-Bass.

Jacoby, B. (2015). *Service-learning essentials.* San Francisco, CA: Jossey-Bass.

Jay, G. (2008). Service learning, multiculturalism, and the pedagogies of difference. *Pedagogy, 8*(2), 255–281.

Keeter, S., Zukin, C., Andolina, M., & Jenkins, K. (2002). *The civic and political health of the nation: A general portrait.* College Park, MD: Center for Information and Research on Civic Learning and Engagement.

Kellogg, W. (1999). Toward more transformative service-learning: Experiences from an urban environmental problem-solving class. *Michigan Journal of Community Service Learning, 6*(1), 63–73.

Kiely, R. (2005). A transformative learning model for service-learning: a longitudinal case study. *Michigan Journal of Community Service Learning, 12*(1), 5–22.

Marullo, S. (1998). Bringing home diversity: A service-learning approach to teaching race and ethnic relations. *Teaching Sociology, 26*(4), 259–275.

McCrillis, R. R. (2013). Civic responsibility development in African-American and Latino students: A mixed methods study to understand the effects of service (Ph.D. dissertation). University of Nebraska, Lincoln, NE. Retrieved from: ProQuest Dissertations. (1431508881)

Morgan, W., & Streb, M. (2001). Building citizenship: How student voice in service-learning develops civic values. *Social Science Quarterly, 82*(1), 155–169.

Mpofu, E. (2007). Service-learning effects on the academic learning of rehabilitation services students. *Michigan Journal of Community Service Learning, 14*(1), 46–52.

National Youth Leadership Council. (2013). What is service-learning? Retrieved on December 1, 2015 from: www.nylc.org/sites/nylc.org/files/wisl/index.html.

New England Resource Center for Higher Education. (2015). Carnegie Community Engagement Classification. Retrieved on December 1, 2015 from: http://nerche.org/index.php?option=com_content&view=article&id=341&Itemid=601.

Nokes, K. M., Nickitas, D. M., Keida, R., & Neville, S. (2005). Does service-learning increase cultural competency, critical thinking, and civic engagement? *Journal of Nursing Education, 44*(2), 65–70.

Plater, W. M. (2004). Civic engagement, service-learning, and intentional leadership. In M. Langseth & W. M. Plater (Eds.) *Public work and the academy* (pp. 1–22). Bolton, MA: Anker.

Reitenauer, V. L. (2013). Becoming community: Moving from I to we. In *Learning through serving: A student guidebook for service-learning and civic engagement across academic disciplines and cultural communities* (2nd ed.). Sterling, VA: Stylus.

Rockquemore, K. A., & Schaffer, R. H. (2000). Toward a theory of engagement: A cognitive mapping of service-learning experiences. *Michigan Journal of Community Service Learning, 7*(1), 14–25.

Sax, L. J., & Astin, A. W. (1997). The benefits of service: Evidence from Undergraduates. *Educational Record, 78*, 25–32.

Sedlak, C. A., Donehy, M. O., Panthofer, N., & Anaya, E. (2003). Critical thinking in students' service-learning experiences. *College Teaching, 5*(3), 99–103.

Simonet, D. (2008). *Service-learning and academic success: The links to retention research.* St. Paul, MN: Minnesota Campus Compact.

State University of New York Faculty Senate (SUNY). (2009). Service-learning: A toolkit. State University of New York. Retrieved on December 1, 2015 from: www.suny.edu/facultysenate/Service_Learning_Toolkit_Final_2009_01_26.pdf.

Van Cleave, T. J. (2013). Short-term international service-learning: Faculty perceptions of and pedagogical strategies for the design and implementation of successful learning experiences (Ed.D. dissertation). Portland State University, Portland, OR.

Vogelgesang, L. J., & Astin, A. W. (2000). Comparing the effects of community service and service-learning. *Michigan Journal of Community Service Learning, 7*(1), 25–34.

Vogelgesang, L. J., Ikeda, E. K., Gilmartin, S. K., & Keup, J. R. (2002). Service-learning and the first-year experience: Learning from the research. In *Service-learning and the first year experience: Preparing students for personal success and civic responsibility* (pp. 15–26). Columbia, SC: University of South Carolina, National Resource Center for the First Year-Experience and Students in Transition.

Wang, Y., & Jackson, G. (2005). Forms and dimensions of civic involvement. *Michigan Journal of Community Service Learning, 11*(2), 39–48.

Faculty Engagement and Targeted Student Programs

5

FACULTY INVOLVEMENT IN ACADEMIC ADVISING

Mitchell A. Levy and Bernard A. Polnariev

Why Does This Matter?

In the media, professional literature and conversations with both Student Affairs and Academic Affairs colleagues from across the nation, it is apparent that those who work in higher education are continually being "asked to do more with less" (see Levy, 2010 in a *Community College Times* interview, Dembicki, 2010), while under increased scrutiny from various stakeholders—all with varied agendas. Unfortunately, this is occurring while there is an upsurge of impediments to student success. One factor which often has a deleterious impact on student achievement is the need for students to manage multiple concurrent responsibilities, including their education (O'Connor, Levy & Polnariev, 2012). This is occurring simultaneously with continued substantial increases in tuition at both two- and four-year institutions. In a paper on *Strategic Advising* (2013), leaders from the Community College Research Center state:

> For many community college students—a significant portion of whom are the first in their family to attend college—these tasks (completing financial aid applications, choosing a major, registering for the "right" courses, trans-ferring) appear to be insurmountable hurdles. The sheer number of choices students face can lead them to stumble. Students may waste time and money on unnecessary course; they may miss a financial aid deadline. These stumbles can contribute to a sense they do not "belong" in college (p. 1).

Given the increasing financial burden college attendance places on many students, it is not surprising that an increased impediment to student success is the need for college students to work while attending school. Often students work more hours per week than their counselors, advisors and faculty would recommend while taking a full-time credit load to maximize financial aid support. In the NSHSS Scholar 2014 Millennial Career Survey Report, Dr. Susan Thurman (2014) indicates that of the 12,000 high school students, college students and young professionals surveyed:

- A number of respondents expect to work while in college, 66% indicating that they do or will work while attending college (up from 43% in 2013).
- 26% of those indicating that they will need to work in college not only to meet their own expenses, but to help them meet their family's expenses.

Another significant impediment to student achievement is lack of college readiness. While college readiness of entering freshmen is a *top priority* for community colleges looking to improve completion rates, the most recent scores from the National Center for Education Statistics' annual Nation's Report Card analysis indicate there is still much work to do (http://nationsreportcard.gov, see below):

- 2013 average score in Math is *unchanged* from last assessment in 2009.
- 2013 average score in Reading *unchanged* from last assessment in 2009.

Given the cumulative impact of students having to work to finance the rising cost of their education which limits their availability for engagement, their continued lack of preparation for college and limited institutional resources given current economic trends, we believe it is essential that colleges capitalize on extant structures. Lowenstein (2013) emphasized that "advisors help students make a coherent whole out of their entire education in a manner analogous to that in which a classroom instructor helps students make sense of the material in a single course" (p. 254). Specifically, we contend that colleges must utilize the primacy of student engagement within a collaborative framework to promote success via developmental advisement (see www.nacada.ksu.edu). Consequently, in this chapter we introduce examples of our research in which we successfully utilized Student Affairs methodology to increase faculty engagement in developmental advising, leading to paradigm shifts in institutional culture. Additionally, we will provide information and resources necessary for readers to begin to introduce methodology promoting Student Affairs and Academic Affairs collaboration at their respective institutions.

Unfortunately, despite the best efforts of many dedicated staff and faculty over the many years, measures of student success remain discouraging. As Mangan (2014) states, "low completion rates continue to plague two-year colleges, despite a flurry of high-level efforts aimed at pushing more students through to the finish line." In *A Matter of Degrees: Practices to Pathways* (Center for Community College Student Engagement, 2013), one of the key findings is that "student success courses work. Developmental students who participate in such courses, which cover topics such topics study skills, test-taking strategies, and time management, were nearly four times more likely to pass an introductory, college-level English class" (p. 4).

This finding clearly illustrates the importance and value of providing students with the "tools" necessary to impactful messages regarding "student success." However, given that both two-year and four-year institutions are charged with increasing student success outcomes (including retention, graduation rates, transfer, job placement, among others key metrics) while faced with diminishing budgets and resources, it is incumbent upon institutions to capitalize on resources they currently possess. As illustrated in Chapter 3, for example, we have found that the curricular infusion of student success initiatives such as career development (see Buoy, DePhilippis, Flemming-McCall, Kammer, Levy, Marler, & Otterburn-Martinez, 2014 in NASPA's *Synergy* newsletter) is an effective strategy for utilizing the existing classroom structure to promote increases in student learning and motivation. Similarly, we have found that the effective integration of faculty members within a model of developmental advising can lead to observable increases in student motivation, satisfaction and learning. Additionally, as illustrated in the promising practices section of this chapter, our research (e.g. Polnariev, Levy, & McGowan, NASPA 2010 conference presentation) indicates that utilizing Student Affairs-based methodologies within Academic Affairs programming often fosters increases in both student retention and enrollment. However, as we will address next, achieving this level of institutional synergy requires a genuine willingness to address some often long-held assumptions and develop a revised perspective with respect to who is responsible for advising. For more than 30 years, researchers have consistently illustrated the primacy of the role in which faculty members can have with respect to the college students' achievement:

- "The more time faculty give to their students . . . the more likely are students to complete their educations" (Tinto, 1982).
- "Regular faculty contact is the most important factor in student involvement, motivation" (Chickering & Gamson, 1987).
- When a student is certain of his or her major and close to graduation, the major advisor has the potential to make the most important contributions to advising (Bean, 2005).
- Academic advising is the very core of successful institutional efforts to education and retain students (Nutt, 2003).
- The common denominator in all of the efforts outlined in the report (*A Matter of Degrees: Practices to Pathways*) is the importance of strong advisors "who give accurate, timely and consistent information." "You don't have to have the title of advisor," Waiwaiole adds. "Secretaries, faculty members, front-desk people, and cafeteria workers can all serve that role" (Waiwaiole, E., cited by Mangan, 2014, in *Uncluttering the Pathway to the Diploma*).

Accordingly, the interaction between faculty and students should be viewed as an essential factor impacting the quality of student experience in higher education. It is essential that both community colleges and four-year institutions capitalize on the faculty–student relationship to promote student goal attainment. Unfortunately, many institutions continually struggle to effectively engage faculty in student success initiatives. In conversation with our colleagues across the nation we find there often exists an invisible, yet no less powerful, divide between Student Affairs and Academic Affairs, impeding effective collaboration. While the cultural, historical, economic and socio-political reasons for these divides are many and vary by region and institutional culture, the common result is a diminished capacity to develop effective collaboration (see Polnariev, Levy, & McGowan 2010 NASPA presentation). This lack of "true" collaboration ultimately restricts the development of an institutional culture predicated on systemic focus on student success. What often results are a diverse array of programs and initiatives developed by well-meaning and dedicated professionals occurring in bureaucratic silos (Bean, 2005). As Bean (2005) articulates, "whether lower division academic advising should be done by a professional advising staff or by faculty members is an unnecessary debate. Advising should be done well so students recognize their full abilities and make informed academic choices" (p. 226). To increase student success, Mangan (2014) states: "It is time for colleges to step-up from small scale, discrete practices to rethinking how they use their resources and make high-impact practices inescapable for all students." Clearly, this speaks to the need for a synergistic educational institution that places student attainment central within the organizational mission.

With respect to increasing cross-divisional collaboration via faculty engagement in developmental advising, researchers have identified a number of challenges that can limit effectiveness of such an initiative. For example, we have found attempts to involve faculty in developmental advising are often ineffective and poorly planned. Dr. Wes Habley, one of the leaders in higher education advisement and student retention practices, stresses "training, evaluation, recognition and reward have been, and continue to be, the weakest links in academic advising throughout the nation. These important institutional practices in support of quality advising are at best unsystematic and at worst nonexistent" (as cited by Cuseo, 2006, p. 4).

Consequently, the lack of true organizational support often contributes to an unwillingness among faculty and staff to participate in advising interventions, impeding the possibility of a standardized and systemic focus on students' success. Within our research, we have refused to view this reluctance as a form of "resistance"—which would have implied a lack of motivation to assist students, leading to negative assumptions regarding the commitment of many of our faculty colleagues. Rather, we have rejected the long-held assumption that the majority of faculty don't want to advise students. We instead "reframed" this traditionally held assumption and realized through numerous conversations with faculty members that their "non-participation" was really apprehension due to uncertainty of key institutional advisement information, especially as it possibly involved financial aid. We realized that faculty wanted training and support before they felt some level of comfort advising students on curricula and career pathways—they simply did not want to make errors in advisement—they essentially wanted to avoid mis-advisement. Utilizing a client-based approach typically employed in Student Affairs, we adopted a "faculty-based" perspective (Polnariev, Levy, & McGowan, 2010; Levy & Polnariev, 2012; Buoy et al., 2014).

When charged (in 2008) with increasing faculty participation in academic advising via institutional mandate at LaGuardia Community College (CUNY),[1] we chose to believe that most of our faculty colleagues were in fact very interested in assisting students in their programs, but needed to be placed in a position to do so successfully (Cuseo, 2006; Polnariev, Levy, & McGowan, 2010; Buoy et al., 2014). To address the need for enhanced faculty training and support with respect to academic advising, we decided to design a comprehensive professional development opportunity titled *The Art of Advising* faculty development seminar (Polnariev, McGowan, & Levy, 2010), which incorporated perspectives traditionally utilized within Student Affairs. With a full endorsement from the dean for Academic Affairs, the recruitment letter we sent faculty body included the following paragraph:

> In response to the growing need (to strengthen advisement and provide enhanced training), we are offering a seminar series that goes beyond traditional definitions of "advising as course selection" to address holistic factors critical to successful academic advisement. Specifically, participants will be exposed to what NACADA and Vowell and Farren (2003) refer as "conceptual elements (student development theory and ethical Concerns), informational elements (policies, facts, and information needed to advise effectively), and relational elements (rapport building and active listening)."

To emphasize that the seminar would be informed by student development perspectives and *not* the traditional view of advisement as simply *course selection*, we also included the following paragraph in the recruitment letter:

> Topics will include similarities between teaching and advising; the role of advising in student retention; advising from a multicultural perspective; and special advising needs for underprepared students and special populations.

In the next section, we describe how we successfully increased faculty involvement in developmental advisement based on *voluntary* participation, leading to an institutional paradigm shift (Polnariev, Levy, & McGowan, 2010). We also illustrate how we employed formative and summative outcomes assessment within feedback-loop methodology to inform further program revisions.

Promising Practices

a) "Art of Advising" Professional Development Seminar

With the premise that faculty members indeed want to advise students after being properly trained and supported, we created the *Art of Advising* faculty development seminar—an introduction to developmental student advisement. We developed this award-winning program after identifying gaps in advisement at our institution—which happens to be regrettably typical around the nation. We consequently designed this seminar with the following approach and perspective (based on the research of Vowell & Farren, 2003):

> Without understanding [i.e. *conceptual elements*], there is no context for the delivery of services. Without information [i.e. *informational elements*], there is no substance to advising. And, without personal skills [i.e. *relational elements*], the quality of the advisee–advisor relationship is left to chance.

Given faculty member time constraints and the great institutional need for student advisement which engages faculty members, we decided that the *Art of Advising* seminar would be limited to three sessions (6 hours in total)—one session to address each of the following key overlapping and overarching parts of advisement: 1) *conceptual*; 2) *informational*; and 3) *relational* elements (see Vowell and Farren, 2003). Faculty were required to participate in three face-to face meetings, plus post online "reflections" after each meeting in response to seminar discussions and/or articles that we disseminated during that workshop session. The expectation for participation was 100% attendance, completion of the reflections via *Blackboard* platform and a two-hour participation in the newly developed College-Wide Advising Day. Utilizing available Title V grant funding from Academic Affairs, the initial iteration of the seminar provided the first 20 participants a stipend of $500, a $200 fund to purchase supplies or equipment in support of advising and a one-year membership in National Academic Advising Association (NACADA)—as we wanted them to appreciate that they were part of a larger body of commitment and expertise. Later seminar offerings did not include the latter two financial incentives given budget restrictions.

The *Art of Advising* faculty development seminar curriculum included:

1. a number of interactive advisement-related ice-breaker exercises;
2. advisor–student role-plays using NACADA training videos;
3. review of NACADA advising *ethical tensions* (see www.NACADA.ksu.edu);
4. presentations by Student Affairs advising staff regarding academic planning information and frequently asked questions;
5. preparation for Advising Day including a Faculty Guide to Academic Advising developed by advisors with tips and strategies;

6. reflective exercises that we asked participants to complete between meetings one and two and two and three (meetings were scheduled 2–3 weeks apart) based on articles we distributed such as Lowenstein (2005).

In order for faculty members to more fully appreciate advisement as a valuable tool for student success, we grounded our work in something that they could relate to given their work in academia, focusing on scholarship and research. We presented research demonstrating the value of faculty members' role in developmental advisement via collaboration with professional advisors and counselors. For more specific descriptions of the curriculum, see *The Art of Advising: Reframing the Issues, Promoting Faculty Success* (Magna Publications, 2012, www.magnapub.com).

b) Linking New Student Orientation to the "Art of Advising" Seminar

In addition to developing the *Art of Advising* seminar and College-Wide Advising Day, both chapter authors supervised the revision of the institutional New Student Orientation model. Data collected via the revised New Student Orientation program (Levy, 2015) was utilized to inform discussion during the seminar meetings. For example, the authors introduced reflective activities (e.g. *Values Auction, Values Bingo, Values Dialogue*) into the New Student Orientation program, providing students with an opportunity to identify their reason for attending college and how to achieve their goals (see Chapter 6 regarding orientation programming). It is important to note that between 30 to 40 faculty members volunteered to facilitate reflective activities during the revised orientation programs. The student responses (n = 1500+ responses) to their priorities for attending college were utilized within the *Art of Advising* to compare faculty values regarding higher education with the student responses. This led to very interesting dialogue regarding differences in the beliefs and values we hold as educators which informs our programming decisions and potentially disconnects with respect to "why students are attending college." The dialogue was often transformational with participating faculty left agape.

To assess the effectiveness of the *Art of Advising* seminar based on feedback of the faculty participants, we developed an assessment instrument that contained the following items employing a five-point Likert scale, see Box 5.1 overleaf.

Faculty responses to the *Art of Advising* seminar assessment across fall 2009, spring 2010 and fall 2010 iterations yielded the following promising results. Below are two key responses with respect to promoting faculty engagement in developmental advising:

1. Did you learn something today that you believe will help you work with students more effectively? n = 32 responses yielded mean of 4.67.

BOX 5.1

1 = not at all; 2 = to a minimum extent; 3 = unsure; 4 = somewhat; 5 = to a great extent

1.   Today we discussed _____ elements. Is this a worthwhile topic for this seminar series?
2.   How effectively did we present the topic today?
3.   Did you learn something today that you believe will help you work with students more effectively?
4.   Please rate how valuable each of the following components of today's session were?

---

2.   The stated goal for today's meeting was to introduce how informational or relational or conceptual elements impact developmental advising. Is this a worthwhile topic for this seminar series? n = 32 responses yielded mean of 4.78.

Clearly, faculty participants in the *Art of Advising* seminars found the workshops quite valuable. An interesting though unexpected outcome was that 100% of the participating faculty requested further training. In consultation with the faculty and senior college leaders, we developed the *Art of Advising II* program for those who completed the initial seminar. We viewed this as an "advising internship" and provided faculty with the opportunity to "shadow" a professional advisor within the Advising Center and eventually advise students within their own program (i.e. major) with the assistance of advising staff—again, focusing on the importance of helping faculty feel prepared and supported to provide effective advising services.

We received two very encouraging letters of support to continue offering our *Art of Advising* faculty development seminar series. The letters are from two well-respected faculty members and capture the essence of our goal. We used the letters as part of the package sent to in support of our nomination for the 2011 NASPA award referenced above. Large portions of the letters are proudly shared below:

I was a participant in one of the first groups of the *Art of Advising* faculty development seminar. This was truly an excellent learning experience. We learned the importance of really listening to students, paying attention to not only to the words they were saying, but also the non-verbal clues as to what their body language and/or cultural upbringing were trying to convey. It is imperative that we partner with students to give them the information they need to make sure we give them the most appropriate advice we can about their academic future.

In closing, many of my colleagues have taken the *Art of Advising* faculty seminar, and we all agree that this conference has opened many discussions regarding how the advisement process helps with both student retention and student success. This seminar has helped to increase the number of faculty who volunteer for College-Wide Advising Day.

Professor Deborah McMillan-Coddington

(Health Sciences department)

I have been a participant in this seminar myself during the fall of 2010, and I have participated in the faculty advising day the last four semesters. These experiences have been instrumental in regards to both heightening my awareness of the need for active faculty participation in student advising, and in acquiring the necessary skills, information, and overall mindset that is required to do the job well.

I was hired by LaGuardia in the fall of 2009 and when I entered the college I did not have any background in how to advise students. Through the *Art of Advising* seminar, I was able to interact with our college's full-time advisors and received a lot of information about how to advise, and more importantly, I learned the value of empowering students to take control over their own advising process. A focus of these seminars was the importance of teaching students how to use the same online tools (such as *DegreeWorks*) that we the faculty and staff use to guide them. This seminar indeed stressed the developmental aspects of advising. Similarly, I learned the value of listening to students and figuring out what their goals are before giving advice on how they should proceed.

I would also like to note that the training that I received through this seminar enabled me to become a voice within my own area (philosophy) and department (humanities) on the importance of faculty participation in advising. I have participated in recruiting efforts that have resulted in more than a third of my department's professor's turn out for faculty advising day.

Furthermore, the philosophy area has recently decided to advise all of the students in our major and it is my responsibility to facilitate this initiative with my peers and be a source of information and advice for them. I am only able to serve my area in this manner because of the training that I received in the *Art of Advising* seminar.

Professor Aaron Rizzieri (formerly of

the Humanities department)

c) College-wide Advising Day

Clearly, as Dr. Bernard Polnariev was quoted in NASPA's Synergy newsletter, the *Art of Advising* seminars "supported a cultural shift that was needed on campus to connect developmental advising and assessment of those efforts intentionally to campus learning and other student outcomes" (Bonous-Hammarth, 2011, p. 13). Our next goal was to utilize a *faculty-centered approach* (Polnariev, Levy, & McGowan, 2010) based on student-centered considerations, to provide faculty with an opportunity to engage students in a supportive and comfortable environment. In collaboration with the academic programs and departments, the Center for Counseling, Advising, and Academic Support (housed in Academic Affairs) developed College-Wide Advising Day only for students who had completed 30+ credits and all basic skill requirements. As stated previously, rather than requiring faculty to participate in advising via contractual mandates, the authors utilized Student Affairs perspectives in creating a faculty-centered approach. The overarching goal was to remove faculty from the isolation of their offices, where they received neither technical support nor assistance for providing academic advising after having received minimal training. It was, and remains, our belief that by empathically understanding their "perceived resistance" rather than fighting against it, the majority of faculty who want to assist students would be more comfortable doing so. Several essential components of effectively running such an advising event include:

1.   Holding the event in a large, open venue, removing the isolation of being alone in faculty offices without support.
2.   Having the professional advising staff available at the event to assist faculty whenever they had a question or needed the expertise of the advising staff.
3.   Faculty members were provided additional training in using the *DegreeWorks* software *prior* to the event (advisement software log-in and passwords were also prepared in advance of the event). Multiple workshops were offered at varied times leading up to the advisement event; faculty could (and did) attend as many times as desired.
4.   Students who participated were segmented by program/major, allowing faculty to work with upper-level students in their programs.
5.   All students had to proceed to a "check-out" table before leaving. At this table, an expert advisor reviewed every registration form and made necessary revisions. Additionally, students completed an evaluation survey regarding their experiences.

These five strategies allowed us to minimize the anxiety and pressure faculty felt regarding making advisement-related mistakes. In essence, we told them "it was ok to make a human error, we will correct it and there will be no negative student consequences." In addition, before the students left the event, we asked each student to complete a *Developmental Advising Assessment Form* (Levy, Polnariev, & McGowan, 2009) that we had created to capture program outcomes. Data collected during the first four College-Wide Advising Days held between fall 2009 and fall 2010 yielded the following key result via the *Developmental Advising Assessment Form*:

1. A total of 1,567 students *chose* to participate (that is, they weren't required to attend).
2. 94.7% of the students stated that they "benefited from the event the way they had hoped."
3. 91.5% of the students stated they "were motivated to take action due to the session." We asked them to indicate what their next actions steps were. One of the most frequent responses (32% of respondents) was to go to the Office of Transfer Services. Consequently, employing assessment-loop methodology we revised the Advising Day program to include the presence of Transfer Services staff and resources—we found this an excellent way to connect student needs and resources.
4. 70.2% of respondents stated the "learned something new." Again, we asked students what they learned and used this information to inform future program revisions. We shared with the college community the importance of this finding, specifically students who had completed approximately 50% of their graduation requirements were still learning something about academic planning due to their engagement with faculty.
5. One of the success strategies we wanted students to learn was the importance of registering early to create a schedule that accommodates their multiple responsibilities. Consequently, we were pleased to find that there was a 48.2% increase in "earlier enrollment" for the same date in January in 2010 vs. 2009.
6. Faculty volunteer participation in Advising Day rose from an initial baseline of 48 in fall 2008 to 84 in fall 2009, then 96 in fall 2010 and eventually 100+ faculty by fall 2011 and beyond.
7. When faculty were asked in fall 2010 if they would participate again, of the 30 respondents, the mean response was 4.63 on a five-point Likert scale: 1= Not Very Much, 3 = Somewhat, 5 = Very Much.

When we presented these results at several major national conferences, including both NACADA and NASPA 2010 and 2011 national conferences, and via webinars (including *Paperclip Communications*, 2011 and *Magna Publications*, 2012), we consistently received the same amazed feedback. Our colleagues from around the country were surprised at the number of faculty who were willing to participate in the College-Wide Advising Day initiative. They were equally surprised that we did not have to "force" or cajole anyone to participate in advising students and that we did not engage in any "battles." We proudly feel that these results vindicate our stance that the vast majority of faculty genuinely want to assist students; however, consistent with basic human nature, they want to feel supported and prepared to do so effectively by their institution. Consequently, we are confident professionals in Student Affairs, with similar beliefs and commitment, can collaborate with colleagues from Academic Affairs in the provision of effective advising services. The relationships we established by utilizing a faculty-centered approach, similar to how we attempt to support student development, allowed us to develop other initiatives, such as having faculty volunteers to participate in New Student Orientation and a series of career development workshops we developed. We felt further vindication of our approach when we received the 2011 NASPA *Student Affairs Partnering with Academic Affairs Promising Practices Award.* We have no doubt that readers can utilize a similar approach, regardless of their divisions or department, and develop successful collaborative initiatives which further promotes a network of student support and success.

Moving Forward

Colleges must continue to review models of efficacious collaboration between Student Affairs and faculty members to ensure that student success is fully supported. If higher education institutions truly value faculty members who serve as effective advisors and want to expand the number and strength of faculty as advisors, then the infrastructure should demonstrate such value. One specific recommendation for Academic Affairs leaders and college presidents to seriously consider is the role of developmental student advisement as part of faculty's tenure and promotion process. Critically, this would not be a simple checkbox of advisement "participation." Rather, faculty should be recognized based on agreed metrics of advisement success as it ties to the college's mission. Several examples that your institution may want to consider include the following:

- Formative assessment of learning outcomes after meeting with the faculty member?
- How many students returned to receive advisement from that faculty member? (not just for a signature!)
- How many of those students stayed "on-track" with recommended courses with the program of study?
- How many co-presented &/or co-authored students research with the faculty members?
- How many went on to graduate?
- To transfer?
- Jobs in their field of study?

A collaborative structure that provides opportunities for faculty to receive institutional support and training via interaction with Student Affairs professionals is an excellent framework from which to replicate the concepts presented in this chapter. Additionally, the development, implementation and assessment of this synergistic approach should be incorporated into ongoing institutional assessment of advising in relation to key performance indicators such as retention, persistence, credit accumulation, transfer and graduation. Additionally, this assessment should possess a significant place within institutional strategic planning (see Chapter 9 for additional recommendations).

Note

1. The LaGuardia Community College advisement model and outcomes that we discussed in this chapter were in effect from 2008 through 2012.

References

Bean, J. P. (2005). Nine themes of college student retention. *College Student Retention: Formula for Student Success*, 215–243.

Bonous-Hammarth, M. (2011, April). The Art of Advising faculty development seminar at LaGuardia Community College. *Synergy: Newsletter of the NASPA SAPAA Knowledge Community*. Retrieved on December 1, 2015 from: www.naspa.org/images/uploads/events/SAPAAApr11Newsletter.pdf.

Buoy, J., DePhilippis, S., Flemming-McCall, M., Kammer, M., Levy, M., Marler, J., & Otterburn-Martinez, J. (2014, December). Curricular infusion of career development. NASPA Student Affairs Partnering with Academic Affairs Knowledge Community Knowledge Community newsletter, *Synergy*. Retrieved on December 1, 2015 from: www.naspa.org/images/uploads/kcs/SAPAA_Synergy_2014_December.pdf.

Center for Community College Student Engagement. (2013). *A matter of degrees: Engaging practices, engaging students (high-impact practices for community college student engagement)*. Austin, TX: The University of Texas at Austin, Community College Leadership Program.

Chickering, A. W., & Gamson, Z. F. (1987). Seven principles for good practice in undergraduate education. *AAHE Bulletin, 3*, 3–7.

Community College Research Center. (2013). Designing a system for strategic advising. Teachers College, Columbia University. Retrieved on December 1, 2015 from: http://ccrc.tc.columbia.edu/media/k2/attachments/designing-a-system-for-strategic-advising.pdf.

Cuseo, J. (2006). Academic advisement and student retention: Empirical connections & systemic interventions. Retrieved on December 1, 2015 from: www.uwc.edu/admin istration/academicaffairs/esfy/cuseo/Academic%20Advisement%20and%20Student%20 Retention.doc.

Dembicki, M. (2010, June 25). Counselors see more severity, complexity among student cases. *The Community College Times*. Retrieved on December 1, 2015 from: www.cc daily.com/Pages/Campus-Issues/Counselors-see-more-severity-complexity-among-student-cases.aspx.

Frost, S. H. (1991). *Academic advising for student success: A system of shared responsibility*. ASHE-ERIC Higher Education Report no. 3. Washington DC, George Washington University, School of Education and Human Development.

Howe, N., & Strauss, W. (2007). *Millennials go to college*. Great Falls, VA: LifeCourse Associates.

Levy, M. A. (2015, June). Assessment driven orientation: 5 key components for success. Presented at 2015 NASPA Assessment and Persistence Conference. Boston, MA.

Levy, M. A., & Polnariev, B. A. (2012). *The art of advising*. Madison, WI: Magna Publications.

Levy, M. A., Polnariev, B. A., & McGowan, L. (2009). Developmental advising assessment form. Assessment survey utilized during LaGuardia Community College Advising Day programs, 2009–2012.

Levy, M. A., Polnariev, B. A., & Thomas, M. (2011). Student orientation: Assessment and strategic planning. Paperclip Communications, Webinar.

Lowenstein, M. (2005). If advising is teaching, what do advisors teach? *NACADA Journal*, *25*(2), 65–73.

Lowenstein, M. (2013). Envisioning the future. In J. K. Drake, P. Jordan, & M.A. Miller (Eds.) *Academic advising approaches: Strategies that teach students to make the most of college* Chapter 14 (pp. 243–258). San Francisco, CA: John Wiley & Sons.

Mangan, K. (2014, September 18). Uncluttering the pathway to the diploma. *The Chronicle of Higher Education*. Retrieved on December 1, 2015 from: http://chronicle.com/article/Uncluttering-the-Pathway-to/148849/.

Nutt, C. L. (2003). Academic advising and student retention and persistence. NACADA Clearinghouse of Academic Advising Resources website.

O'Connor, S., Polnariev, B.A., & Levy, M.A. (2012, March). Five core considerations for counseling non-traditional students. Student Affairs News (eSAN). Retrieved on December 1, 2015 from: www.studentaffairsnews.com

Polnariev, B. A., Levy, M., & McGowan, L. (2010). Reframing faculty resistance to academic advising. Program ID-149. Half-Day Pre-Conference Workshop, NASPA Annual Conference. Chicago, IL.

Polnariev, B. A., Levy, M., & McGowan, L. (2011). Reframing faculty resistance to academic advising. Program code—465. NACADA Annual Conference, October 2010, Orlando, FL.

Thurman, S. (2014). National Society of High School Scholars (NSHSS) Scholar 2014 Millennial Career Survey Results. Retrieved on December 1, 2015 from: https://www.nshss.org/media/25555/2014-NSHSS-Milennial-Career-Survey.pdf.

Tinto, V. (1982). Limits of rheory and practice in student attrition. *Journal of Higher Education*, *53*(6), 687–700.

Vowell, F., & Farren, P. J. (2003). *Expectations and training of faculty advisors*. Bolton, MA: Anker Publishing Company.

6

FACULTY COMMITMENT IN ASSESSMENT-BASED ORIENTATION

Yevgeniya Granovskaya, Mitchell A. Levy and Bernard A. Polnariev

Why Does This Matter?

New Student Orientation programs are offered in nearly all colleges and universities in the United States (Frost, Strom, Downey, Schultz & Holland, 2010; Mayhew Vanderlinden, & Kim, 2010). Orientation programs provide students with opportunities to learn the college-specific "norms, attitudes, values, and behaviors" (Braxton, Hirschy & McClendon, 2004 as cited by Braxton, Doyle, Hartley, Hirschy, Jones, & McClendon, 2014, p. 89). Successful transition to college is essential for student success and retention (Mayhew et al., 2010). Susan Aud, from the National Center for Education Statistics, and her colleagues report that "only about 60 percent of first-time, full-time degree-seeking college students at four-year colleges actually earn a degree within six years, and only about 30 percent of first-time, full-time students at two-year colleges earn a certificate or associate degree within three years" (as cited in Karp & Bork, 2012). Almost 50 percent of students who drop out of college do so during or after their first year (Morrow & Ackermann, 2012, as cited in Blau & Snell, 2013).

An impactful orientation is an integral part of an effective first-year experience program. The goals of college orientation often include setting the tone for the upcoming year and creating a welcoming environment for incoming students, assisting with personal and social integration into the institution, facilitating academic integration, aligning student and faculty expectations and introducing available support services, clubs and organizations (Robinson, Burns, & Gaw, 1996). It is also important to address students' concerns regarding finances, registration and living options as well as to introduce rules, policies, behavioral norms and expectations pertaining to personal and social issues during orientation activities (Robinson et al., 1996). Since feeling connected to other students, faculty members and the campus community has been shown to correlate to college persistence, academic achievement and graduation, orientation is the perfect time and setting to begin developing social relationships and networks (Astin, 1993; Robinson et al., 1996; Tinto, 2002).

As discussed in other chapters in this book, student participation in a number of quality high-impact practices (HIP) identified by the Center for Community College Student Engagement (CCCSE) contributes to higher levels of engagement and college persistence (2013). College orientation is recognized as one of the HIP, but it could also serve as a vehicle for raising students' awareness about, and possibly engaging students in, some of the other HIP, including academic goal-setting and planning, accelerated or fast-tracked developmental education (e.g. the Accelerated Learning Program (ALP) courses discussed in Chapter 3), first-year experience, student success courses, learning communities, experiential learning beyond the classroom, tutoring, supplemental instruction, assessment and placement, registration before classes begin, class attendance, alert and intervention (CCCSE, 2013). Although research supports the link between HIP and college persistence, each institution faces the challenge of figuring out which practices to implement on their campus and how to approach the orientation program design, resource allocation, implementation and assessment in a way that would address the needs of their specific student population and the goals of their institution (CCCSE, 2013).

One example of "unify[ing] the campus around shared goals and outcomes" is Columbia College's Integrated First-Year Initiative (IFYI), a Silver Winner of NASPA's *2012 Excellence Award*. The revamped orientation program grew out of campus-wide efforts around student success, co-led by the vice presidents of Academic and Student Affairs. This program was developed around learning outcomes based on identified student success principles, placed an emphasis on student-faculty connections during and after the program and included a peer mentoring component, in addition to informing students about campus resources and academic expectations. As seen in this example, faculty members, alongside Student Affairs staff and peer mentors, can facilitate orientation program activities, engage students as unified and supportive partners in learning, share exciting experiences and success stories related to students' participation in HIP and then continue to serve as resources to students in their first semester of college and through graduation.

Successful orientations are characterized by "total campus commitment, orientation activities prior to beginning of classes, freshmen-year orientation activities, and program assessment and improvement methods" (Robinson et al., 1996). Tinto (2002) identifies *five conditions* that best promote student persistence and retention: 1) high expectations of students to succeed; 2) clear and consistent academic and career advice; 3) academic, social and personal support; 4) campus involvement with peers, faculty and staff, especially during the first year of college; and 5) involvement in active learning experiences. The implementation of these collective conditions must introduced and reinforced during orientation and continue throughout students' first year on campus, and beyond. Collaborations between members from Academic and Student Affairs divisions create invaluable opportunities for students to become academically connected, involved on campus and more inclined to interact with faculty and other students, thereby contributing to increased student engagement, learning and retention (Frost et al., 2010). Abel, Bice and Cox (2007) state that "orientation is perhaps the first, and among the most valuable, opportunities for an institution to intentionally shape new student perceptions of the faculty . . . as active, engaged, and caring members of the campus community" (p. 25).

Studies have linked out-of-classroom faculty support offered to students experiencing stressful circumstances to increased student satisfaction, motivation, academic performance and persistence (Jones, 2008). Furthermore, "institution-level orientation programs are most successful if accompanied by department or faculty based initiatives designed to support students within their disciplinary subgroups" (Krause, 2006, p. 2). Faculty involvement in new student orientation may contribute to students' comfort level in approaching faculty members outside of class and establish the feelings of connectedness and belonging to the institution. "A spirit of campus cooperation and commitment to student learning and professional development projects a strong sense of the campus as a learning community to incoming students" (Robinson et al., 1996, p. 61). The National Orientation Directors Association Databank 2004 Summary Report identifies academic advisement and evaluation of orientation leader applicants as two traditional avenues of faculty involvement in new student orientation (as cited in Abel et al., 2007). Additional ways that a number of institutions, highlighted by Abel et al. (2007), involve faculty in orientation activities include academic programming, such as presentation of model classrooms and mock lectures, panel presentations on student success topics and summer reading seminar discussions, as well as less formal social programming such as hosting dinner events, serving as greeters, providing assistance during move-in day and attending student organization fairs.

The likelihood of students' success is compromised when there is confusion or lack of transparency about academic and behavioral expectations placed on them by faculty and the institution, which often leads to poor academic perform-ance, lack of feeling of belonging to the campus community and eventually to dropping out (Karp & Bork, 2012). These adverse effects are even more detrimental for low-income, minority, non-traditional and first-generation college students, as can be seen from lower than average college completion rates for students in these categories and community college students (Karp & Bork, 2012). According to the American Association of Community Colleges data for the time span between years 2011 and 2013, there were approximately 7.4 million students pursuing degree programs at 1,123 community colleges in the United States— representing 46% of all undergraduates (2015); thus, nearly half of all college students begin higher education at a community college. Among these students, 61% attended college part-time, 58% of students received some form of financial aid, 36% were first-generation college students, 17% were single parents and 4% were veterans (American Association of Community Colleges, 2015).

Role theory concerns one of the most important features of social life, characteristic behavior patterns or *roles*. It explains roles by presuming that persons are members of social positions and hold expectations for their own behaviors and those of other persons. Karp and Bork (2012) borrow from role theory research to suggest that the lack of clear expectations about what it takes to be a community college student makes it that much harder for these students to integrate into college, as well as to balance responsibilities and success behaviors pertinent to this new role with their already complicated lives and other multiple roles such as full-time parent, employee and/or caretaker. Orientation activities aimed at clarifying students' life roles, along with their values and professional goals, serve to reinforce students' commitment to college and facilitate the development of students' sense of ownership of their college experience. These types of activities can also contribute to students' sense of urgency in mastering successful "academic habits, cultural know-how, balancing multiple roles and time constraints, and help seeking" behaviors, identified by Karp and Bork (2012) as the four community college *student role* components.

Almost 25 years ago, Pascarella and Terenzini (1991) pointed to a wealth of research that supports a "statistically significant positive link between exposure to various orientation experiences and persistence, both from freshman to sophomore year and from freshman year through attainment of the bachelor's degree" (as cited in Robinson et al., 1996). However, Matthew Mayhew and his colleagues (2010) found that most research on orientation effectiveness is embedded into studies of first-year programs, and that very little research addressing orientation-specific student learning outcomes for both first-year and transfer students has been published. Implementation of assessment-based orientation programs allow institutions to more seriously engage in an ongoing process of program evaluation and revision (the ideal feedback loop), to ensure continuous improvement in student transition services—thereby contributing to an increase in student retention, persistence and graduation rates. Moreover, going beyond satisfaction surveys and creating orientation-specific learning outcome assessments and rubrics will afford institutions the opportunity to strengthen the empirical support for effective campus-specific orientation practices, revise or eliminate less-effective practices and justify institutional investment of resources in quality programming; regional accrediting bodies would be quite impressed (see Chapter 9).

It would be impractical to suggest a *one-size-fits-all approach* to developing a successful orientation program. With that said, program creation, evaluation and revision should be guided by professional standards set forth by the Council for the Advancement of Standards in Higher Education (CAS), that were revised in 2011 to reflect Professional Competency Areas for Student Affairs Practitioners, outlined by the American College Personnel Association (ACPA) and the National Association of Student Personnel Administrators (NASPA). Based on their review of literature, Gerstner and Finney (2013) identify six core action steps that are in line with the above-mentioned standards and appear in many outcomes assessment cycle models used for program development and evaluation in higher education. The six steps are: "establishing objectives/outcomes, mapping programming to these objectives/outcomes, selecting or designing measures of the outcomes, collecting outcomes data, analyzing and maintaining outcomes data, and using outcomes information" to modify programs as necessary (Gerstner & Finney, 2013, p. 17). This approach to program implementation and assessment allows institutions to respond to the unique needs of their student population, while taking advantage of available campus resources and addressing campus-specific challenges.

Gerstner and Finney (2013) further suggest that the program evaluation cycle needs to be expanded to include "implementation fidelity assessment," to certify that the assessed program was implemented *as intended*, and that the measured learning outcomes (whether positive or negative) could really be attributed to the program as it was designed. Although the concept of implementation fidelity hasn't received much attention in the assessment literature until recently, Gerstner and Finney (2013) remind us that "program drift," or deviation from planned programming during implementation, does frequently occur, thus limiting administrators' ability to accurately interpret the outcomes assessment results and make program modification decisions since there could be major differences between what actually occurred during the program and what was planned to take place. Effective execution of large-scale collaborative efforts like new student orientation depends on committed program facilitators across divisions and departments, who understand the planned program objectives, are trained in implementation of program activities, are invested in the program assessment efforts and most importantly are committed to student success. The use of implementation fidelity assessment may serve as a reminder to facilitators to avoid program drift and may provide the groundwork for developing a shared sense of ownership for program implementation, assessment and modification among the involved faculty and staff.

Additionally, Mayhew and his team (2010) uncovered differences in student orientation learning outcomes based on gender, race, transfer and international student status. Since the goal of effective orientation programming is to assist all incoming students with college transition, it is recommended that colleges implementing assessment-based orientations monitor student learning outcomes for various student subgroups and strategize to eliminate any possible disparities in learning based on student group affiliation.

Outcomes assessment is the "common ground" and a great foundation for collaborative efforts for the divisions of Student and Academic Affairs, as it focuses on student learning (Banta & Kuh, 1998). Pope (2001) strongly recommends that Student Affairs leaders include faculty members into orientation program planning, and provide professional development activities and guidance on student development strategies and student advocacy. Trudy Banta and George Kuh (1998) highlight six themes that undergird and bolster effective collaborations across these two divisions:

1. administrative commitment to collaborative assessment;
2. joint curriculum and assessment planning;
3. shared understanding of student development;
4. coordination or curricular and co-curricular experiences;
5. development and implementation of appropriate outcome assessments; and
6. use of assessment data to enhance student experience (Banta & Kuh, 1998).

Faculty reward structures centered on research and scholarship have received much attention in the literature as an obstacle in securing faculty buy-in and participation in student development activities outside of the classroom setting (Abel et al., 2007). Abel et al. (2007) suggest that because of this perception, and in the manner of a self-fulfilling prophecy, Student Affairs administrators may not actively seek out faculty participation in their programs. These researchers urge institutions to rethink the parameters of compensation and promotion practices to reward and encourage collaborative efforts between divisions, as well as to involve part-time faculty in student development efforts, especially since part-time faculty hiring has been increasing over the last few decades (Abel et al., 2007).

Promising Practices

To increase student engagement in exploration of their academic and career goals via interactive methodology, while decreasing the passive and didactic nature of previous orientation programs, the authors of this chapter and colleagues utilized a collaborative, assessment-driven approach to redesign the LaGuardia Community College (LAGCC)[1] New Student Orientation (NSO) program in 2009. The following list of five institutional *challenges* and systemic *responses* illustrates how faculty participation in partnership with Student Affairs was utilized to enhance the LAGCC NSO experience contributing to stronger student preparedness and success (adapted from Levy, Polnariev, & Thomas, 2011; Polnariev, Levy, & McGowan, 2010 a & b; Levy, 2015).

Challenge #1: Due to large number of students attending fall 2009 NSO (n = 1440), and based on student feedback requesting more interactions with faculty and staff (students stated on evaluation forms that some of the workshops were "too crowded" and "required more space"), LAGCC implemented the following two programmatic revisions:

Response #1a: For spring 2010, the NSO was replicated on two separate days, thereby decreasing the number of students engaged with a member of the faculty and/or staff. In turn, faculty and staff could have spent more (quality) time with the students instead of rushing them off "the assembly line."

Response #1b: Needs-assessment determined workshops were offered in more comfortable, multiple sites, providing greater access. Workshops topics were based on student feedback rather than staff assumptions of student need or interest.

Challenge #2: Provide increased opportunity for students to identify and discuss individual goals via interactive exercises.

Response #2: Activities (each faculty facilitator was trained to implement one the following interactive goal-clarification exercises: *Values Auction, Values Bingo, Values Dialogue*). The faculty facilitators were able to choose the activity they felt most comfortable implementing. Each activity afforded students the opportunity to identify and prioritize their academic and career goals while interacting with other students and faculty in their chosen programs of study.

Editors' Note: In essence, rather than telling students what they should be doing to be successful while they listened passively, we wanted to connect students to faculty in their majors who gave them the opportunity to interact and reflect on their reasons for attending college. It is our belief, and finding, that students will be more motivated to listen to information regarding how to be successful and where to go for help if this message is connected to the achievement of the goals they have individually identified. In other words, the messages regarding student success and help seeking are now personally relevant for each student.

Challenge #3: Increase sense of "belonging and community" among new students via engagement within the academy structure (groupings of majors and programs of study).

Response #3: Students are provided color-coded T-shirts representing one of the three academic academies; these students were invited to sit in a specific section of the theater with other members of the academy. After a general welcome, students directed to specific classrooms in their "Academy Wing" with other students in their major to meet with a faculty member from their major or program of study.

Challenge #4: Provide students with workshops addressing their greatest concerns as opposed to menu of workshops predicated on assumptions of what students want or need.

Response #4: Drs. Levy and Polnariev conducted ten *Values-Auction Goal Clarification* workshops across the curriculum over a period of six months prior to orientation. This was done to determine what information current students wanted during their previous NSO. The student data (n = 235 responses) was then utilized to develop NSO workshops that aligned with the topics identified by students as having the greatest priority. Of course the NSO workshops were assessed and revised for future orientation programs.

Challenge #5: Incorporate a longitudinal, developmental model of NSO by providing strong linkages between the program and other campus support initiatives.

Response #5: To more closely align post-orientation initiatives with the NSO program, LAGCC's Center for Counseling, Advising and Academic Support revised its spring semester workshop schedule to a) address topics relevant for a first semester student based on data collected during the ten Values Auction activities conducted in-class (see challenge #4 above), and b) offer workshops earlier in spring 2010 vs. previous semesters, promoting a greater connection with the NSO program and framework. Clearly, it was easier to promote the workshops (time management, career planning, study skills) when they more closely followed the NSO rather than being advertised two months later as had been previously done.

Program Assessment: To go beyond simple measures of *satisfaction*, Drs. Levy and Polnariev developed assessment instruments which investigated students' sense of belonging, motivation, learning and help-seeking—atypical evaluation metrics for college orientation based on our experience and research findings. In addition, LaGuardia's Office of Institutional Research tracked the persistence of NSO-attendees vs. non-attendees. The data was utilized within assessment feedback-loop methodology to inform continued program revisions and enhancements (see Polnariev, Levy, & McGowan, 2010 a & b).

Spring 2009

The NSO committee conducted a standardized assessment of the spring 2009 Opening Sessions for New Students. Data analysis yielded the following mean responses across all three Academy orientation presentations (n = 383 respondents):

- 100% felt "welcome[d] at today's events."
- 99% "strongly agreed" or "agreed" that "based on my experiences here today, I am glad that I decided to attend LaGuardia."
- 97.7% "strongly agreed or agreed" that "based on my experiences here today, I feel like a member of the campus community."
- 95.7% "strongly agreed" or "agreed" they "learned a lot about my [their] academy."

Fall 2009

Of 165 completed surveys:

- 96.3% of students said they did "benefit from today's NSO the way [they] wanted or expected."
- 91.5% responded that they did "learn something to help [them] feel more prepared for college."
- 87.9% of respondents said they were willing or very willing to "seek help with academic, career or personal concerns from the appropriate office on campus during your [their] first semester."
- Of the 118 students completing evaluations after attending one of the 28 student support workshops, 96.6% reported "strongly agreeing" or "agreeing" that they "found the workshop valuable in preparation for college."

Spring 2010

Data indicated that 705 students attended the spring 2010 NSO sessions, which represented 33% of the incoming new student cohort.

- When asked: "How valuable was the opportunity to think about and discuss your goals and reasons for attending college?" 98.9% of respondents (n = 523) stated "very" or "somewhat."
- When asked: "Did the workshop change the way you think about your goals?" 80.2% of respondents stated "completely" or "somewhat." Upon review of the qualitative data, it was apparent that many students interpreted the second question as asking "Did you change your goals?" The NSO committee revised this item for the fall 2010 NSO evaluation to more accurately reflect changes in students' cognitive experience with respect to the activity.
- When asked: "How prepared are you to use the online resources at the college?" 95.2% of respondents (n = 585) answered "very" or "somewhat."

- When asked: "How beneficial was the discussion with faculty and students within your academy?" 97.8% of respondents answered "very" or "somewhat."
- When asked: "How valuable was the information provided in the workshops?" cumulatively 97.5% of respondents (n = 344) answered "very" or "somewhat" with respect to the following topics: *Time Management & Study Skills; Finding Money for Education & Living Expenses; What Can I Do With a Major In . . . Career Planning, e-Portfolio Introduction; and Alumni Affairs Panel Discussion.* Cumulatively 88.4% of students responded "completely" or "somewhat" when asked, "Did this workshop change how you will approach the particular issues addressed?"
- The NSO committee disseminated a survey to the Session I faculty and staff facilitators and 93.3% of respondents (n = 15) stated: "Yes, the activities and ensuing discussion were valuable for new students," while 100% of respondents stated they would consider participating in the fall 2010 NSO program.
- The Center for Counseling, Advising and Academic Support continued to train faculty to facilitate the *Values Auction, Values Bingo or Values Dialogue* activities during fall 2010 NSO. The data collected during spring 2010 NSO regarding student goals and objectives for attending college (n = 523 responses) were used to contextualize the faculty training and increase the relevance of faculty-to-new student engagement with the fall 2010 NSO cohort. For example, many of the student values identified as having the highest priority were related to "career" and "lifestyle success." Consequently, the fall 2010 NSO program engaged students in dialogue regarding how their academic and career decisions while attending college can positively impact their identified career goals and objectives.
- Additional data analysis conducted by the Office of Institutional Research indicated the students who attended the fall 2009 NSO were 10% more likely (82%) to register for the spring semester than those students who did not attend the NSO program (72%).
- In fall 2009, students participating in the NSO utilizing the interactive goals clarification activities were 16% more likely to be retained the next semester as opposed to students who did not participate. This is an increase of 6% vs. the previous year, when students participating in the previous orientation model (less interactive, no goal-clarification activities) were 10% more likely to be retained vs. non-participants.
- In 2010, there was a 47% increase in early enrollment (a key success message stressed by the faculty and staff) vs. the same date the previous year.

The LaGuardia Community College Middle States Evaluation Team Report (April 9, 2012), chaired by the President of Community College of Philadelphia, Dr. Stephen M. Curtis contained the following citation:

> The College is to be commended for a robust new student orientation
> ... (p. 15).

Another noteworthy reference regarding our revised NSO is the following
from two brilliant and well-respected City University of New York (CUNY)
Institutional Research directors, Drs. Nate Dickmeyer and Sam Michalowski, who
presented their research at the 52nd *Annual Forum of the Association for Institutional
Research* (2012):

> Researchers rarely get a chance to assign students randomly to an
> intervention but some promising local demonstration studies are underway.
> Students, randomly assigned to orientations using Values Auctions, had
> higher retention after the first semester than those from other orientations
> (see Levy, M. A., Jones, V., McGowan, L., & Polnariev, B., 2011 for a
> description of this activity).

Moving Forward

One subsequent step that we would recommend to our readers is an honest
assessment of their current orientation program. We suggest using the following
template to illuminate the objectives of the program. We have found that often
orientation programs continue to "roll-out" from year to year, and as personnel
change over time, the original objectives and goals for the program are often
"lost." It is essential that institutions candidly ask themselves if they are
implementing an orientation program because they have either:

a)   always done so;
b)   feel the need to "keep up with other schools";
c)   want to be able to document that they had a program; or
d)   there is a true commitment to student success across the institution (our hope).

Having clarified the mission and objectives of the orientation program, a second
next step would be to invite faculty members, staff, alumni and current students
to engage in program planning (Levy, 2015).

With respect to increasing faculty involvement, we recommend our colleagues
share our assumption that many, if not most, faculty members at each institution
genuinely *want* to engage with students, especially within their programs (Polnariev
et al., 2010 a & b). However, faculty members are often are *not* adequately
trained or supported to do so; they are therefore understandably reluctant to "go
advise" without being prepared to properly do so (Polnariev et al., 2010 a & b).
Consequently, orientation programs are an excellent opportunity to train faculty
to interact with new students in their programs and provide students with an
opportunity to identify their academic, career and personal goals, and learn what

Orientation Assessment Template questions:

a) Why are we doing this orientation—what are we hoping to accomplish?
b) What do we want students to gain? Learn?
c) How would we like students to be different?
d) What are the goals of faculty and staff for the orientation?
e) How will we know if we accomplished our objectives?
f) How can we assess the program and use the data within a feedback-loop to make improvements?

resources are available to support their success. Additionally, this is an excellent opportunity for faculty to learn more about the needs and concerns of their students, and use this information to collaborate with Student Affairs to develop initiatives that meet their needs. Both faculty members and Enrollment Management staff should also view this as an excellent opportunity to determine how to market various programs with respect to identified needs and goals. For example, at Atlantic Cape Community College (ACCC), the Division of Student Affairs has shared the goals identified by over 250 students, and their reasons for attending college obtained via curricular infusion of career development research (see Chapter 3) with the division of Enrollment Management. The ACCC Office of Marketing and Community Relations is using this data to revise its marketing messages to more closely align with identified student goals and needs.

Clearly, efforts to improve cross-divisional communication should include sharing of data from successful program outcomes as well as the challenges that arose in order to formulate a comprehensive institutional response to bolster student success.

Note

1. The LaGuardia Community College orientation program and outcomes that we discussed in this chapter were in effect from 2008 through 2012.

References

Abel, M. J., Bice, A., & Cox, B. E. (2007). Importance of faculty involvement in orientation. *Journal of College Orientation and Transition*, *14*(2), 25–31.

American Association of Community Colleges. (2015). 2015 community college fast facts. Retrieved on December 1, 2015 from: www.aacc.nche.edu/AboutCC/Documents/FS_2015_2.pdf.

Astin, A. W. (1993). *What matters in college? Four critical years revisited*. San Francisco, CA: Jossey-Bass.

Banta, T. W., & Kuh, G. D. (1998). A missing link in assessment. *Change*, *30*(2), 40–46.

Blau, G., & Snell, C. M. (2013). Understanding undergraduate professional development engagement and its impact. *College Student Journal*, 4(4), 689–702.

Braxton, J. M., Doyle, W. R., Hartley III, H. V., Hirschy, A. S., Jones, W. A., & McLendon, M. K. (2014). *Rethinking college student retention*. San Francisco, CA: John Wiley & Sons.

Bresciani, M. J., & Todd, D. K. (2010). ACPA/NASPA professional competency areas for student affairs practitioners. (Eds.) American College Personnel Association, National Association of Student Personnel Administrators.

Center for Community College Student Engagement (CCCSE). (2013). *A matter of degrees: engaging practices, engaging students (high-impact practices for community college student engagement)*. Austin, TX: The University of Texas at Austin, Community College Leadership Program.

Columbia College's Integrated First-Year Initiative Award. (2012). Retrieved on December 1, 2015 from: www.naspa.org/images/uploads/main/Silver1180.pdf.

Council for the Advancement of Standards in Higher Education. (2011). General standards: CAS standards and guidelines. Retrieved on December 1, 2015 from: http://standards.cas.edu/getpdf.cfm?PDF=E868395C-F784-2293-129ED7842334B22A.

Dickmeyer, N., & Michalowski, S. (2012, June). The relationship between student time allocation decisions and outcomes: an interactive simulation model. Paper presented at the 52nd Annual Forum of the Association for Institutional Research. New Orleans, LA.

Frost, R. A., Strom, S. L., Downey, J., Schultz, D. D., & Holland, T. A. (2010). Enhancing student learning with academic and student affairs collaboration. *The Community College Enterprise*, 16(1), 37–51. Retrieved on December 1, 2015 from: http://search.proquest.com/docview/340291342?accountid=11946.

Gerstner, J. J., & Finney, S. J. (2013). Measuring the implementation fidelity of student affairs programs: A critical component of the outcomes assessment cycle. *Research & Practice in Assessment*, 8(2), 15–28.

Jones, A. C. (2008). The effects of out-of-class support on student satisfaction and motivation to learn. *Communication Education*, 57(3), 373–388.

Karp, M. M., & Bork, R. H. (2012). They never told me what to expect, so I didn't know what to do: Defining and clarifying the role of a community college student (Working Paper No. 47). Teachers College Community College Research Center (CCRC). Retrieved on December 1, 2015 from: www.compact.org/wp-content/uploads/2012/05/they-never-told-me-what-to-expect1.pdf.

Krause, K. (2006). Transition to and through the first year: Strategies to enhance the student experience. Retrieved on December 1, 2015 from: www.griffith.edu.au/__data/assets/pdf_file/0008/39275/USCKeynoteFinal2006.pdf.

Levy, M. A. (2015). An assessment based approach to orientation. Mini-Institute presented at NASPA Assessment and Retention Conference. Boston, MA. June 26, 2015.

Levy, M. A., Jones, V., McGowan, Levy, M. A., Jones, V., & Polnariev, B. A. (2011, March). Purposeful student leadership: A goals clarification activity. Program ID-255. Workshop presented at NASPA Annual Conference. Philadelphia, PA.

Levy, M., Polnariev, B. A., & Thomas, M. (2011). Student orientation: Assessment and strategic planning. Paperclip Communications, Webinar.

Mayhew, M. J., Vanderlinden, K., & Kim, E. K. (2010). A multi-level assessment of the impact of orientation programs on student learning. *Research in Higher Education*, 5(4), 320–345.

Polnariev, B. A., Levy, M., & McGowan, L. (2010a, March). Reframing faculty resistance to academic advising. Program ID—149. Half-Day Pre-Conference Workshop, NASPA Annual Conference. Chicago, IL.

Polnariev, B. A., Levy, M., & McGowan, L. (2010b, October). Reframing faculty resistance to academic advising. Program code—465. NACADA Annual Conference, Orlando, FL.

Pope, M. (2001). Faculty involvement in Student Affairs: Legitimate claim or latest fade? *Journal of College Orientation and Transition*, 8(2), 7–15.

Robinson, D. G., Burns, C. F., & Gaw, K. F. (1996). Orientation programs: a foundation for student learning and success. *New Directions for Student Services*, (75), 55–68.

Tinto, V. (2002). Taking student retention seriously. Speech presented at the annual meeting of the American Association of Collegiate Registrars and Admission Officers, Minneapolis, MN. April 15, 2002. Retrieved on December 1, 2015 from: http://survey. csuprojects.org/gedocuments/taking-student-retention-seriously--rethinking-the-first-year-of-college.

7

DEVELOPING SUCCESSFUL COLLABORATIVE BRIDGE PROGRAMS

Sharon O'Connor, Bernard A. Polnariev and Mitchell A. Levy

Why Does This Matter?

The main goal of summer bridge programs is to more effectively transition students into college, especially those students believed not academically or socially prepared for college (Sablan, 2014). Collaborative college bridge programming helps create more seamless pathways, increases access, reduces redundancy of efforts and thus more efficiently manages resources (Bragg, Kim, & Barnett, 2006). Using Beyond Postsecondary transcript data and extensive data from a large university system, Daniel Douglas and Dr. Paul Attewell (2014) researched the effects of "summer bridge" programs on students. These students began coursework prior to the beginning of their college experience. Their (2014) results were quite encouraging, they found that students who participated in summer bridge programs, from both two-year and less selective four-year colleges, were 10 percentage points more likely to graduate within six years (a typical measure of student graduation success for both types of colleges). Drs. Thomas Bailey and Sung-Woo Cho from Columbia University's Teachers College Community College Research Center (CCRC) suggest that "intensive bridge programs that take place in the summer before college starts have the potential to make up for weaknesses and allow students to start college at the college level" (2010, pp. 2–3). Many institutions provide more than one type of bridge program given their diverse student body and needs (Kezar, 2000).

Purpose and Need

To more effectively support students who may be at-risk academically, we must first seek to better understand the actual challenges that our students face. With first-to-second-year retention rates at 55.5% for two-year colleges (ACT, 2012a,

p. 4) and 65.2–80.2% for four-year colleges (ACT, 2012a, p. 5), the attrition rate among new students is considerable. Identifying student populations which are the most vulnerable to attrition can assist us in more effectively targeting our approach to help these students remain in school and complete their desired levels of education. Students who are at-risk academically are often the ones with the least amount of access to resources and support outside of school. For example, lower-income students are more likely than their peers to be unprepared or underprepared for higher education, and more likely to drop out before completing their degrees (Lorah & Ndum, 2013). For students who have little financial support from families, or for those who must financially support themselves completely while attending college, managing school while also struggling to meet essential expenses of living makes it more difficult to persist to graduation. Couple these factors with family responsibilities such as caring for children, younger siblings and/or aging parents, and the difficulties are clearly compounded. To ensure that students are able to persist and complete their educations, they must not only have the opportunity and flexibility to work while attending school, but to also have access to sufficient financial aid resources to assist with tuition and expenses during their time in higher education (Seidman, 2005).

Dr. Adrianna Kezar, Professor of Higher Education at the University of Southern California, suggests "students in summer bridge programs are often first generation college students" (2000, p. 2). For students who are among the first-generation in their families to attend higher education, there are many challenges to be confronted. Not only are these students navigating new territory without the benefit of the ability to draw from the experience of past generations, they are more likely to arrive at college less prepared than their peers whose parents had obtained postsecondary degrees. According to the Department of Education (2010), students whose mothers had more education were more likely to engage in "early childhood education programs and home literacy activities." (U.S. Department of Education, 2009, as cited in U.S. Department of Education, 2010, p. 20). Additionally, students whose parents had *not* attended college were also found to score *lower* on the SAT College Admission Exams (Saenz, Hurtado, Barrera, Wolf, & Young, 2007, p. 4). The U.S. Department of Education (2010) also found that children whose parents are more educated scored better in both mathematics and reading on the National Assessment of Educational Progress as compared to their peers whose parents had less education (U.S. Department of Education, 2009, as cited by U.S. Department of Education, 2010, p. 20). These findings highlight the importance of building a strong educational foundation early in life, and suggest that students who have not had access to such opportunities are more likely to struggle later on in life.

Our college student population continues to become more ethnically and racially diverse. As such, identifying and addressing the unique issues and challenges that present as barriers to persistence is essential. At-risk populations include, among others, African American and Hispanic populations, who were found to "start with the lowest scores and grow at the slowest pace" (ACT, 2012a, p. 2) compared with their White and Asian counterparts. These disparities begin long before college, and indicate not only "achievement gaps," but also "growth gaps," as African American and Hispanic students were found to make slower progress than their Asian and White peers (ACT, 2012a, p. 2). According to the ACT foundation (2012a), "[o]n average, neither Hispanic nor African American students meet the ACT College Readiness Benchmarks" (p. 2) with the exception of Hispanic students who "just met the English Benchmark" (p. 2). African American and Hispanic students are also less likely to attend college as opposed to many other demographic groups. Hispanic students have consistently represented one of the largest ethnic groups among first-generation college students (Saenz et al., 2007, p. 10). According to the U.S. Department of Education (2010), the percentages of African American and Hispanic students who complete high school and move on to college immediately afterward are substantially lower than that of White students. In 2008, 71.7% of White students moved on to college immediately after high school, while 63.9% of Hispanic students, and 55.7% of African American students who graduated that same year enrolled in college (U.S. Department of Education, 2010, p. 118). Also in 2008, 32.6% of White Americans over the age of 25 years were found to have "at least a bachelor's degree," while these numbers were only 19.7% for African Americans and 13.3% for Hispanic Americans (U.S. Department of Education, 2010, p. 141), further highlighting the disparity among ethnic groups in not only in rates of enrollment in college, but also in degree attainment.

Although female students tend to fare better than male students across lines of race and ethnicity, the disparity is especially apparent among African American students. In 2008, African American men earned less than half the amount of degrees earned by African American women (U.S. Department of Education, 2010, p. 136). According to Seidman (2005), major barriers faced by African American students include financial challenges, limited family support, "low self-esteem, and low social expectations for going to college and completing a college degree" (p. 16). Seidman (2005) also posits that "many African American students are first-generation and from single-parent homes" (p. 16) and may be lacking in role models within their families on which to model their academic pursuits.

Minority students often arrive at college without sufficient academic preparation (Simon, 1993; Thomason & Thurber, 1999, as cited by American Speech-Language Hearing Association (ASHA), 2015). This disparity is partially due to minority students attending schools in areas with fewer financial resources, as well as the increased likelihood that minority students will be placed in remedial or non-college preparatory courses (NCES, 1996; Simon, 1993, as cited by ASHA, 2015). As we continue this chapter, we will explore best practices for creating bridge programs that address the challenges and meet the needs of our most at-risk student populations to most effectively support our students' persistence and success.

One example of a well-organized and collaborative bridge program is the California State University's Summer Bridge program, which focuses of *four* key elements:

- the experience is designed to develop student self-efficacy;
- the experience takes place face-to face on campus before the incoming semester/quarter;
- the program has an academic component that leads into the incoming semester/quarter;
- the program has assessment and accountability.

Promising Practices

Practice #1—Suffolk County Community College (SUNY) College Success Program (CSP)

An example of a promising "bridge/transition" program for students who are considered at-risk, both academically and financially, was the Suffolk County Community College (State University of New York, SUNY) College Success Program (CSP). The primary objective of the program was to provide students who had financial need and placed into two or three levels of remediation via the ACCUPLACER test with the support necessary to successfully transition to, and ultimately succeed in, college. The following description speaks to the design, implementation and assessment outcomes achieved by Dr. Levy (program director on the Michael J. Grant campus of Suffolk County Community College) and colleagues from 2006 to 2008.

Recruitment

Because participation was voluntary, freshman students who placed into two or three levels of remediation were provided with program information when meeting with an advisor to register for their first semester classes. It is interesting to note that many of the students who were eligible for the CSP were simultaneously eligible for the Education Opportunity Fund (EOF) program. Consequently, it was decided that the most ethical action in these instances was to explain all the available options to the students and support them in making the most positive and informed decision for themselves. The program was able to achieve the recruitment goal of 60 new students each year.

Summer Bridge Component

Students who chose to participate in the CSP program were required to complete a three-week summer transition component before the start of their first semester.

Students would participate in the program for three weeks in August, Monday through Friday, from 9 am to 1 pm. The students were divided into cohorts of 25, with each grouping of 25 representing the enrollment of one section of the program-based freshman seminar course. Consequently, each section of freshman seminar, which was to continue for one hour per week in the fall, remained intact throughout the summer program. Each cohort was led by a freshman seminar instructor who was responsible for working with the students in the summer and the fall. In addition, a program counselor was assigned to each section, with these students forming a case-load. A key factor in the positive outcomes of the program, we believe, was the extensive collaboration between faculty and staff in not only developing program curricula, but in implementing all aspects of the program.

Curriculum

The summer curriculum included the following interventions developed jointly by the Student Affairs staff and faculty members:

- 4 to 6 hours per week in the Writing Lab using self-paced learning software in preparation for their fall semester reading and writing coursework.
- 4 to 6 hours per week in the Math Lab using self-paced learning software in preparation for their fall semester math coursework.
- Introduction to college success strategies such as time management, effective note-taking strategies, how to effectively learn from a text-book and introduction to campus resources such as the library, tutoring and counseling services.
- In addition, two initiatives which focused on psycho-social development were introduced and had a significant impact as evidenced by the experiences of students and staff, promoting community and focus on non-cognitive factors.

Promoting Community

To help students feel a part of the college campus and reduce any sense of academic shame (Levy, 2015) due to their developmental placements, the program implemented a series of community-building exercises. For example, on the first Friday of the summer program, students participated in on-campus service projects such as assisting in the clean-up of the community food pantry housed at the Grant campus. On the second Friday, each cohort/class was given the opportunity to develop a Coat-of-Arms identifying their group and a presentation explaining their identity. The third Friday (last day of the program) a luncheon was held commemorating their successful completion of the summer component. The college president, campus deans and faculty members were present. Each cohort/ class then presented their Coat-of-Arms, sometimes using art, music and/or performance to explain to the audience "who they were" and "why they were in college." Their Coat-of- Arms was eventually memorialized by being displayed in the Grant campus CSP program office. The campus staff found the presentation truly inspiring and incredibly powerful.

Addressing Non-cognitive Factors

In addition to providing the students with the necessary information and engagement with resources to promote success, we made a conscious decision to address the issue of help-seeking (Levy, 2015). It has been our experience that all too often students do not effectively avail themselves of campus resources regardless of how much assistance we offer or how many different ways we advertise those services (O'Conner, Polnariev, & Levy, 2012). We believe for many students, especially those who are first generation and underrepresented, the suggestion that they seek help often causes confusion, anxiety and discomfort. Consequently, the counselors and faculty asked students: "Now that you know of all the help that is here for you, would you go for help? If no, what would keep you from getting help? What can we do to make it easier?" This led to some very profound and enlightening conversations. The program staff utilized this qualitative data to revise the program—for example, Dr. Levy asked the directors of the Writing and Math Labs to meet individually with each student to get a sense of their individual experiences and needs with Writing or Math, and develop a "file for each student." The program staff believed that the students would be more comfortable seeking help in the fall now that they formed a personal relationship with the director, who was a faculty member, and the staff now had individualized information regarding each student to be utilized. A review of lab attendance in the fall indicated students in fact were more likely to seek services from the lab as opposed to developmental students not in the program.

Results

From 2006–2008, the Grant campus CSP students attained a 2.7 cumulative GPA in college-level courses as opposed to a non-CSP control group matched for academic placement level, which attained a 1.9. The retention rate for the CSP students for fall to spring was 92%, and fall to fall was 88%, both exceeding the non-program control group.

Practice #2—Accelerated Study in Associate Programs (ASAP) at City University of New York (CUNY)

> *Make it happen!* Each time I see this phrase, I think to myself, this is not just a cluster of simplistic words, but a philosophical way of life . . . I am

so proud to be a member of ASAP. . . . As I get ready to leave LaGuardia, I look ahead and see clearly what ASAP has done for me. The program has provided warmth and a fabric of memories that will remain in my heart forever.

2009 ASAP alumni

Another example of a successful bridge program for at-risk students is Accelerated Study in Associate Programs (ASAP) (see also Chapter 2 to learn more about the program). Although ASAP began in 2007 with students who were remedial-free,[1] only 50%[2] of the cohort (originally comprised of 208 LaGuardia Community College students) graduated within the three-year period. The program eventually attained graduation rates which increased 100% or more when compared to similar LaGuardia students who started at the College in 2006[3] (see Linderman & Kolenovic's 2012 report for greater details of this approach as it applied to ASAP's outcomes).

Clearly, having remedial needs is only but one major barrier to community college student success. The ASAP program accepted 100 new students in fall 2009. However this time almost three-quarters of the students had placed into at least one level of developmental[4] need (the program accepted students with no more than two developmental placements by the fall of 2009). The retention rates for this group were significant—with 88% re-enrolling after one year and 75% within two years.[5] Within three years, the ASAP team helped to graduate 56 students (or 56%) from this cohort. When compared to the ASAP cohort graduation outcomes, a comparable control group who started LaGuardia in 2008 attained a graduation rate of only 27% (94 out of 348 students). As compared to our remedial-free cohort 1, the ASAP cohort with remedial needs improved graduation by 6 percentage points. It was truly exhilarating to demonstrate continued improvement through refined efforts in a host of retention initiatives— including the summer orientation and curricular infusion via ASAP seminar (see details and outcomes in Chapter 2).

Another significant phase of the ASAP initiative was the experimental random-assignment research design conducted by MRDC over a five-year period. The study involved ASAP students from three colleges: Borough of Manhattan Community College (BMCC), Kingsborough Community College, and LaGuardia Community Colleges. Scrivener and colleagues (2015) emphasize that "ASAP's effects are the largest MDRC has found in any of its evaluations of community college reforms. The model offers a highly promising strategy to markedly accelerate credit accumulation and increase graduation rates among educationally and economically disadvantaged populations" (Scrivener, Weiss, Ratledge, Rudd, Sommo, & Fresques 2015, p. iii). The program (across all three participating colleges) almost doubled the percentage of students who received an associate's degree within three years: 40.1% for ASAP students vs. 21.8% for the control group. In addition, because ASAP produced significantly more graduates than most college initiatives, the "cost per degree was lower despite the substantial investment required to operate the program" (p. iii). The MDRC research team further stressed that ASAP was well executed and is scheduled for significant continued scaling as mentioned in Chapter 2, to help an even greater number of students succeed.

Overall, MDRC's evaluation of ASAP found that CUNY developed and successfully implemented a program that generated large, meaningful changes for low-income students with developmental education needs at three urban community colleges. With an investment in the right combination of enhanced services, requirements and messages, community college students can succeed at far higher rates than usual. After a five-year evaluation, MDRC researchers concluded that the "ASAP model offers a promising strategy to markedly increase graduation rates and build human capital among disadvantaged populations" (Scrivener et al., 2015, p. 95). ASAP substantially improved students' academic outcomes over three years, almost doubling graduation rates. ASAP increased continued enrollment in college and had especially large effects during the winter and summer intersessions. On average, program group students earned 48 credits in three years, nine credits more than the control group students achieved. By the end of the study period, 40% of the program group had received a degree, compared with 22% of the control group. At that point, 25% of the program group was enrolled in a four-year school, compared with 17% of the control group.

In his 2015 State of the Union Address, President Barack Obama stated that:

> Colleges must also adopt promising and evidence-based institutional reforms to improve student outcomes, such as the effective Accelerated Study in Associate Programs (ASAP) programs at the City University of New York which waive tuition, help students pay for books and transit costs, and provide academic advising and supportive scheduling programs to better meet the needs of participating students, resulting in greater gains in college persistence and degree completion.

It's amazing that this 2007 boutique program has caught the attention of the President of the United States and has been utilized in his speeches. This higher education program continues to be a huge success! New York City and CUNY are investing another $42 million to scale and support ASAP. CUNY's Chancellor J. B. Milliken stated that "the $42 million in city funds will allow ASAP to expand from 4,000 students to 25,000 students across all CUNY associate programs by 2018" (as cited by Colangelo & Chapman, 2015; see Chapter 9 for further info on Milliken).

Several CUNY specific ASAP programs have connected with Hunter College School of Social Work, a CUNY graduate school, to place second-year social work interns (SWI) with ASAP programs to provide counseling and support to program students. Most academic years since 2008, LaGuardia's ASAP program has an on-site, part-time (typically three days per week) SWI to meet with students individually on an as-needed basis. Meeting with the SWI is entirely voluntary, but the service has been utilized consistently by students seeking support to manage a range of issues including stress, anxiety, depression, family dynamics and social challenges. Students may meet with SWIs at various points throughout the academic year for support in addition to the existing support from their advisors. SWIs may also conduct presentations related to mental health, stress management and life skills, and conduct groups pertaining to various issues relevant to student concerns such as stress management, relationships and wellness.

Co-author Sharon O'Connor served as LaGuardia's ASAP SWI during academic year 2009–2010 when enrolled in Hunter's MSW program. The students were extremely receptive to obtaining counseling. The SWI was an integral part of the program and as such was "infused" into the program—she would attend bi-monthly staff meetings and led ASAP-specific seminar workshops. Additionally, the SWI met with the college's counseling department director, Dr. Mitchell Levy, who is a licensed mental health counselor. ASAP students were frequently referred and introduced to the SWI by their ASAP advisors, with whom they met twice per month (as part of the program's mandate). ASAP advisors and students quickly developed relationships with the SWI—this was key to her work and success. Advisors were able to identify students who might benefit from counseling, and then make an immediate introduction to the SWI in the convenience of the ASAP office. Due to the SWI's physical proximity and general involvement with ASAP, students were able to become familiar with the intern before engaging in counseling, which likely facilitated a smoother transition into a counseling relationship, and made the process less intimidating. ASAP students also seemed less likely to "fall through the cracks," and more likely to follow through with a referral as the counseling was being facilitated *in-house*. Following counseling with the SWI as part of the larger ASAP program, students expressed feeling increased support and stability, as well as greater hope that they would achieve their academic and life goals.

Moving Forward

One next step that we would recommend to our colleagues is an assessment of your bridge program efforts with respect to help-seeking. As previously stated, it does *not* matter how many pages are in the student handbook or if we try to utilize intrusive practices via email, text, blog, tweet, post-card and the latest social media. If students are not taking advantage of the services and assistance we are offering, then we believe there is a disconnect. Too often, we have heard colleagues lament that their students are not motivated or don't care because when they suggest that they seek tutoring, the student does not attend. Rather than assume that the student behavior is evidence of their level of motivation or commitment, we would instead ask the following questions:

- Does the student understand what you mean by "tutoring?"
- Has the student had negative experiences when they sought additional help before at this or other institutions?
- Is it the culture norm of the student to not seek help—is it shameful to admit difficulty?
- Is asking for help perceived as a sign of weakness within the student's culture?
- How welcoming are your support services?

Clearly, we strongly recommend that before promoting the latest trend (or fad) in student success literature regarding communication with student's staff and faculty, institutional leaders in addition to community stakeholders should "take a step back" and learn from students how our efforts are being perceived and what barriers (often invisible) exist for students seeking the help and support their need.

Another next step recommendation would be to consider offering counseling and support within the bridge program, tailored to the needs of the program's specific student population. One effective way to offer this service is to utilize graduate school-level student interns in psychology, social work and/or mental health counseling if the college is somehow connected with a graduate school that offers these disciplines. Student clinicians can assist bridge program students by providing support related to stress management, life skills, self-care, depression screening and overall wellness, especially when there are budgetary restrictions regarding hiring counseling professionals within the program. Interns may also provide connections and referrals to external mental health resources in the community for more long-term or intensive counseling. Intern clinicians should also link with existing on-site mental health professionals at the institution's general counseling/health center for on-site supervision and guidance to ensure continuity of care during summers and breaks for example, as well as to provide a necessary framework for emergency protocol, safety and best practices. In addition, the intern can provide aggregate, non-identifying data regarding the emerging psycho-social themes which are being addressed in the counseling. This information can be utilized to inform the development of programming, which more effectively addresses student needs with respect to proactive prevention and management.

Notes

1. The 2007 ASAP group was only accepted into the program if they were remedial-free by the start of the fall 2007 semester. Almost half of them had remedial needs prior to their start.
2. We actually graduated 50.5% of the 208 cohort—yielding 105 graduates!
3. Student groups were matched from years that we did not accept students in order to more fully control for variables such as motivation. Hence the comparison group for cohort 1 and cohort 2 started College in 2006 and 2008, respectively.
4. The term *developmental needs* are used interchangeably with *remedial needs* in much of the literature and in this book. Students' placement into such no-credit courses is based on scores on the CUNY Assessment Test.

5. Note that 24% of the 75% two-year re-enrollment rate accounts for graduation; thus 51% continued at LaGuardia in the fall 2011 semester.

References

ACT (2012a). Do race/ethnicity-based student achievement gaps grow over time? Retrieved on December 1, 2015 from: www.act.org/research/policymakers/pdf/Race EthnicityReport.pdf.

ACT (2012b). National collegiate retention and persistence to degree rates. Retrieved on December 1, 2015 from: www.act.org/research/policymakers/pdf/retain_2012.pdf.

American Speech-Language Hearing Association (ASHA). (2015). Minority student recruitment, retention and career transition practices: A review of the literature. Retrieved on December 1, 2015 from: www.asha.org/practice/multicultural/recruit/litreview.htm.

Bailey, T., & Cho, S. W. (2010). Developmental education in community colleges. Issue brief prepared for the White House Summit on Community Colleges. New York: Teachers College, Columbia University.

Bragg, D. D., Kim, E., & Barnett, E. A. (2006). Creating access and success: Academic pathways reaching underserved students. *New Directions for Community Colleges, 135*, 5–19.

California State University's Summer Bridge program. Retrieved on December 1, 2015 from: www.csustan.edu/eop/program-summer-bridge.

Colangelo, L., & Chapman, B. (2015, October 16). CUNY unveils $42M plan to boost graduation rates. *New York Daily News*. Retrieved on December 1, 2015 from: www.nydailynews.com/new-york/exclusive-cuny-42m-plan-boost-grad-rates-article-1.2399541.

Douglas, D., & Attewell, P. (2014). The bridge and the troll underneath: Summer bridge programs and degree completion. *American Journal of Education, 121*(1), 87–109.

Kezar, A. (2000). Summer bridge programs: Supporting all students. ERIC Digest. Retrieved on December 1, 2015 from: http://files.eric.ed.gov/fulltext/ED442421.pdf.

Levy, M. A. (2015, June 26). Assessment driven orientation: 5 key components for success. Presented at 2015 NASPA Assessment and Persistence Conference. Boston, MA.

Linderman, D., & Kolenovic, Z. (2012). Results thus far and the road ahead: A follow-up report on CUNY Accelerated Study in Associate Programs (ASAP). CUNY Accelerated Study in Associate Programs.

Lorah, J., & Ndum, E. (2013). Trends in achievement gaps in first-year college courses for racial/ethnic, income, and gender subgroups: A 12-year study. ACT. Retrieved on December 1, 2015 from: www.act.org/research/researchers/reports/pdf/ACT_RR2013-8.pdf.

Obama, B. (2015, February). White House Unveils America's College Promise Proposal: Tuition-Free Community College for Responsible Students. Retrieved on December 1, 2015 from: www.whitehouse.gov/the-press-office/2015/01/09/fact-sheet-white-house-unveils-america-s-college-promise-proposal-tuitio.

O'Connor, S. K. (2010, May). Knowing what works for you. Elephant in the Room. ASAP Program, LaGuardia Community College. LIC, New York.

O'Connor, S, Polnariev, B. A., & Levy, M. (2012, February). Five core considerations for counseling non-traditional students. Student Affairs eNews. Retrieved on December 1, 2015 www.studentaffairsnews.com/five-core-considerations-for-counseling-non-traditional-students.

Sablan, J. R. (2014). The challenge of summer bridge programs. *American Behavioral Scientist*, *58*(8), 1035–1050.

Saenz, V. B., Hurtado, S., Barrera, D., Wolf, D., & Young, F. (2007). First in my family: A profile of first-generation students at four-year institutions since 1971. Cooperative Institutional Research Program/Higher Education Research Institute, University of California, Los Angeles. Retrieved on December 1, 2015 from: www.heri.ucla.edu/PDFs/pubs/TFS/Special/Monographs/FirstInMyFamily.pdf.

Scrivener, S., Weiss, M. J., Ratledge, A., Rudd, T., Sommo, C., & Fresques, H. (2015). Doubling Graduation rates three-year effects of CUNY's Accelerated Study in Associate Programs (ASAP) for developmental education students. New York: MDRC. Retrieved on December 1, 2015 from: www.mdrc.org/sites/default/files/doubling_graduation_rates_fr.pdf.

Seidman, A. (2005). Minority student retention: Resources for practitioners. *New Directions for Institutional Research* (125). Wiley Periodicals. Retrieved on December 1, 2015 from: www.dso.iastate.edu/sites/default/files/files/success/minority-retention-seidman.pdf.

U.S. Department of Education (2010). Status and trends in the education of racial and ethnic groups. Institute of Educational Sciences/National Center for Education Statistics. Retrieved on December 1, 2015 from: http://nces.ed.gov/pubs2010/2010015.pdf.

8

ACADEMIC SUPPORT SERVICES

Janet Marler

Why Does This Matter?

Community colleges often pride themselves on being open access institutions, which provide the opportunity to attend higher education. The unique nature of community colleges necessitates a strong network of support between Academic Affairs and Student Affairs. As Ozaki, Hornak and Lunceford (2014) note, "the demographics of students entering community colleges shows that higher percentages of these student come from schools that are less likely to academically prepare students for higher education, have lower socio-economic backgrounds, have parents with lower education levels, and require more developmental coursework" (p. 79). They note the absolute necessity of collaboration between Student and Academic Affairs in order for all students to achieve success.

Purpose and Need

One way to strengthen the bond between the academic support services (the library) and Student Affairs would be to create specific staff liaisons to student services using the *library faculty liaison model* (i.e. libraries having a social sciences librarian who works with social sciences faculty to plan library instruction, do collection development in the social sciences, etc.). Improving collaboration between Student Affairs and Academic Affairs often means educating the two areas about what the other area does. Even in a collaborative effort, such as the presentations that preceded this chapter, the research component for curricular infusion of career development was largely limited to the United States Department of Labor's *Occupational Outlook Handbook (OOH)*.[1] By limiting the students' searching to one resource, students learned to refine their searches by selecting occupations by median pay, entry-level education, new job projections and growth rate. The *OOH* website offers drop-down menus for each of these areas which makes searching relatively easy. Students can also search careers through a static vertical menu that groups careers into categories such as "Healthcare" and "Computer and Information Technology." These links then further break down occupations within a given category and gives students a comprehensive view of directions within the field.

While the *OOH* is a fine resource, part of the academic mission of colleges is to improve information literacy, so it is important for students to have a sense of the incredible gamut of career resources available to them both online and in print; this repeats the theme presented by editors Maxine Melling and Margaret Weaver in their collection of essays, *Collaboration in Libraries and Learning Environments* (2012). Numerous examples are given of collaboration between departments in library and information settings and also extending that model to include creating strategic alliances with outside organizations.

Stephen Bell's article, "Building Creative Space for Entrepreneurs" (2015), addresses the need for academic libraries to rethink how services are offered to students in an entrepreneurial business environment. Some public libraries such as the Lancaster Public Library began economic gardening programs more than 15 years ago to foster a climate of economic development. Entrepreneur resource lists were formed, "Business Start-Up Book Bags" with books and business support materials were created and material resources such as a fax machine, scanner and computers were made available to the small business community. As student services look to expand Career Services to students and community members, entrepreneurial career resources are a natural area for the academic library and student services to partner in providing services to students and the community.

Opportunities for collaboration between student services and libraries range from simple to complex. Several colleges are making space available for students to meet with student services professionals in a discreet, comfortable setting. There is no stigma to going to the library as opposed to the potential discomfort a student might feel in visiting the counseling services of a college. It's also more convenient; students go to the library or information commons of a college or university to study, use the computers, obtain information and meet with friends. By providing space to student services professionals, the library extends the reach of its services and tightens the collaborative bonds between the academic and student services functions of a college.

Ozaki, Hornak and Lunceford (2014) also review the concept of *institutional excellence* and advocate for "rigorous" assessment by institutions of their programs. On a practical level, they advocate for "collaborations, cross-training, information sharing, and partnerships" (p. 81) between Student and Academic Affairs in formal and informal ways.

Promising Practices

Practice #1—Atlantic Cape Community College

While developing our collaborative curricular infusion research paradigm, it occurred to us that we were not simply employing a linear Student Affairs to Academic Affairs linkage. Rather, there was a third "corner within a triangle" to be engaged. This is when we realized that it was vital to incorporate academic support services and tutoring into "the conversation" (Levy & Marler, 2015).

For our colleagues interested in creating a synergy between Student Affairs, faculty and academic support services, our first recommendation is training of tutors and academic support personnel. At Atlantic Cape Community College we have found that having tutors participate in the same Values Auction (see Chapter 3) that was utilized in various courses not only provided them with an understanding of what was transpiring in the curriculum, but it also motivated and engaged them. It was evident to us that they truly appreciated the opportunity to assist students beyond their typical interactions. When we asked if it "made sense" to train them to refer students to the college library Career Resources LibGuide we had created, they overwhelmingly said "yes." In addition, when we asked them for their ideas and recommendations regarding how academic support personnel could assist students with their career development, they provided us with an excellent array of potential programs and activities.

An example of how to create linkage between various campus resources and the external community is illustrated by the fact that the two counties that support our community college both have large public library systems whose online resources include Job & Career Accelerator (part of Learning Express) which encompass over 5 million job postings and the option to create professional-looking resumes and cover letters. Training in computer software is offered through Learning Express, and the Tutor.com service can offer job seekers the option to connect with an online tutor. Many of our students already have public library cards with the county libraries. In demonstrating not just the college's resources but also the resources available to the students through their public libraries, we enable them to both test drive and learn to navigate a wider variety of online resources. This is true not just in the geographic area we serve but in many library systems throughout the United States.

One of the library's web-based services is a subject guide utilizing LibGuides, a product created by Springshare. As part of the library's contribution to career-infused instruction, my predecessor at Atlantic Cape Community College, Grant Wilinski, worked with Student Affairs to create a Career Resources LibGuide. This Career LibGuide offers everything from links to relevant databases to tutorials on how to create a LinkedIn account. Student services staff send information to academic support staff, which then gets posted to the Career LibGuide. It has been an asset to have a single location to send students to on our webpage where they can access multiple resources.

Unfortunately, the process has not always been as smooth as it should be. This is largely because we only have four people with access to the LibGuides: two of whom are part-time. Because of legitimate concerns regarding what information was posted on a publicly available website, only the library dean and three reference librarians had access to creating and editing LibGuide site content. For the LibGuide content to be responsive to postings of student services and other college division or departmental events, those restraints need to be loosened and a generic LibGuide request email created so content changes or addition requests are not dependent on individual staff.

At Atlantic Cape Community College, we continue to partner with Student Affairs in providing a Career LibGuide with links to both internal and external online and print resources. In order to address this at Atlantic Cape, Student Affairs requested the library's assistance with creating a career information sheet that could be used as a handout. The library already subscribed to a service, LibGuides from Springshare. LibGuides is the most popular content management system available to libraries. There are currently over 400,000 LibGuides extant that have the option of being shared within the LibGuide community. It enables libraries to provide online topic guides on specific subjects or for specific courses. Tabs can provide links to everything from websites to databases or content sites such as Learning Express. Content can range from these links to RSS feeds that maintain currency. Atlantic Cape's LibGuide included a link to a single sheet listing various career development resources. The sheet was created within Student Affairs by a counselor in consultation with the library staff and was distributed during embedded career training sessions within English as a Second Language (ESL) and developmental English classes. As Atlantic Cape Professor Maryann Flemming-McCall noted (see Chapter 3): "The career planning activities addressed numerous course objectives: develop computer and information literacy skills; choose a program of study based on informed decisions; and, become familiar with college culture and resources." Through the Career LibGuide, students were introduced to the LibGuide page whose content ranges from a LibGuide that teaches MLA and APA citation skills to our Holocaust and Genocide Resources LibGuide.

The Career Resources LibGuide itself includes links to the Myers-Briggs Trait Indicator Test, the Holland Codes personality quiz, print and e-book title links, a video link that explains the *OOH* website, and links to information regarding potential career paths for different majors. In addition, there is information and videos on professional social networking sites such as LinkedIn. The versatility of the LibGuide platform includes the ability for us to have direct links to our content providers such as Ebsco and other vendors. Counseling and other support services at our college have also utilized the Career Resources LibGuide to market upcoming career events to students.

In the spring of 2014, the LibGuide created by library staff supported tutors' efforts in assisting English department faculty implementing curriculum career development goals. For example, in an English 101 (Composition I) course at

Atlantic Cape's Cape May Campus, students wrote cover letters with the assistance of the tutoring staff. Professor Jennie Buoy and Cape May Campus Director Tammy DeFranco (see Chapter 3) spoke at the NASPA Region II Conference in June 2014 about the real-life skills some students acquired, providing these student comments as examples:

> I will feel more confident in applying for positions with my professional-looking cover letter.
> I really liked the cover letter assignment because it is something I will need in the real world one day.

Through aligning the career component with course goals and objectives, students left with a tangible, life-enhancing tool that evidenced the practical applications of essay development. Mike Sargente, Program Coordinator of the Atlantic City and Cape May County's Learning Assistance Center and Support Services of Atlantic Cape Community College, visited Professor Buoy's Composition 1 class.

The purpose of this visit was to:

- inform the students about our tutoring services;
- introduce the students to tutoring staff;
- invite the students to see us for help outside of class;
- give tutors the opportunity to attend a class session;
- give tutors the opportunity to participate in the cover letter writing workshop.

The goals of this visit was to:

- directly assist students with their cover letter writing assignment;
- increase the likelihood that students will view tutoring as a regular component of their academic experience.

As a result of the collaboration between Professors Buoy and DeFranco and the director of the campus academic support center, Michael Sargente, the center staff were able to explain to the students the range of assistance available to them and were able to reinforce that students avail themselves of the support available. The students stated that they were now more likely and willing to go to the academic support center given that they had met the staff and interacted with them.

At a May 2014 focus group meeting with tutors, suggestions for the future direction of continuing collaborative efforts included:

- more aggressive outreach;
- potentially use career assistance as a means of attracting students to tutoring services;

- making tutoring part of the classroom culture;
- enhanced tutor training;
- maintain career LibGuides;
- future assessment of outcomes: are we having a positive effect on GPA, retention and graduation rates?

Practice #2—National Initiatives

Career counseling libraries and centers are at times based in a library setting or in an independent setting. Depending on the college, they may be part of student services or considered as either a library collection or independent library. At Essex County College in New Jersey, it takes the form of a Career Resource Center that has career software, texts and videos. Harvard University's Office of Career Services offers an eResource Library and suggested career pathways. Myplan.com, a web resource that has "over 150,000 pages of content, including articles, statistics, images, and videos," is provided to Harvard students and alums free of charge but is also available to anyone and has a mixture of free and fee-based content. Harvard's Office of Career Services also has a "Making Connections" link that includes the "Crimson Compass," an "online database of Harvard University alumni who have volunteered to talk about their career experiences with students and other alumni. The database is intended to assist in developing professional networking relationships." Some schools may respond, "Well, we're not Harvard." However, within any given career path, there are obvious advantages for students to have access to alumni and others who are willing to act as mentors to a college's students and graduates.

For those students interested in entrepreneurial information and activities, library information can be further enhanced by collaborative partnerships with local Small Business Development Centers (SBDCs). Funded in part by the U.S. Small Business Administration, the centers are spread throughout the United States with "hundreds of delivery service points." The SBDCs and their advisors:

> provide aspiring and current small business owners a variety of free business consulting and low-cost training services including: business plan development, manufacturing assistance, financial packaging and lending assistance, exporting and importing support, disaster recovery assistance, procurement and contracting aid, market research help, 8(a) program support, and healthcare guidance.

At the University of California San Diego, the library offers "Academic Partnership Consultations," a simple but useful and effective one-stop shopping option for students. Any "Campus Departments or Programs which support or enhance student learning and success may arrange to meet with students, regularly or occasionally conduct satellite office hours, enrichment activities, or outreach activities in the library." The advantage of utilizing the library in this manner is that the library's hours are more extensive than student services departments and programs; for the fall 2015 semester, the Geisel Library Building was open from 7:30am to midnight.

Unfortunately, many libraries face space constraints that mean this is not a viable option. However, even with limited space, libraries may still be able to accommodate the needs of student organizations. For example, at Atlantic Cape we are making available to our chapter of the Phi Theta Kappa International Honor Society a study room for the chapter's advisors to schedule regular meetings.

The UC San Diego library also offers a "study room specifically intended for use by student parents accompanied by young children." The room—which must be reserved in advance—incudes materials for the students to study (computer, whiteboard and a large table) but also "child-sized furniture, manipulatives, and a collection of works by Dr. Seuss" as well as the opportunity to obtain everything from blocks to "creativity boxes" from nearby service desks. UC San Diego's library is aptly named after the beloved author of the Dr. Seuss books; its attention to the needs of students with young children is commendable.

At Atlantic Cape, we are taking small steps to provide space for student parents to utilize the library. At the Mays Landing Campus, coloring books and crayons are available as are picture books. A small children's collection from the Atlantic County Library System has recently been established, and a cooperative library visit program has been recently launched at the Mays Landing Campus with the on-site Head Start program that will include a storytime. There is room here for cooperative efforts with student services for outreach to student parents to meet their study needs when they have young children in tow. Our hope is that at some point we may be able to cooperatively find space for parents to be able to work on computers to do their school work while electronically connected to such academic support services as tutoring and library reference/research assistance in a space that enables student parents to be close to their children who will have access to safe toys, art supplies and books.

Practice #3—Advising

Librarians and tutors often do informal advising in the sense of assisting students with accessing information on a college's website. Some schools have taken this a step further; in a November 2015 issue of *College and Research Library News* Judy Williams and Claire Wiley discuss how it came about that faculty librarians at Belmont University in Tennessee are advisors to undeclared students. They describe historical precedents for library faculty serving as advisors noting, however, that it's still unusual. What is interesting is that the librarians at Belmont have taken the standard library "reference interview" concept and applied it to eliciting information about the undecided students' interests (pp. 545–546). They note that librarians' cross-disciplinary positions give them a unique perspective and knowledge of course content and methodologies. A key component not noted by Williams and Wiley is the research skills of the librarians that can be applied to assisting students in discerning their future career directions.

Practice #4—Tutoring

Tutoring "is the oldest of all learning assistance approaches and nearly universal at every postsecondary institution" (Gordon & Gordon, 1990 in "Access at the Crossroads"). At a presentation in the spring of 2014, "The Curricular Infusion of Career Development," a team of educators from Atlantic Cape Community College demonstrated how the interaction between Academic Support Services, Curriculum and Faculty, and Student Affairs led to demonstrable gains in student achievement. Grant Wilinski, then Associate Dean of Academic Support (and now retired) spoke of tutoring as the "missing component" in the triad. Dean Wilinski saw "tutors as guides, not counselors" and advocated an "ongoing assessment" of tutors in tutoring sessions. He also spoke of the value of information literacy to improve students' lives as they embraced lifelong learning. Consequently, the Atlantic Cape Community College Academic Support Services program collaborated with Student Affairs to train tutors regarding how to direct students who were completing course assignments that were infused with career development components. The tutors were trained to make students aware of career resources on campus and career information available via the Library Career Resources LibGuide.

Practice #5—Information Literacy across the Curriculum and Student Services

Libraries provide the resources for e-learning via the provision of databases, data banks, subject guides and links to external resources such as authenticated websites. There is an idealistic goal such as that posited by John Seely Brown (2014), Director of Xerox's Palo Alto Research Center that: "The real literacy of tomorrow entails the ability to be your own personal reference librarian—to know how to navigate through confusing, complex information spaces and feel comfortable doing so. 'Navigation' may well be the main form of literacy for the twenty-first century." Even some library directors subscribe to the mythology that students who routinely struggle with the most basic of research tasks will be empowered by the magic of the web to wade easily through a morass of data.

Student services personnel offer workshops aimed at empowering students to learn study skills and time management skills. Similarly, academic support staff at many institutions offer writing workshops, time management workshops and study skills workshops to students. There is often a duplication of efforts between the two areas of academic support and student services; each offering some of the same information and services but often with a slightly different emphasis. The future ideal would be for academic support (tutoring) and student services to work together to utilize the strengths of each area. At Atlantic Cape Community College, we are working to do that through a new initiative, the Career and Success Program (CASP), through which students will acquire needed skills and an academic/career-planning portfolio which will demonstrate those skills to potential employers and give the student concrete evidence of their ongoing successes.

Moving Forward

The first recommendation to our colleagues hoping to replicate collaboration between faculty members, Student Affairs and academic support services is training with all of the parties involved. It was clear to us that the academic support and tutoring staff at Atlantic Cape Community College were very excited to be asked for their input and be involved in program development. Clearly, to create a network of seamless student support it is essential that all parties "are on the same page" and working toward a common strategic goal. One suggestion is to provide training in which small teams of faculty within a specific program meet with tutors and a Student Affairs professional to generate ideas regarding how to link curricular infusion within their programs with both academic support services and Student Affairs.

Another recommendation is to "build" assessment into the development of linkages between academic support services, Academic Affairs and Student Affairs. Beyond formative assessment capturing student feedback "in the moment," we encourage institutions to "track" the outcomes achieved via these initiatives. For example, at Atlantic Cape Community College, we are tracking student engagement in both Student Affairs programming and academic support services. Consequently, we will investigate the impact of tutoring in combination with other initiatives on student outcomes with respect to credit accumulation, persistence, retention, academic performance and graduation rates. This data will be used to inform future program development and resource allocation in Student Affairs and the Academic Support Services Center.

Note

1. United States Department of Labor's *Occupational Outlook Handbook:* www.bls.gov/ooh (accessed on December 1, 2015).

References

Bell, S. (2015). Building creative space for entrepreneurs. *Library Journal, 140*(15), 14.

Brown, J. S. (2000). Growing up digital: How the web changes work, education, and the ways people learn. *Change: The Magazine of Higher Learning, 32*(2), 11–20.

Gordon, E. E., & Gordon, E. H. (1990). *Centuries of tutoring.* New York: University Press of America.

Levy, M. A., & Marler, J. (2015, March). The curricular infusion of career development. Presented at 2015 NASPA National Conference. New Orleans, LA.

Melling, M., & Weaver, M. (Eds.). (2012). *Collaboration in libraries and learning environments.* London: Facet.

Ozaki, C. C., Hornak, A. M., & Lunceford, C. J. (2014). *Supporting student affairs professionals.* San Francisco, CA: Jossey-Bass.

Springshare. LibGuides. Retrieved on December 1, 2015 from: www.springshare.com/libguides/.

U.S. Small Business Administration. Local assistance: Small Business Development Centers. Retrieved on December 1, 2015 from: www.sba.gov/tools/local-assistance/sbdc.

Weaver, M., & Melling, M. (2013). *Collaboration in libraries and learning environments.* London: Facet Publishing.

Williams, J., & Wiley, C. (2015). Academic advising. *College & Research Libraries News,* 76(10), 544–559.

SECTION III

Creating Collaborative Synergy

9

COLLABORATIVE STRATEGIC PLANNING

Bernard A. Polnariev and Mitchell A. Levy

> Take nothing on its looks; take everything on evidence. There's no better rule.
> Charles Dickens, *Great Expectations* (Chapter 40)

Why Does This Matter?

The collection of all objectives, from all departments and divisions, adds a unique vantage point for appreciating an institution's coordination, integrity and dedication. Strategic planning is a mechanism that begins from "the college mission and provides a blueprint for unified and methodological movement of an organization toward a congruent goal. The primary benefit of an organizationally aligned plan rests in its ability to increase the likelihood of seizing opportunities and anticipating threats" (Garza Mitchell & Maldanado, 2015, p. 113). It's wonderful to witness how strategic plan targets develop in alignment with the college's mission and priorities, and then consequently observe how their implementation and results impact student success. Based on our varied experiences both within Academic Affairs and Student Affairs, we believe that an effective strategic planning process is inherently collaborative, goal-oriented and affords a systemic approach toward institutional effectiveness. Institutional success can only materialize from true institutional collaboration. The key question is really how do faculty, staff and senior administrators align goals that engage members with varied contextual agendas—creating synergy between various institutional programs, initiatives and policies to ensure a high level of coherence and impact?

The strategic or institutional[1] planning process is an opportunity to collaboratively reflect and assess the "successes" and "challenges" (as defined by the college and/or the governing boards) of identified goals based on institutional priorities. From our perspective, not attaining a specific numerical target is *not* necessarily a failure. By the same token, setting a "low-bar," and consequently surpassing it does not necessarily imply success! Strategic planning is an opportunity to re-examine the organization's values, current status and the environment; the strategic plan should be intimately linked to the college's mission, internal and external environments, and also take into account the dynamic environmental trends (Burkhart & Reuss, 1993).

Strategic planning is neither a goal in and of itself, nor an actual product; rather, the true benefit of strategic planning is the *sine qua non* opportunity for collaboration in order to continuously assess and improve specific institutional priorities. This improvement should go beyond departmental and divisional goals and when possible place the student at the center of the college's mission. The strategic plan is an ideal forum to more cohesively unite activities—pulling them further away from silos and strengthening their connections to other departments and divisions. Effective strategic planning necessitates broad participation and reflects a continuous commitment to collaboratively lead the institution toward achieving its aspirations (Mina, 2014). We maintain that an inclusive strategic planning process with many diverse stakeholders affords a more authentic sense of ownership and potentially a greater sense of responsibility with respect to goal attainment. The strategic planning process and the implementation of the plan itself is the opportunity to develop and utilize a systemic approach that is both holistic in focus and informed by assessment feedback loops (Lopez, 2004).

As the visionary Peter Senge stated over 25 years ago, "systems thinking shows us that there is no outside: that you and the cause of your problems are part of a single system" (1990, p. 67). Nearly a decade ago, Cook, Ghering, and Lewis (2007) indicated that "colleges and universities—academic and student affairs divisions in particular—must operate as single systems with 'no outsiders' if they are to educate successfully 21st Century students and deliver on the changing demands society places on them" (p. 6). In *Learning Reconsidered* (2004) a clear "call to arms" was sounded: "presidents and senior offices in both academic and student affairs must adopt a partnership model that expects and rewards collaborations among all campus educators for student learning" (p. 33). Learning experiences, for example:

> need to be integrated into a coherent whole for each and every student. And this integration needs to occur as a result of enhanced collaboration among faculty across departments, as well as closer collaboration between faculty and student affairs professionals—including academic advisors, career counselors, and other campus educators who work every day to help students make sense of their educational experiences.
> (Humphreys, 2013, para. 13" as cited by Suskie, 2015, p. 81).

The following passage succinctly sums up our perspective on the value of such partnership:

One of the best ways to make student learning come alive on campuses is to improve collaborations between student and academic affairs staffs. These collaborations need to go beyond relating out of class activities to the curriculum. They need to be true, substantive partnerships, across administrative lines, which serve to implement the goals of liberal education.
(Brady, 1999, p. 33).

Unfortunately for many institutions, the development of, and commitment to, a strategic plan that promotes success via collaboration and assessment across the institution remains a significant challenge. Clayton-Pederson and Dungy (2007) identified one variable influencing this challenge: increased role specialization; they contend that:

As a result of the level of specialization and separation within the academy today, faculty members often interact more with members of their own discipline in other states and around the world than with their colleagues on campus. Given the modern intellectual divide between academic disciplines, this lack of collaboration within institutions is not surprising (p. 266).

Additionally, in *The Student Learning Imperative* (Calhoun, 1996, p. 119), the schism that often exists between institutional divisions and the deleterious impact of this "dichotomy" is described:

Higher education traditionally has organized into "academic affairs" (learning, curriculum, classroom, cognitive development) and "student affairs" (co-curriculum, student activities, residential life, affective or personal development). However, this dichotomy has little relevance to post-college life, where the quality of one's job performance, family life, and community activities are all highly dependent on cognitive and affective skills (p. 119).

Often compounding the impact of the institutional dichotomies, or "silos," described above is the impact on institutional works roles and the focus developed by different offices or divisions. Brady (1999) further claims that while "some student affairs professionals might" become less directed or focused on cognitive development of students, "it could equally be stated that student affair professionals are seldom invited, and perhaps are not welcome at the table where serious educational issues are discussed" (p. 19). In *Learning Reconsidered* (2004), Keeling and his colleagues address the importance of having a common language with respect to what they term "student development education" (p. 12). As articulated by Dr. Levy in a (Dembicki, 2010) *Community College Times* interview, the importance of having a shared "language" used to pursue a common goal cannot be underestimated, especially with respect to how colleges and universities have evolved to meet the increased amount and diversity of student needs (Dembicki, 2010).

While the aforementioned research speaks to the value of cross-divisional collaborative efforts in pursuit of mutually agreed upon goals, we see why this can be so challenging. The institutional silos and isolation that frequently develop only serve to impede effective collaboration. We can thus appreciate how imperative it is "to get everyone on the same page." Throughout our research and consultation with colleagues, it is clear that a culture of true collaboration must permeate the institution both vertically and horizontally. Kuh (2013) contends that changing campus culture is more *art* than *science*. Reframing institutional assumptions and norms that shape assessment work in colleges and universities need to occur through intentional and strategic processes. We view the process of strategic planning and institutional assessment in accordance with accreditation standards as the most substantive methodology for developing a "strong, coherent institutional culture that features talent development, academic achievement, and respect for differences and is congenial to student success" (Kuh, Kinzie, Schuh, & Whitt, 2005).

Kuh (1998) further describes institutional culture as "a combination of influences that encompass the entire college experience, including how people behave and what is (and is not) important to administrators, faculty, staff and students." We fully agree with the assertion made by Clayton-Pederson and Dungy (2007) that the "cornerstone of effective collaboration is *a common vision*." They further submit that "senior leaders can 'foster collaboration' in many ways, one important process for accomplishing this is the creation of formal structures promoting collaboration among faculty and student affairs professionals" (Clayton-Pederson & Dungy, 2007). As Baker (2004) describes the relationship between institutional mission and accreditation:

> Regional accrediting organizations do not determine institutional missions or goals, nor do they specify institutional, program, or student learning outcomes, because those decisions are properly the domain of the institution and its stakeholders. However, they do require each accredited or pre-accredited institution to define its mission clearly, set goals that lead to fulfillment of the mission, and identify indicators of mission and goal achievement. Thus institutional mission is the kernel of regional accreditation and one of the major considerations when making an accreditation decision regarding institutional quality, effectiveness, and compliance with accreditation criteria (p. 7).

In addition, accrediting bodies require institutions to have an increased commitment to using evidence-based data to inform institutional decision making. As one of the national leaders in this field who, among other qualifications, served as an accreditation commissioner with the MSCHE, Dr. Michael F. Middaugh

(2009) highlights that "a feedback loop that informs institutions how effective those plans are in moving them forward toward the realization of their institutional mission and planning goals" is unfortunately *lacking* at most colleges (p. 5). He (2009) further stresses that there is a "disconnect between the planning and assessment processes at colleges and universities . . . The problem is that the planning and assessment processes all too often do not talk to each other" (p. 5). Dr. Karen Hinton (2012), a leading authority regarding the importance of effective strategic planning in higher education, acknowledges that "the costs of engaging in a poor planning process range from disillusioned faculty, staff, and students, to poor use of vital resources, to failed accreditation reviews which, in turn, cause an institution to lose funding and prestige. The stakes are high, but the rewards are higher" (p. 5). A well-developed and applied institutional planning process can afford an institution with a forum for campus-wide discussions about critical choices.

Given how essential effective strategic planning is for institutional functioning, and the challenges often present when trying to develop a "culture" of collaboration, some of the guiding principles for this chapter will be the following:

- In a classic book on the topic, the authors affirm that "strategic planning is the single most important function of the CEO"—as the key decision maker (Below, Morrisey, & Acomb, 1987, p. 1).
- "Collaborative deliberations are at the heart of good strategic planning" (Morrill, 2013 as cited in Suskie, 2015).
- In a review of best practices regarding strategic planning, the authors note "regional accreditors discourage top-down planning and instead emphasize collaborative, participatory planning processes" (Sanaghan & Hinton, 2013, p. 4).
- A long-standing expert in this field asserts "a well designed and implemented strategic planning process can provide an institution with a forum for campus-wide conversations about important decisions" (Hinton, 2012, p. 5).
- CUNY's Brooklyn College's President Karen L. Gould powerfully exclaims "student success is central to all elements of our strategic plan" (2011, p. i).

Consequently, we will present two in-depth case examples in which our current institutions use strategic planning to foster increased collaboration in support of student success and greater institutional effectiveness. Additionally, we will demonstrate how this methodology was implemented in support of institutional accreditation efforts.

Promising Practices

Authentic collaboration is the bedrock for effective strategic planning. Specific strategic plan targets and their feedback loops from both authors' current institutions (both part of the Middle States Commission) are illustrated below. In addition, strategic planning's pivotal role is provided as part of six other regional accreditors. Although there are several common threads, one main link across all of the seven American regional accrediting bodies is that they require evidence of effective strategic or institutional planning. In their soon-to-be seminal book on refining higher education, Dr. George Kuh and his colleagues argue "accreditation of academic institutions has become the federal government's engine for change in higher education" (Kuh, Ikenberry, Jankowski, Reese Cain, Ewell, Hutchings, & Kinzie, 2015, p. 22).

Kuh and his colleagues (2015) also emphasize that evidence "requires interpretation, integration, and reflection in the search for holistic understanding and implications for action" (Kuh et al., 2015, pp. 2–3). Furthermore, the "push from accrediting bodies for institutions to gather and use information about student learning has been reinforced by demands from policymakers at both the federal and state levels" (p. 3). They (Kuh et al., 2015) further underscore that the need for accountability has often overshadowed the need and opportunity for continuous improvement; there must be a balance between these sides of the same coin. Certainly, providing evidence of institutional effectiveness to stakeholders and external accrediting bodies for the purpose of accountability is appropriate. Nevertheless, the importance of faculty and staff improving teaching and learning and the legitimate interest of

> ... external bodies for accountability can be reconciled if college and university presidents, provosts, assessment professionals, and faculty members take ownership of assessment and align assessment work with campus needs and priorities in ways that focus on compelling questions and issues of student success and the myriad challenges to institutional effectiveness. Far more important than activity for mere accountability is the effective and productive use of student learning outcomes data by partners and end users inside the institution—faculty, staff, students, campus leaders, and governing board members. Failure to do so undermines the credibility and trust that is crucial in any system of accountability.
>
> (Kuh et al., 2015, p. 6).

Connecting resource allocation to the strategic planning and decision making is essential for today's institutional success and accreditation. In her book on advancing quality in higher education, Dr. Linda Suskie (2015) cogently notes that all regional accreditors focus on the quality to which institutions "link goals, plans, evidence, and resource development decisions. Goals inform assessment strategies and resource allocations, while evidence informs goals, plans, and resource allocations" (p. 31). Moreover, "linking strategic planning to other operations of the college, such as assessment, can help the institution foster collaboration and communication across its divisions and departments" (Young, 2011, p. 44).

Dr. Paul Gaston III (2013) brilliantly argues that increased consensus and collaboration in all arenas of assessment would improve the public's understanding of accreditation, promote greater creativity and advance resoluteness and transparency; this approach would make it possible for assessment and accreditation to advance student success (also review Suskie, 2015 for a comprehensive review of accreditation). Gannon-Slater and her colleagues note "similarities in assessment practices across accreditation regions outweigh the differences" (2014, p. 3).

Our review of *strategic planning* and *accreditation* is far from exhaustive. Rather, this chapter is geared to help colleagues from *any* college better understand how the two are implicitly connected in order to more fully unite collaborative activities and ultimately support students while helping institutions attain and/or retain accreditation status. As a disclaimer, both of us are far more familiar with Middle States accreditation standards—we have participated and significantly contributed to four major accreditation self-studies. We are also certain that the evidence presented below, vis-à-vis the two major case study examples provided, will help illuminate successful approaches for strategic planning at your home institution. We hope that you also realize that we are offering crucial institutional information with somewhat of a limited framework—often disconnected from its socio-cultural and historical context (see Stetsenko & Arievitch, 2004 for a deeper review of this theoretical perspective). Please take these factors into perspective as you continue reading and thinking about how certain approaches presented below may be useful for your institution's and students' success. A summary of key recommendations will be included at the end of this chapter to help you through your accreditation self-study. The following section on strategic planning is grounded in the seven regional accrediting bodies.

I—For the *Middle States Commission on Higher Education*[2] (MSCHE), Standard 2—*Planning, Resource Allocation, and Institutional Renewal* addresses strategic planning written for Middle States accreditation purposes, The *Characteristics of Excellence in Higher Education* (2006, 12th edition) states:

> An institution conducts ongoing planning and resource allocation based on its mission and goals, develops objectives to achieve them, and utilizes the results of its assessment activities for institutional renewal. Implementation and subsequent evaluation of the success of the strategic plan and resource allocation support the development and change necessary to improve and to maintain institutional quality (p. ix).

Boldly, and with significant broad input, the MSCHE has recently (circa 2013) re-evaluated its own accreditation process and standards, in part due to the societal tensions for increased accountability. As such, there are several major MSCHE changes fully taking effect by 2018 including: streamlined language, fewer standards (14 vs. 7) and assessment built into all standards as part of their revised accreditation approach. MSCHE has approved a plan to implement the revised 13th edition standards through a unique *Collaborative Implementation Project*. Over a period of two years, more than two dozen institutions that are scheduled to submit their self-studies during the 2016–2017 academic year will undergo a "high touch" experience in which they will communicate frequently with one other and Commission staff, as they participate in self-study utilizing the revised standards. Note that self-studies beyond 2017 (i.e. under the revised approach, strategic planning, will fall under Standard VI—*Planning, Resources, and Institutional Improvement*:

> The institution's planning processes, resources, and structures are aligned with each other and are sufficient to fulfill its mission and goals, to continuously assess and improve its programs and services, and to respond effectively to opportunities and challenges.
>
> (MSCHE, 2015, p. 12).

Case #1: LaGuardia Community College

The City University of New York (CUNY) is considered to be the largest urban public institution in the nation with over 500,000 students across 1,400 academic programs.[3] All 24 CUNY colleges currently utilize the Performance Management Process (PMP) which links planning and goal-setting by the University, measuring annual progress toward key goals. Many CUNY colleges use the PMP interchangeably with their "strategic plan." McDonnell and his CUNY colleagues (2013) note that the "PMP follows an annual cycle of goal-setting, implementation of policies, programs, and practices that are intended to move the institution closer to the established goals, progress measurement, and consequences in the form of a monetary reward for good performance" (McDonnell, Chellman, Littman, & Crook, 2013, p. 4). With a new CUNY Chancellor James B. Milliken,[4] the University began re-evaluating its vision and has launched a new strategic planning effort for a "21st Century CUNY."[5]

Although there has been some structural variation of CUNY's PMP over the past decade, little has changed conceptually—the University's priorities remain stalwart. There are generally three overarching *goals* within the PMP framework: I) Raising Academic Quality; II) Improving Student Success; and III) Enhancing Financial and Management Effectiveness. More specific than the PMP goals, the objectives form a category for evaluation. There tends to be nine interconnected objectives including, to "ensure that all students receive a quality general education and effective instruction" or "increasing retention and graduation rates . . ." Finally, there are both university-specific and college-specific *targets* which are even more detailed than the objectives.

LaGuardia Community College's (LAGCC) strategic plan[6] is in-line with CUNY's PMP multilayered organization and directive; the goals are driven by the college's mission, values and priorities as well recommendations made from the 2012 Self-Study for Middle States accreditation. LaGuardia's 2012 Self-Study stresses that the "structure of the strategic plan . . . makes the core priorities clear to the college community and focuses attention, energy, and resources on priority areas" (p. xii). The number of divisional targets varies based on the division's size and priorities. One of the most valuable connections demonstrated in the LAGCC strategic plan is its alignment to the college mission and the collaborative nature of its development given the parameters set forth by CUNY at large. Every target identifies mechanisms to assess goal achievement.

In 2012, an extensive task force effort led by institutional leaders from both Student Affairs and Academic Affairs at LaGuardia realized that with "an effective and cohesive 'first-year experience' program, students can get help early on from faculty and professional staff who will teach them the importance of planning, accomplishment and success" (Insalaco-Egan & Engel, 2012). Based on research gathered by Brown, King, and Stanley (2011), the goal of all first-year endeavors will be to link new students' early experiences to the courses and activities that serve as the culmination of their academic and developmental learning and result in graduation" (Insalaco-Egan & Engel, 2012, p. 2). LaGuardia's *new* First-Year Seminar (FYS) integrates an introduction to essential college terms, concepts and careers in the major with proactive advisement, co-curricular engagement, peer mentoring and a primer to the college's technology suite. One clear LAGCC Strategic Plan Goal, which demonstrates the above point, is the following edited example over a period of five years:

Goal II—Improving Student Success
    Objective 4: Increase retention and graduation rates and ensure students make timely progress toward degree completion.
    Fiscal Year (FY) 2012–13 College Target # 3.3.04:[7] *As part of the Academic Affairs-Student Affairs alignment initiative, redesign the "first-year experience" program, including development of learning objectives for the first year.*
    Target Outcomes: Identified design members in summer 2012. Attended John Gardner's Institute for Excellence; reviewed strategic plan and aligned key initiatives; defined the "first-year experience" scope/student success and key learning objectives in fall 2012; completed framework design for the "first-year experience" program. Task Force Report completed and submitted in February 2013. The College is already moving forward on implementation of 10 of the Task Force 14 recommendations, and will advance on multiple fronts in 2013–14.
    Funding resources: Approximately $145,000[8] *(from LaGuardia's Coordinated Undergraduate for Education [CUE] budget).*
    Involved parties: This was a campus-wide initiative, involving more than 100 faculty and staff, which took many months to construct and implement.
    FY 2013–14 College Target # 4.1.05: Launch and assess the implementation of FYE Task Force recommendations, including strengthening pre-term activities;

developing the credit-based First-Year Seminar; advancing the integration of co-curricular with curricular learning.

Target Outcomes: Launched a new FYS with 17 sections; serving 289 students from two academic departments. Effectiveness of the revised FYS courses were measured by comparing course completion and next-semester retention rates with prior college baselines.

Funding resources: Approximately $132,000 (from LaGuardia's CUE budget).

FY 2014–2015 College target # C1g:[9] *Launch and assess the implementation of over 60 sections of a First-Year Seminar for the Business & Technology, Health Sciences, and Natural Sciences departments, and also for the Liberal Arts programs; prepare select faculty for an Engineering specific First-Year Seminar.*

Involved parties: (for FY 2012–2016): Academic Affairs (with direct support from both Student Affairs and Institutional Technology divisions).

Funding resources: Approximately $162,000 (from LaGuardia's CUE budget; additional support is likely to have been provided from various grants including the Federally funded *First-in the World* grant, LaGuardia's *Project COMPLETA, Comprehensive Support for Student Success*; see Mellow, 2014 for more information about the grant and initiative).

Target Outcomes: In FY 2014–2015, 78 FYS faculty served 4,270 students in 198 sections. Preliminary data show that students who participated in FYS achieved an average higher cumulative GPA than students who were eligible but did not take the course, 2.69 vs. 1.60 respectively. Encouragingly, we found that students who took a spring 2014 FYS were retained after one year by nine percentage points greater than those who did not take the FYS course; these students also earned 3.6 more credits by spring 2015 than did the comparison group (FYS course credits did not count towards the total credits for the purpose of data sharing). Student experiences from 1,264 students in the FYS via qualitative surveys showed great promise as well. For example,

- 92% said that the course "helped them learn about LaGuardia."
- 91% said that they "learned about their major and possible careers."

Use of Results: For FY 2015–2016, 65 additional faculty, representing the additional programs, will complete their FYS training and begin to teach the course in the coming academic year. Research and planning aimed at continual engagement of the FYS trained faculty has begun. Formative data gathered from surveys of students in the FYS courses and faculty participants from a college professional development seminar will be used to revise course syllabi and seminar activities.

FY 2015–2016 College target goal # C1e: Implement and assess the implementation of over 260 sections serving 6,000 students of a First-Year

Seminar for the Business & Technology, Health Sciences, Engineering & Computer Sciences, Natural Sciences, Criminal Justice, Psychology, Social Sciences, Liberal Arts (AA and AS) programs.

(CUNY, n.d.)

The above strategic plan feedback loop gracefully articulates how the outcomes were assessed and used to continue to build and enhance the college's FY experience that helped strengthen student success. (A slightly modified version of) LaGuardia's 2016 Strategic Plan template (provided below) places the College's mission front and center of the document; the priority areas and instructions follow. All proposed targets from the various divisions and departments must associate with a specific college priority area (provided on LaGuardia's template) and must align to the College's mission (also provided on the template)—which is "to educate and graduate one of the most diverse student populations in the country to become critical thinkers and socially responsible citizens who help to shape a rapidly evolving society." Below is a strategic planning template with key categories (with several prompts to help facilitate deeper strategic thinking). We encourage you use and modify this template in Table 9.1 for your campus, as appropriate,

Case #2: Atlantic Cape Community College

Atlantic Cape Community College is a public, two-year institution located in southern New Jersey, encompassing Atlantic and Cape May counties. The college has three campus sites, with a full complement of academic and student support services on each campus. College enrollment in 2014–2015 was approximately 6,500 students, with over 50% of new students requiring remediation.

In 2014, in response to a request by MSCHE, Atlantic Cape Community College developed a comprehensive Enrollment Management Plan (EMP) which incorporated a focus on retention in support of Strategic Planning *Goal #1: Maximize Student Success*. The steps taken to utilize cross-functional committee methodology to advance the institutions' strategic planning are described below.

Progress and status (as of November 2015):

Action Step I:

- Consistent with the Enrollment Management and Student Success Cross-Functional Committee (EMSS/XFC) Mission Statement to address emerging issues and trends which impact college enrollment and student success, the EMSS/XFC co-chairs facilitated discussion regarding development of an EMP focused on student retention. The faculty, staff and students in the committee provided input into the initial framing of the EMP, identifying the issues and factors needing to be addressed.

TABLE 9.1 LaGuardia Community College Strategic Plan Template (2016)

Strategic Planning Template (YEAR)

Department or Unit: _____   Division: _____

Target #1:
Identify a target explicitly connected to your College's mission statement and aligned to a specific institutional policy, as appropriate. When possible, use specific quantitative goals in developing your target statement.

Objective:	*Activities and Timeline:*	*Assessment (Planned Mechanisms)*	*Resources to be Used*	*Connection to Other Areas of the College*	*Accreditation*
• What do you want to accomplish? Why? • How does it link to a specific College focus area?	• Describe up to three specific actions that will be undertaken to achieve this goal.	• Be explicit with how the target will support/enhance student learning and/or employment	• Identify which funding and other resources will be used to further advance the targets	• Identify divisions and/or other departments that will either be impacted and/or	• Specify how this will help support specific accreditation standards or criterion.

- Reference evidence (i.e. data) relevant to establishing your specific target.
- How does this objective address the college and/or department's mission?
- Include two or three clear and measurable outcomes that can be achieved by DATE?

- Who will take responsibilities for these tasks? How do these tasks lead to achieving the objective within the identified time? How and when will these actions be completed?
- Include intermediate benchmarks.
- Be specific with what will be achieved and by when.

- opportunities.
- How will you assess or determine that the objective has in fact been achieved?
- Identify measures which will provide evidence related to your activities.
- Identify one or two clear assessment activities. Who will lead the assessment efforts?

- ones whose support will be needed—either way, these units should be aware of your target. Be sure to obtain consent from any division and/or dept. that may be affected by the proposed target before submitting your work plan.

- you have identified.

- How does the above goal align to and support the college's mission? *Add below* . . .

- Identify two or three challenges? What would you do differently next time? *Add below* . . .

- Recommendations for colleagues at other institutions to repeat your work or ideas. *Add below* . . .

Action Step II:

• After discussion within the EMSS/XFC, the committee co-chairs, Dean of Enrollment Management Andre Richburg and Vice President of Student Affairs Dr. Mitchell Levy met with the directors in their respective areas to initiate development of the first iteration of the EMP. In these meetings, the directors were asked to identify the key components of a comprehensive Enrollment Management and Retention Plan utilizing the following principles culled from literature within the fields of Enrollment Management and Student Affairs:

   a)   The EMP should be *just in time*—providing students what they need at crucial junctures rather than "giving them too much or everything all at once" (Dickmeyer & Michalowski, 2012; Levy, Polnariev & Thomas, 2011).

   b)   The plan should be *holistic*—addressing academic, career, social and psychological considerations (Seidman, 2005).

   c)   The plan is predicated on the belief that increased engagement will yield increased motivation (Tinto, 2000).

   d)   Not every student starts at the same place with respect to their motivation, maturity, readiness or self-concept (Seidman, 2005).

   e)   There are no *one-size-fits-all* interventions (Levy, Polnariev, & McGowan, 2011).

   f)   There are no *magic or one-shot* interventions (Levy, Polnariev, & McGowan, 2011).

   g)   Continued assessment must be utilized within *feedback loops* to inform continued program revision and enhancement (Dickmeyer & Michalowski, 2012; Gardner, 1994; Levy, Polnariev, & Thomas, 2011).

Action Step III:

• To augment the feedback obtained in Action Step II, Dr. Levy created a *Comprehensive Enrollment Management Plan Design Template* and disseminated it to all of the Student Affairs directors. Utilizing the template, Vice President Levy asked the Student Affairs directors to meet with their respective staff and identify the key variables necessary to promote enhanced enrollment management and student success.

Action Step IV:

• Incorporating the feedback obtained via the EMSS/XFC meetings, discussions with Enrollment Management and Student Affairs directors, and meetings held by directors with Enrollment Management and Student Affairs staff, Dean Richburg and Vice President Levy created the first iteration of the EMP model.

Action Step V:

- Given that action steps I through IV and institutional engagement in the Achieving The Dream (ATD) initiative were occurring simultaneously, Dean Richburg and Vice President Levy felt it essential to link the two initiatives, creating a more holistic and integrated institutional approach to enrollment management and student success. A major priority was the development of a seamless process by which enrollment management and student success "pilots" which showed promise could be "ramped up" and institutionalized.

As a result, Dean Richburg and Vice President Levy convened a student success retreat planning committee comprising faculty and administrators to develop a program which increased awareness of the various enrollment management and student success initiatives while providing an opportunity for enhanced project collaboration among faculty, staff and students.

The initial student success retreat was held August 20, 2014 with 70 participants including ten student leaders and alumni, members of the EMSS/XFC, the program coordinator and at least one representative from every academic department (departments were invited to have one full-time and adjunct attend), academic deans, the Vice President of Academic Affairs, the Dean of Finance and President Peter Mora. In addition to an introduction by President Mora and a number of interactive exercises, participants were introduced to a developmental timeline illustrating the actions steps taken (I—IV above) to revise the initial draft of the comprehensive EMP, utilizing input from the EMSS/XFC, Student Affairs directors, Enrollment Management directors and staff from both Enrollment Management and Student Affairs. This iteration of the EMP identified unique developmental phases or critical junctures (Dickmeyer & Michalowski, 2012) essential for student success. Participants at each table were then directed to discuss how to best support effective enrollment management and increase student success relative to a specific developmental phase.

Qualitative data from the ensuing discussions were collected and forwarded to Dean Richburg and Vice President Levy to inform continued EMP development. The final EMP was forwarded to the MSCHE for review and was accepted as an effective progress report response.

A recommendation is to utilize the Atlantic Cape Community College Project Implementation Planning Template (Levy, Richburg, Montefusco, & Marzelli, 2015), which follows:

Atlantic Cape Community College

AtD/SSI (student success initiative) Project Institutionalization Planning Template

1)   Vision for "Scaling-Up" of Project

In your vision of the project when fully implemented, what does it look like? How many total students are your serving (approximate)? What are the different populations/cohorts being served? How many staff members involved? What equipment being utilized? How much space is being utilized?

2) Institutional Support

To fully institutionalize your vision, what support do you need from the institution with respect to the following variables?

- Financial/Personnel—hourly staffing? Coordinator on salary or reduced load? New staff?
- Training—staff and/or students?
- Recruiting—staff and/or students?
- Marketing?
- Equipment?
- Space?
- Scheduling?
- Continued and/or increased collaboration with Student Affairs, Academic Affairs, IT, Institutional Effectiveness, other areas?

3) Assessment

Which assessment efforts should be continued or newly designed to ensure that initiatives are "scaling up" with the desired outcomes? *Specifically, what do you want to know and/or need to know about your project's outcomes?* Two considerations:

1)   *Formative (Process) Assessment*: comprises evaluation of implementation and progress.

   a)   Implementation evaluation—seeks out discrepancies between the original plan and what is actually taking place; allows for modifications while program being implemented.
   b)   Progress evaluation—observes indicators of progress toward objectives; make mid-program revisions if appropriate.

2)   *Summative (Outcome) Assessment*: determine if the ultimate objectives have been attained. Review program strengths and weaknesses, make recommendations for future program revisions. Supports decision making re: program quality and value, program expansion, revision, reduction or suspension.

The other six regional accrediting bodies' emphasis on strategic planning are highlighted below (see Suskie, 2015).

II—For the New England Association of Schools and Colleges Commission on Institutions of Higher Education[10] (NEASC-CIHE), Standard 2 addresses Planning and Evaluation. The Standards of Accreditation Commission on Institutions of Higher Education New England Association of Schools and Colleges (2011) states that:

> The institution plans beyond a short-term horizon, including strategic planning that involves realistic analyses of internal and external opportunities and constraints. It plans for and responds to financial and other contingencies, establishes feasible priorities, and develops a realistic course of action to achieve identified objectives. Institutional decision-making, particularly the allocation of resources, is consistent with planning priorities (p. 4).

The University of Massachusetts (UMass) is one of the top public research universities in America.[11] UMass' Strategic Plan approach is quite collaborative and effectual. One key point made in a recent community communication message from Dr. Kumble Subbaswamy[12] (n.d.), University of Massachusetts Chancellor, is: ". . . one uncommon feature of this planning process is its collaborative nature from beginning to end."

III—For the *Higher Learning Commission of the North Central Association of Colleges and Schools*[13] (HLC), Criterion Five—Resources, Planning and Institutional Effectiveness addresses strategic planning:

> The institution's resources, structures, and processes are sufficient to fulfill its mission, improve the quality of its educational offerings, and respond to future challenges and opportunities. The institution plans for the future.

Specifically, Core Component 5.C. (especially points 3, 4 and 5) addresses institutional planning most directly:

> The institution engages in systematic and integrated planning.
> 3. The planning process encompasses the institution as a whole and considers the perspectives of internal and external constituent groups.
> 4. The institution plans on the basis of a sound understanding of its current capacity. Institutional plans anticipate the possible impact of fluctuations in the institution's sources of revenue, such as enrollment, the economy, and state support.
> 5. Institutional planning anticipates emerging factors, such as technology, demographic shifts, and globalization (website).

IV—For Northwest Commission on Colleges and Universities[14] (NWCCU), Standard Three—Planning and Implementation:

> The institution engages in ongoing, participatory planning that provides direction for the institution and leads to the achievement of the intended outcomes of its programs and services, accomplishment of its core themes, and fulfillment of its mission. The resulting plans reflect the interdependent nature of the institution's operations, functions, and resources. The institution demonstrates that the plans are implemented and are evident in the relevant activities of its programs and services, the adequacy of its resource allocation, and the effective application of institutional capacity. In addition, the institution demonstrates that its planning and implementation processes are sufficiently flexible so that the institution is able to address unexpected circumstances that have the potential to impact the institution's ability to accomplish its core theme objectives and to fulfill its mission (p. 34).

V—For the Southern Association of Colleges and Schools[15] (SACS):

> The institution engages in ongoing, integrated, and institution-wide research-based planning and evaluation processes that (1) incorporate a systematic review of institutional mission, goals, and outcomes; (2) result in continuing improvement in institutional quality; and (3) demonstrate the institution is effectively accomplishing its mission (Institutional effectiveness) (p. 16).

VI—For Western Association of Schools and Colleges—Accrediting Commission for Senior Colleges and Universities[16] (WASC-ACSCU), Criterion 10: Institutional Planning and Evaluation:

> The institution must systematically evaluate and make public how well it is accomplishing its purposes, including the assessment of Schoolwide Learner Outcomes. The institution must provide evidence of planning for improvement of institutional operations and processes, student achievement of educational goals, and student learning levels (p. 12).

VII—For Western Association of Schools and Colleges—Accrediting Commission for Community and Junior Colleges Western Association of Schools and Colleges (WASC-ACCJC), Standard I: Mission, Academic Quality and Institutional Effectiveness, and Integrity:

> The institution demonstrates strong commitment to a mission that emphasizes student learning and student achievement. Using analysis of quantitative and qualitative data, the institution continuously and system-

atically evaluates, plans, implements, and improves the quality of its educational programs and services. The institution demonstrates integrity in all policies, actions, and communication. The administration, faculty, staff, and governing board members act honestly, ethically, and fairly in the performance of their duties (p. 1).

Promising Collaborative Strategic Plan (SP) Recommendations

1. Develop your SP with broad input, including students and alumni when possible. Genuine buy-in is crucial!
2. Clearly demonstrate how your SP connects to and supports your college's mission.
3. Help all stakeholders better understand why various parties are engaged in specific SP activities.
4. Student success should be the foundation of your SP.
5. Validate how your SP is aligned to the specific standard(s) of your accrediting body.
6. Communicate your SP with your stakeholders, periodically.
7. Utilizing quantitative and qualitative data is essential.
8. Monitor and assess your SP regularly.
9. An inclusive assessment of the SP should help it move toward even greater transparency, accountability and commitment.
10. Use the outcomes of the SP to develop a revised plan for the following SP, etc.
11. Your SP goals should be reasonably high, though realistically attainable—don't set yourself up for failure.
12. Align your SP activities with resources based on the institution's priorities to help attain these goals.
13. Keep the SP relatively focused based on your priorities instead of addressing all of your intuitional issues in any given year.
14. Keep in mind that the SP is used for many purposes and for a wide array of audiences—limit jargon when possible.
15. The SP is a living document—be prepared to re-evaluate and revise as necessary.
16. Don't set process-focused targets (such as to form committees or attend a meeting); instead, set a target about the expected outcome (the reason for the committee or meeting).

Moving Forward

The purpose of strategic planning is ultimately to produce useful results (not simply plans) based on the "agreed upon" or prescribed metrics—this requires full institutional commitment (Below et al., 1987). Strategic planning is a transformational process that affords a community forum and a method for producing and implementing an institutional vision. Some have argued that the hardest part of strategic planning is successfully implementing the plan after all stakeholders have agreed.

Sharing evidence of student learning with various stakeholders is crucial for implementing changes leading to greater student and institutional success. Moreover, "meaningfully communicating actionable information to those who can use it, most of whom, in the case of learning outcomes assessment, are internal partners and end users: faculty, students, campus committees, provosts, deans, department chairs, budget officers, president, and members of governing boards" (Kuh et al., 2015, p. 23). The strategic planning process is an ideal forum to revisit institutional priorities and goals, strategies to achieve and assess the goals and communicate both success and shortcomings. Although strategic planning and evaluation are critical components of the "academic planning process, its value is realized only when the assessment data are used to improve programmatic offerings and student performance" (Hollowell, Midddaugh, & Siboloski, 2006, p. 102). We hope that you have found the above case examples of various strategic plans useful as you consider enhancing your own planning and assessment process. Realize that the work of a collaborative college is never complete. Find a meaningful way to collaborate with colleagues from other areas. Keep all partners and constituents engaged and focused on the real institutional priorities, and you will succeed.

Notes

1. *Strategic Planning* is used interchangeably with *Institutional Planning* in the literature, across the regional accreditors, and thus this chapter.
2. Middle States Commission for Higher Education covers educational institutions from the following areas: New York, New Jersey, Pennsylvania, Delaware, Maryland, the District of Columbia, Puerto Rico and the US Virgin Islands (we're sure there's a fair reason). Read more: www.msche.org/ (accessed December 1, 2015).
3. Explore CUNY: www.cuny.edu/academics.html (accessed December 1, 2015).
4. J. B. Milliken was appointed Chancellor and Distinguished Professor of Law at the CUNY Law School by the CUNY Board of Trustees, effective June 1, 2014.
5. See initial details regarding CUNY's vision for strategic planning: www1.cuny.edu/sites/21stcenturycuny/ (accessed December 1, 2015).
6. Review Chapter 2 of LaGuardia's 2012 Self-Study for a fuller review of their approach to strategic planning: www.laguardia.cuny.edu/uploadedFiles/T2/middlestates/PDFs/Chapter2%281%29.pdf (accessed December 1, 2015).
7. The impetus for LaGuardia's redesigned *First-Year Experience* came out of years of internal evaluation.
8. CUE funding, which comes from CUNY Central, supported the development and implementation of LaGuardia's new FYS; other funds from various grants and/or the College's Academic Affairs budget may have also supported this initiative.
9. Explore LaGuardia's Strategic Plan along with a downloadable current template that you may find useful: http://Wp.laguardia.edu/strategicplan (accessed December 1, 2015).

10. New England Association of Schools and Colleges covers educational institutions from the following six states: Connecticut, Maine, Massachusetts, New Hampshire, Rhode Island, and Vermont. Read more: www.neasc.org/(accessed December 1, 2015.

11. Explore the University of Massachusetts: www.umass.edu/gateway/about (accessed December 1, 2015).

12. Community message by UMass' Chancellor regarding Strategic Plan approach: www.umass.edu/provost/sites/default/files/uploads/Chancellor%27s%20Message.pdf (accessed December 1, 2015).

13. The accreditation work of the North Central Association (NCA) is undertaken by two independent corporations. The Higher Learning Commission (HLC) oversees higher education accreditation for NCA, providing institution-level accreditation of degree-granting colleges and universities. They cover educational institutions from the following 19 states: Arkansas, Arizona, Colorado, Iowa, Illinois, Indiana, Kansas, Michigan, Minnesota, Missouri, North Dakota, Nebraska, New Mexico, Ohio, Oklahoma, South Dakota, Wisconsin, West Virginia and Wyoming. Read more: www. northcentralassociation.org/ (accessed December 1, 2015).

14. Northwest Commission on Colleges and Universities covers educational institutions from the following seven states: Alaska, Idaho, Montana, Nevada, Oregon, Utah and Washington. Read more: www.nwccu.org/ (accessed December 1, 2015). Note that the northwestern region has responsibility divided between two separate accreditation agencies (Northwest Accreditation Commission for primary and secondary schools, and the Northwest Commission on Colleges and Universities for colleges and universities). For our purposes, we have focused on the latter.

15. Southern Association of Colleges and Schools accreditation covers educational institutions from the following 11 states: Virginia, Florida, Georgia, Kentucky, Louisiana, Mississippi, North Carolina, South Carolina, Alabama, Tennessee and Texas. Read more: www.sacs.org/ (accessed December 1, 2015).

16. Western Association of Schools and Colleges covers educational institutions from the following areas: California, Hawaii, Guam, American Samoa, Micronesia, Palau and Northern Marianas Islands. Read more: www.wascsenior.org/ (accessed December 1, 2015).

Contact information for each of the seven regional accreditors

Higher Learning Commission (HLC)
(Formerly the Higher Learning Commission of the North Central Association of Colleges and Schools)
Barbara Gellman-Danley, President
230 South LaSalle Street, Suite 7–500
Chicago, Illinois 60604–1411
Phone: (312) 263–0456
info@hlcommission.org

Middle States Commission on Higher Education (MSCHE)
Elizabeth H. Sibolski, President
3624 Market Street, 2nd Floor West
Philadelphia, PA 19104

Phone: (267) 284–5000
info@msche.org

New England Association of Schools and Colleges, Commission on Institutions of Higher Education (NEASC-CIHE)

Barbara E. Brittingham, President/Director of the Commission
New England Association of Schools and Colleges, Inc.
3 Burlington Woods Drive, Suite 100
Burlington, Massachusetts 01803
Phone: (781) 425–7700
www.neasc.org

Northwest Commission on Colleges and Universities (NWCCU)

Sandra E. Elman, President
8060 165th Avenue N.E., Suite 100
Redmond, WA 98052
Phone: (425) 558–4224
www.nwccu.org/

Southern Association of Colleges and Schools Commission on Colleges (SACS-COC)

Belle S. Wheelan, President
1866 Southern Lane,
Decatur, GA 30033
Phone: (404) 679–4500
www.sacscoc.org/

Western Association of Schools and Colleges Accrediting Commission for Community and Junior Colleges (ACCJC)

Barbara A. Beno, President
10 Commercial Boulevard, Suite 204
Novato, CA 94949
Phone: (415) 506–0234
www.accjc.org

Western Association of Schools and Colleges Accrediting Commission for Senior Colleges and Universities (WASC Senior)

Mary Ellen Petrisko, President
985 Atlantic Avenue, Suite 100
Alameda, CA 94501
Phone: (510) 748–9001
www.wascsenior.org/

References

Baker, R. (2004). Keystones of regional accreditation: Intentions, outcomes, and sustainability. In P. Hernon and R. Dugan (Eds.) *Outcome assessment in higher education* (pp. 29–71). Westport, CT: Libraries Unlimited.

Below, P. J. Morrisey, G. L., & Acomb, B. L. (1987). *The executive guide to strategic planning.* San Francisco, CA: Jossey-Bass.

Brady, S.M. (1999, Winter). Students at the center of education: A collaborative effort. *Liberal Education*, 14–21.

Brown, T., King, M. C., & Stanley, P. (2011). *Fulfilling the promise of the community college: increasing first-year student engagement and success. The first-year experience monograph series number 56.* National Resource Center for The First-Year Experience and Students in Transition. University of South Carolina, Columbia, SC.

Burkhart, P. J., & Reuss, S. (1993). *Successful strategic planning: A guide for nonprofit agencies and organizations.* Thousand Oaks, CA: Sage.

Calhoun, J. C. (1996). The student learning imperative: implications for student affairs. *Journal of College Student Development, 37*(2), 118–122. Retrieved on December 1, 2015 from: http://co.myacpa.org/wp-content/uploads/2015/01/acpas_student_learning_imperative.pdf.

The City University of New York (CUNY) (2014, July). Performance management report 2013–14 year-end university report final. Office of Institutional Research & Assessment.

The City University of New York (CUNY) (n.d.) 2012–2013 Performance Management Process (PMP). Retrieved December 1, 2015 from: www1.cuny.edu/sites/6/about/administration/chancellor/office/performance-management/#1443534324205-0685 6f34-0223.

Clayton-Pederson, A. R., & Dungy, G. J. (2007). Developing effective collaborations. In J. H. Cook & C. A. Lewis (Eds.) *Student and academic affairs collaboration: The divine comity* (Chapter 13, pp. 265–281). Washington, DC: National Association of Student Personnel Administrators (NASPA).

Cook, J. H., Ghering, A. M., & Lewis, C. A. (2007). Divine comity: The basics. In J. H. Cook & C. A. Lewis (Eds.) *Student and academic affairs collaboration: The divine comity* (Chapter 1, pp. 1–16). Washington, DC: National Association of Student Personnel Administrators (NASPA).

Dembicki, M. (2010, June 25). Counselors see more severity, complexity among student cases. The *Community College Times*. Retrieved on December 1, 2015 from: www.ccdaily.com/Pages/Campus-Issues/Counselors-see-more-severity-complexity-among-student-cases.aspx.

Dickmeyer, N., & Michalowski, S. (2012, June). The relationship between student time allocation decisions and outcomes: an interactive simulation model. Paper presented at the 52nd Annual Forum of the Association for Institutional Research, New Orleans, LA.

Gannon-Slater, N., Ikenberry, S., Jankowski, N., & Kuh, G. (2014). *Institutional assessment practices across accreditation regions.* Urbana, IL: University of Illinois and Indiana University, National Institute for Learning Outcomes Assessment.

Gardner, L. F. (1994). Assessment and evaluation: Knowing and judging results. In J. Stark and A. Thomas (Eds.) *Assessment and program evaluation* (pp. 65–78). ASHE Reader Series. Boston, MA: Pearson Custom Publishing.

Garza Mitchell, R. L., & Maldanado, C. (2015). Strategic planning for new presidents: Developing an entrance plan. *Community College Journal of Research and Practice, 39,* 113–121.

Gaston, P. L. (2013). *Higher education accreditation: How it's changing, why it must.* Sterling, VA: Stylus Publishing, LLC.

Gould, K. (2011, May). 2011–2016 strategic plan for Brooklyn College. Retrieved on December 1, 2015 from: www.brooklyn.cuny.edu/web/abo_president/110501_Strate gicPlan_2011–16.pdf.

Higher Learning Commission (HLC). Retrieved on December 1, 2015 from: www.ncahlc. org/Criteria-Eligibility-and-Candidacy/criteria-and-core-components.html.

Hinton, K. E. (2012). A practical guide to strategic planning in higher education. Retrieved on December 1, 2015 from: http://oira.cortland.edu/webpage/planningandassessment resources/planningresources/SocietyforCollegeUniversityPlanning.pdf.

Hollowell, D., Midddaugh, M. F., & Siboloski, E. (2006). *Integrating higher education planning and assessment: A practical guide.* Ann Arbor, MI: The Society for College and University Planning.

Insalaco-Egan, D., & Engel, D. (2012, March). *A roadmap for student success: The alignment of academic affairs and student affairs at LaGuardia Community College.*

Kuh G. D. (1998). Shaping student character. *Liberal Education, 84*(3), 18–25.

Kuh, G. D. (2013). High-impact educational practices: A brief overview. *Association of American Colleges and Universities.* Retrieved on December 1, 2015 from: www.aacu.org/ leap/hips.

Kuh, G. D., Ikenberry, S. O., Jankowski, N., Reese Cain, T., Ewell, P., Hutchings, P., & Kinzie, J. (2015). *Using evidence of student learning to improve higher education.* San Francisco, CA: Jossey-Bass.

Kuh, G. D., Kinzie, J., Schuh, J. H., & Whitt, E. J. (2005). *Assessing conditions to enhance educational effectiveness.* San Francisco, CA: Jossey-Bass.

LaGuardia Community College (City University of New York) Comprehensive Institutional Self-Study for the Middle States Association of Colleges and Schools Commission on Higher Education. (2012). Retrieved on December 1, 2015 from: www. laguardia.cuny.edu/uploadedFiles/T2/middlestates/PDFs/Self-Study-.pdf.

LaGuardia Community College (City University of New York) Mission Statement. (2015). Retrieved on December 1, 2015 from: www.lagcc.cuny.edu/About/Mission-Statement/.

Levy, M. A., DePhilippis, S., Kammer, M., McCall, M., & Otterbun, Martinez, J. (2014, December). Curricular infusion for career development: Student affairs partnering with academic affairs. Synergy (NASPA).

Levy, M. A., Polnariev, B.A., & McGowan, L. (2011, August). The integration of reality-based programming to address "schizophrenic" support services. Student Affairs News (SAN) website. Retrieved on December 1, 2015 from: www.studentaffairs news.com.

Levy, M. A., Polnariev, B., & Thomas, M. (2011, March). Student orientation: Assessment and strategic planning. Webinar. PaperClip Communications.

Levy, M. A., Richburg, A., Montefusco, L., & Marzelli, S. (2015). Atlantic Cape Community College student success initiative implementation assessment template. Developed March, 2015.

Lopez, C. L. (2003). A decade of assessing student learning: What we have learned and what is next. In P. Hernon and R. Dugan (Eds.) *Outcome assessment in higher education* (pp. 29–71). Westport, CT: Libraries Unlimited.

McDonnell, S., Chellman, C. C., Littman C. B., & Crook, D. (2013). Implementing value-added accountability measures at the City University of New York. City University of New York. Retrieved on December 1, 2015 from: www.aefpweb.org/sites/default/files/webform/20120312_RAPM_AEFP13_McDonnell_et_al.pdf.

Mellow, G. (2014, October). What will it take to be 'first in the world?' *The Huffington Post*. Retrieved on December 1, 2015 from: www.huffingtonpost.com/gail-mellow/what-will-it-take-to-be-f_b_5915636.html.

Middaugh, M. F. (2007). Creating a culture of evidence: Academic accountability at the institutional level. *New Directions for Higher Education, 140*, 15–28.

Middaugh, M. F. (2009). Closing the loop: Linking planning and assessment. *Planning for Higher Education, 37*(3), 5–14.

Middle States Commission on Higher Education. (2006). *Characteristics of excellence in higher education: Eligibility requirements and standards for accreditation* (12th ed.). Philadelphia: Middle States Commission on Higher Education. Retrieved on December 1, 2015 from: www.msche.org/publications/CHX06060320124919.pdf.

Middle States Commission on Higher Education. (2015). *Characteristics of excellence in higher education: Eligibility requirements and standards for accreditation* (13th ed.). Philadelphia: Middle States Commission on Higher Education. Retrieved on December 1, 2015 from: www.msche.org/publications/RevisedStandardsFINAL.pdf.

Mina, J. (2014). Strategic planning: Devising the way of US higher education institutions. In *Survival of the fittest* (pp. 157–173). Heidelberg: Springer.

Northwest Commission on Colleges & Universities (2015, March). Accreditation handbook. Retrieved on December 1, 2015 from: www.nwccu.org/Pubs%20Forms%20and%20Updates/Publications/Accreditation%20Handbook,%202013%20Edition.pdf.

O'Connor, S., Polnariev, B. A., & Levy, M. A. (2012, March). Five core considerations for counseling non-traditional students. Student Affairs News (SAN). Retrieved on December 1, 2015 from: www.studentaffairsnews.com.

Resource Manual for the Principles of Accreditation: Foundations for Quality Enhancement (2012). (2nd ed.). Southern Association of Colleges and Schools Commission on Colleges. Decatur, GA. Retrieved on December 1, 2015 from: www.sacscoc.org/pdf/Resource%20Manual.pdf.

Sanaghan, P., & Hinton, M. (2013, July, 3). Be strategic on strategic planning. *Inside Higher Ed*. Retrieved on December 1, 2015 from: www.insidehighered.com/advice/2013/07/03/essay-how-do-strategic-planning.

Seidman, A. (2005). Where we go from here: A retention formula for student success. In Seidmanc, A. (Ed.) *College student retention* (pp. 295–316). Westport, CT: ACE/Praeger Series on Higher Education.

Senge, P. M. (1990). Catalyzing systems thinking within organizations. In F. Masarik (Ed.) *Advances in organization development*. Norwood, NJ: Ablex.

Southern Association of Colleges and Schools Commission on Colleges. (2012). *Resource Manual for the Principles of Accreditation: Foundations for Quality Enhancement* (2nd ed.). Decatur, GA. Retrieved on December 1, 2015 from: www.sacscoc.org/pdf/Resource%20Manual.pdf.

Standards of Accreditation Commission on Institutions of Higher Education New England Association of Schools and Colleges. (2011). Retrieved on December 1, 2015 from: https://cihe.neasc.org//sites/cihe.neasc.org/downloads/Standards/Standards_for_Accreditation.pdf.

Stetsenko, A., & Arievitch, I. (2004). The self in cultural-historical activity theory: Reclaiming the unity of social and individual dimensions of human development. *Theory & Psychology, 14*, 475–503.

Suskie, L. (2015). *Five dimensions of quality: A common sense guide to accreditation and accountability.* San Francisco, CA: John Wiley & Sons.

Tinto, V. (2000). Linking learning and leaving: Exploring the role of college classrooms in student departure. In J. Braxton (Ed.) *Reworking the student departure puzzle* (pp. 81–94). Nashville, TN: Vanderbilt University Press.

Western Association of Schools and Colleges—Accrediting Commission for Senior Colleges and Universities. (2011). Postsecondary accreditation manual: Western Association of Schools & Colleges. Temulca, CA. Retrieved on December 1, 2015 from: www.acswasc.org/pdf_postsecondary/PostsecondaryManual2011.pdf.

Western Association of Schools and Colleges—Accrediting Commission for Community and Junior Colleges Western Association of Schools and Colleges (2014, June). Accreditation standards. Retrieved on December 1, 2015 from: www.accjc.org/wp content/uploads/2014/07/Accreditation_Standards_Adopted_June_2014.pdf.

Young, R. (2011). Exploring successful strategies for integrating academic assessment and strategic planning in the community college. Dissertation. National Louis University.

10

FINAL THOUGHTS

Bernard A. Polnariev and Mitchell A. Levy

In a powerful 2015 *TEDtalk* on the issue of organizational productivity, Dr. Yves Morieux, an expert in corporate transformation, stresses that our society is preoccupied with accountability instead of cooperation. We are constantly trying to put accountability in "someone's hands" as he puts it. Morieux uses a *relay race* as a great example and metaphor for how accountability can derail our work efforts. There is a clear line of accountability as one runner passes the baton on to the next runner—done at the right time and speed. In this approach to a partnership—passing the baton and responsibility—Morieux argues, "we will know who to blame. But we'll never win the race. If you think about it, we pay more attention to knowing who to blame in case we fail, than to creating the conditions to succeed." This method creates institutions and leaders that are "able to fail, but in a compliant way, with somebody clearly accountable when we fail" (Morieux, 2015).

In an era of increased demand for accountability and compliance, colleges and universities take:

> cues from government, accreditors, and their peer institutions on how to document and improve student and institutional performance, initiatives tend to pile up, multiply, duplicate—and become transitory. Not uncommonly, academic and student affairs faculty feel overwhelmed by the sense of "one more thing" and disenfranchised by someone else's notion of what constitutes improvement and accountability. The result is often pervasive frustration and a fragmented, burdensome, and less effective institutional investment in assessment.
>
> (Kuh et al., 2015, p. 23)

Given the veracity of the adage "what gets measured gets done," logically, most folks will put their significant attention at work to what can get measured, often at the expense of *cooperation*. When the measured outcomes decline, institutions in turn often add further processes and policies to remedy. The real issue that Morieux (2015) helps bring to the forefront is about accountability and cooperation. He asks:

> . . . is it really in their personal interest to cooperate or not, if, when they cooperate, they are individually worse off? Why would they cooperate? . . . We need to create organizations in which it becomes individually useful for people to cooperate . . . Remove most of the quantitative metrics to assess performance . . . Look at cooperation, the "how." How did you pass the baton? Did you throw it, or did you pass it effectively? Am I putting my energy in what can get measured—my legs, my speed—or in passing the baton? You, as leaders, as managers, are you making it individually useful for people to cooperate? The future of our organizations, our companies, our societies hinges on your answer to these questions.

We must find ways to truly collaborate and cooperate if we are to effectively advance student and institutional success. Multiple methods which grant appropriate incentives for organizational professionals to collaborate are paramount in order to avoid running to simply "pass the baton" off to a colleague. The more effectively faculty and staff cooperate and work toward the same goal— whether part of orientation, advisement, curricular infusion, career development and/or strategic planning—the more likely that the measured goals of these areas will be positively and steadily enhanced. Furthermore, institutional leaders must be cognizant to avoid a culture of *initiative overload* which tends to focus on an add-on activity instead of a carefully thought out and systemic approach to advancing college priorities. In fact, FranklinCovey (2015) state that for institutions to be most effective, they must focus on the success of three or four institutional initiatives, not an ever-increasing menu. In essence, "more" is not always better!

Kuh and his colleagues (2015) posit that "enduring confidence in American higher education will be defined by our performance, by the quality of college graduates, and by the impact of the innovation, creativity, and service colleges and universities render society" (p. 12). Since the 1970s, policymakers have become progressively concerned about improving higher education outcomes (Lahr, Pheatt, Dougherty, Jones, Natow, & Reddy, 2014). Massachusetts Senator Elizabeth Warren eloquently and persuasively stated to an educational panel at a June 2015 meeting focused on government initiatives, "this is a critical moment in America, a moment at which we reconsider how to build a future." For students, faculty and staff to thrive in a twenty-first century higher education institution, it is imperative that we re-imagine our roles and approaches to defining, providing and measuring the outcomes of collaborative support services.

As Josh Wyner, Vice President and Executive Director of the Aspen Institute, contends in his recent (2014) book dedicated to *student success*, institutional leaders must create an urgency for student success by refocusing our attention to what matters most—planning for large changes, earmarking sizeable resources for student success and fully embracing that the college is not a destination, but rather a *bridge*. Dr. Jamie Merisotis, the CEO and President of the Lumina Foundation argued (2015) regarding the reauthorization of the Higher Education Act, "meeting the needs of these students requires more than tweaks to the system; it demands a redesign of higher education as we know it."

Our purpose for the creation of this book is directly aligned with these views. Presenting nationally, engaging other leaders in discussions, publishing, and having worked collectively in both Academic Affairs and Student Affairs for 50 years as faculty, advisors, counselors, program directors, researchers and consultants at various levels has afforded us the opportunity to appreciate the value and elegance of true synergy across institutional divisions and boundaries. As described in the chapters regarding faculty involvement in advisement and curricular infusion, we have witnessed first-hand the possibilities inherent via true collaboration and how students can benefit from an institutional commitment to holistic and intentional support. Our goal for this project was to share what we have learned with our many colleagues who continually strive to enhance student success—as defined in various ways. We wanted this volume to go beyond theoretical constructs and philosophical discussions of the importance of a utopian ideal of cross-divisional collaboration, negating the often-inevitable system of "silos." Essentially, we wanted to share the collective thoughts, beliefs and experiences, as grounded in evidence, of the many excellent colleagues that we have had the pleasure to work with. We hope that we have provided you with a "handbook" of ideas, techniques, strategies and recommendations to help these efforts grow beyond our small sphere. It is our genuine hope that after reading this book you have found some useful "takeaways" to inform your collaborative work and continue to spread the message on how to further help students achieve their academic, career and personal goals.

We *challenge* and encourage you to truly partner with others across the divisional walls, develop genuine relationships with faculty and Student Affairs professionals, join vital cross-divisional committees such as the NASPA SAPAA Knowledge Community, collaborate, apply several of the approaches and recommendations presented in this book, assess and publish the outcomes and continuously revise the approach as needed—relentlessly focused on student success and learning. In essence, *help build the bridge*!

Enthusiastically,

Bernard & Mitchell

References

FranklinCovey (2015). Retrieved December 1, 2015 from: www.franklincovey.com/leadership/7-habits.

Kuh, G. D., Ikenberry, S. O., Jankowski, N. A., Cain, T. R., Hutchings, P., & Kinzie, J. (2015). *Using evidence of student learning to improve higher education.* San Francisco, CA: John Wiley & Sons.

Lahr, H., Pheatt, L., Dougherty, K. J., Jones, S., Natow, R. S., & Reddy, V. (2014). *Unintended impacts of performance funding on community colleges and universities in three states.* Community College Research Center. Teachers College, Columbia University.

Merisotis, J. (2015, July). Why rebooting higher education policy could strengthen our nation's economic future. *The Huffington Post.* Retrieved December 1, 2015 from: www.huffingtonpost.com/jamie-merisotis/why-rebooting-higher-educ_b_7849690.html.

Morieux, Y. (2015). How too many rules at work keep you from getting things done. *TEDtalks.* Retrieved December 1, 2015 from: www.ted.com/talks/yves_morieux_how_too_many_rules_at_work_keep_you_from_getting_things_done?language=en.

Warren, E. (2015, June 8). The affordability crisis: Rescuing the dream of college education for the working class and poor. Retrieved December 1, 2015 from: www.warren.senate.gov/files/documents/ShankerInstitute-AFTEducationSpeech.pdf.

Wyner, J. S. (2014). *What excellent community colleges do: Preparing all students for success.* Cambridge, MA: Harvard Education Press.

INDEX